科技英语丛书

# 机械专业英语
# English for Mechanics

主审　余晓流
主编　汪永明
参编　邓　克　单建华
　　　叶　晔　俞金众

中国科学技术大学出版社

## 内 容 简 介

本书为专业英语教材,详细介绍了机械相关专业所涉及的金属材料及热加工、金属切削机床与切削原理、几何公差与配合、机械电子、液压传动、CAD/CAE/CAPP/CAM、先进制造技术、机械工程文献介绍及英文写作等内容,力求使读者既能全面地了解到重要的专业知识,又能切实地提高其专业英语的阅读和应用水平。

本书可作为高等院校机械工程、机械设计制造及自动化、机电一体化、工业工程、材料成型及控制工程等专业的本科生和研究生学习机械专业英语的教材,也可以作为工厂企业从事机械设计、机械制造工作的工程技术人员或管理者的英语学习教材或参考书。

**图书在版编目(CIP)数据**

机械专业英语/汪永明主编.—合肥:中国科学技术大学出版社,2012.2(2023.6重印)

ISBN 978-7-312-02967-7

Ⅰ.机… Ⅱ.汪… Ⅲ.机械工程—英语—教材 Ⅳ.H31

中国版本图书馆 CIP 数据核字(2011)第 270003 号

| | |
|---|---|
| 出版 | 中国科学技术大学出版社<br>安徽省合肥市金寨路 96 号,230026<br>http://press.ustc.edu.cn<br>http://zgkxjsdxcbs.tmall.com |
| 印刷 | 安徽省瑞隆印务有限公司 |
| 发行 | 中国科学技术大学出版社 |
| 开本 | 710 mm×960 mm　1/16 |
| 印张 | 15.25 |
| 字数 | 270 千 |
| 版次 | 2012 年 2 月第 1 版 |
| 印次 | 2023 年 6 月第 5 次印刷 |
| 定价 | 26.00 元 |

# 前　言

本书为科技英语系列教材之一。全书共分为 7 个单元,每个单元包含 4~6 课,每课供 2 个学时使用。各专业可以适当节选内容,以满足各自不同的教学要求。教材内容主要涉及金属材料及热加工、金属切削机床与切削原理、几何公差与配合、机械电子、液压传动、CAD/CAE/CAPP/CAM、先进制造技术、机械工程文献介绍及英文写作等。

本书资料新颖,内容涵盖面广,既可作为高等院校机械工程、机械设计制造及自动化、机电一体化、工业工程、材料成型及控制工程等专业的研究生和本科生学习机械专业英语的教材,也可作为工厂企业从事机械设计、机械制造工作的工程技术人员和管理者的英语学习教材或参考书。

本书课文全部节选自欧美文献原著。为保持原著的语言风格,编者对选材一般只作删节,不作改写。对原著中采用的各种计量单位及图样标注均不作改动。本书原稿曾作为"机械专业英语"选修课校内讲义供高年级本科生和工程硕士生使用了多年,在听取了有关老师和学生的意见和建议后,我们对书稿又作了较大的增删与修改,直至成书。

本书由安徽工业大学汪永明任主编,对全书各章节进行了多次审稿、改稿和统稿。本书的 Unit 1、Unit 2 (Lesson 8)、Unit 5 (Lesson 17~18)、Unit 6 和 Unit 7 由汪永明编写,Unit 2 (Lesson 5~7) 由单建华编写,Unit 3 由叶晔编写,Unit 4 由邓克编写,Unit 5 (Lesson 19~20) 由俞金众编写。全书由安徽工业大学余晓流教授主审,他对教材的编写大纲、编写内容及特点等方面提出了许多宝贵的意见。

本书在编写过程中得到了安徽工业大学机械工程学院领导和同仁的大力支持和帮助，参考了国内外学者、专家的有关文献。在此，谨向他们表示衷心感谢。

限于编者的水平，书中不足或错误之处在所难免，恳请读者批评指正。

编 者

2011 年 9 月

# Contents

**Unit 1　Metallic Material & Hot Working** ……………………………… ( 1 )
　　Lesson 1　Metallic Material ………………………………………… ( 1 )
　　Lesson 2　Mechanical Properties of Metallic Material ………… ( 8 )
　　Lesson 3　Hot working ……………………………………………… ( 15 )
　　Lesson 4　Forming Processes ……………………………………… ( 20 )

**Unit 2　Machine Tools & Cutting Technology** ……………………… ( 36 )
　　Lesson 5　Machine Tools …………………………………………… ( 36 )
　　Lesson 6　Tool Life ………………………………………………… ( 44 )
　　Lesson 7　Tolerances ……………………………………………… ( 49 )
　　Lesson 8　Machining Fundamentals ……………………………… ( 56 )

**Unit 3　Mechatronics** …………………………………………………… ( 61 )
　　Lesson 9　Expert System …………………………………………… ( 61 )
　　Lesson 10　Robot and Robotics …………………………………… ( 70 )
　　Lesson 11　Basics of Microcomputers …………………………… ( 79 )
　　Lesson 12　PLC and FMS ………………………………………… ( 86 )

**Unit 4　Hydraulic Transmission** ……………………………………… ( 94 )
　　Lesson 13　Introduction to Fluid Power ………………………… ( 94 )
　　Lesson 14　Fluid Power Pumps …………………………………… (100)
　　Lesson 15　Hydraulic Cylinder and Rams ……………………… (110)
　　Lesson 16　Industrial Hydraulic Circuits ………………………… (118)

**Unit 5　Computerized Manufacturing** ………………………………… (129)
　　Lesson 17　Computer Aided Design ……………………………… (129)
　　Lesson 18　Computer Aided Engineering ………………………… (137)
　　Lesson 19　Computer Aided Process Planning ………………… (143)
　　Lesson 20　Computer Aided Manufacturing …………………… (149)

## Unit 6　Advance Manufacturing Technology ……………………………………(155)
Lesson 21　Agile Manufacturing …………………………………(155)
Lesson 22　Rapid Prototyping Technologies ……………………(160)
Lesson 23　E-manufacturing ……………………………………(166)
Lesson 24　Concurrent Engineering ……………………………(173)

## Unit 7　Extracurricular Reading …………………………………………………(180)
Lesson 25　Nanotechnology ……………………………………(180)
Lesson 26　Reaching for a Smarter Factory …………………(185)
Lesson 27　Basics of Computer Numerical Control ……………(190)
Lesson 28　Planar Linkages ……………………………………(201)
Lesson 29　Introduction to Mechanical Engineering Literature ……(210)
Lesson 30　English Paper Writing Guide ………………………(218)

## Referrences …………………………………………………………………………(236)

# Unit 1  Metallic Material & Hot Working

## Lesson 1  Metallic Material

## 1  Introduction

### 1.1  Historical Perspective

Materials are so important in the development of civilization that we associate Ages with them. In the origin of human life on earth, the Stone Age, people used only natural materials, like stone, clay, skins, and wood. When people found copper and how to make it harder by alloying, the Bronze Age started about 3000 BC. The use of iron and steel, a stronger material that gave advantage in wars started at about 1200 BC. The next big step was the discovery of a cheap process to make steel around 1850, which enabled the railroads and the building of the modern infrastructure of the industrial world.

### 1.2  Materials Science and Engineering

Understanding of how materials behave like they do, and why they differ in properties was only possible with the atomistic understanding allowed by quantum mechanics, that first explained atoms and then solids starting in the 1930s. The combination of physics, chemistry, and the focus on the relationship between the properties of a material and its microstructure is the domain of Materials Science. The development of this science allowed designing materials and provided a knowledge base for the engineering applications (Materials Engineering).

**Structure:**
- ◆ At the atomic level: arrangement of atoms in different ways. (Gives different properties for graphite than diamond both forms of carbon.);
- ◆ At the microscopic level: arrangement of small grains of material that

can be identified by microscopy. (Gives different optical properties to transparent vs. frosted glass.)

Properties are the way the material responds to the environment. For instance, the mechanical, electrical and magnetic properties are the responses to mechanical, electrical and magnetic forces, respectively. Other important properties are thermal (transmission of heat, heat capacity), optical (absorption, transmission and scattering of light), and the chemical stability in contact with the environment (like corrosion resistance).

Processing of materials is the application of heat (heat treatment), mechanical forces, etc., to affect their microstructure and, therefore, their properties.

### 1.3 Why Study Materials Science and Engineering?

- ◆ To be able to select a material for a given use based on considerations of cost and performance;
- ◆ To understand the limits of materials and the change of their properties with use;
- ◆ To be able to create a new material that will have some desirable properties.

All engineering disciplines need to know about materials. Even the most "immaterial", like software or system engineering depend on the development of new materials, which in turn alter the economics, like software-hardware trade-offs. Increasing applications of system engineering are in materials manufacturing (industrial engineering) and complex environmental systems.

### 1.4 Classification of Materials

Like many other things, materials are classified in groups, so that our brain can handle the complexity. One could classify them according to structure, or properties, or use. The one that we will use is according to the way the atoms are bound together:

**Metals**: Valence electrons are detached from atoms, and spread in an "electron sea" that "glues" the ions together. Metals are usually strong, conduct electricity and heat well and are opaque to light (shiny if polished). Such as aluminum, steel, brass, gold.

**Semiconductors:** The bonding is covalent (electrons are shared between atoms). Their electrical properties depend extremely strongly on minute proportions of contaminants. They are opaque to visible light but transparent to the infrared. Such as Si, Ge, Ga, As.

**Ceramics:** Atoms behave mostly like either positive or negative ions, and are bound by Coulomb forces between them. They are usually combinations of metals or semiconductors with oxygen, nitrogen or carbon (oxides, nitrides, and carbides). Such as glass, porcelain, many minerals.

**Polymers:** They are bound by covalent forces and also by weak Van der Waals forces, and usually based on H, C and other non-metallic elements. They decompose at moderate temperatures (100℃ ~ 400℃), and are lightweight. Other properties vary greatly. Examples: plastics (nylon, teflon, polyester) and rubber.

Other categories are not based on bonding. A particular microstructure identifies composites, made of different materials in intimate contact (Such as fiberglass, concrete, wood) to achieve specific properties. Biomaterials can be any type of material that is biocompatible and used, for instance, to replace human body parts.

## 1.5 Advanced Materials

Materials used in "High-Tec" applications, usually designed for maximum performance, and normally expensive. Examples are titanium alloys for supersonic airplanes, magnetic alloys for computer disks, special ceramics for the heat shield of the space shuttle, etc.

## 1.6 Modern Material's Needs

- ◆ Engine efficiency increases at high temperatures: requires high temperature structural materials;
- ◆ Use of nuclear energy requires solving problem with residues, or advances in nuclear waste processing;
- ◆ Hypersonic flight requires materials that are light, strong and resist high temperatures;
- ◆ Optical communications require optical fibers that absorb light negligibly;

- ◆ Civil construction-materials for unbreakable windows;
- ◆ Structures: materials that are strong like metals and resist corrosion like plastics.

## 2  Metallic Material

It is known that metals are very important in our life. Metals have the greatest importance for industry. All machines and other engineering constructions have metal parts, some of them consist only of metal parts.

There are two large groups of metals:

(1) Simple metals — more or less pure chemical elements;

(2) Alloys — materials consisting of a simple metal combined with some other elements.

About two thirds of all elements found in the earth are metals, but not all metals may be used in industry[1]. (see Appendix of Lesson 30) Those metals which are used in industry are called engineering metals. The most important engineering metal is iron (Fe), which in the form of alloys with carbon (C) and other elements, finds greater use than any other metals. Metals consisting of iron combines with some other elements are known as ferrous metals[2], all the other metals are called nonferrous metals. The most important nonferrous metals are copper (Cu), aluminum (Al), lead (Pb), zinc (Zn), tin (Sn), but all these metals are used much less than ferrous metals, because the ferrous metals are much cheaper.

Engineering metals are used in industry in the form of alloys because the properties of alloys are much better than the properties of pure metals. Only aluminum may be largely used in the form of a simple metal. Metals have such a great importance because of their useful properties or their strength, hardness, and plasticity.

Different metals are produced in different ways, but almost all the metals are found in the form of metals ore (iron ore, copper ore, etc.).

The ore is a mineral consisting of a metal combined with some impurities. In order to produce a metal from some metal ore, we must separate these impurities from the metal that is done by metallurgy.

There are many different material types to choose from when undertaking a project. For the purposes of our discussion, the materials are grouped roughly into two categories, these being "Non-metallic" and "Metallic". In respect to metallic materials these are then subsequently grouped into two groups being ferrous and non-ferrous. Each of the materials has their own characteristics and requires different machining techniques. Careful consideration needs to be given to the correct material selection for its application. (Definition: ferrous as in containing iron, e.g., steel Non-ferrous as in not containing iron, e.g., aluminum, copper.) A simple test for ferrous/non-ferrous materials is to use magnet as a magnet will sick to ferrous materials due to its iron content.

### 2.1 Aluminum Alloy

There are many kinds of alloys to choose from but often, aluminum is chosen as it is lightweight (about 2700 kg/m$^3$ density), it is comparatively soft and its process-ability is good. From a machining viewpoint pure aluminum (JIS A1000) greatly differs from Al-Cu alloy (JIS A2000).

Pure aluminum is easy to bend but it is difficult to process as it is too soft and easily clogs cutting tools. On the other hand, the Al-Cu alloy, such as A2011 or A2017 (as shown in Fig. 1.1) is easy to handle and cut with several of the grades having strength similar to that of steel. However, one of the drawbacks of aluminum is that it is difficult to weld, solder and bend.

Fig. 1.1　Aluminum Alloy (JIS A2017)

It is very difficult to distinguish between the pure aluminum, the Al-Cu alloy, etc. When they are cutting with a machine, we may recognize the material.

### 2.2 Stainless Steel

A typical stain less steel is JIS SUS304, as shown in Fig. 1.2. The benefits of stainless steel is that it has high strength, great heat-resistance, and it resists staining e.g. rust. Due to its high resistance to heat it makes an ideal material for mechanical parts that are subjected to heating such as a heater of a stirling engine. Also, due to the materials resistance to rusting, it is ideal for use where

Fig.1.2 Stainless Steel(JIS SUS304)

it is exposed to water. Other examples of its use is in drive shafts where both strength and corrosion resistance is needed.

Stainless steel tends to be a bit sticky in respect to cutting and machining and as it is a relatively hard material it tends to shorten the life of the cutting tools being used. Such cutting tools need to be sharpened often particularly in prolonged cutting operations. Stainless steel can usually be identified by its glossy silver colour.

### 2.3 Carbon Steel

Typical carbon steel materials are JIS S45C (as shown in Fig. 1.3) and JIS SS400. They are very cheap, excelling in weld ability, and they can be subjected to various heat treatments. Since many machine tools are designed to cut mild steel material, it is very rare to encounter problems while machining.

I hardly use mild steel apart from cases where welding is required as I mostly make experimental models as therefore issues such as low manufacturing costs are not a consideration in the work that I do.

Generally, mild steel has a black surface and this surface is very hard, if possible, this surface should be left intact as it offers additional protection.

Fig.1.3 Carbon Steel (JIS S45C)

### 2.4 Brass

Brass is an alloy which is made from a combination of copper and zinc as the main ingredients, as shown in Fig. 1.4. In compared with carbon steel or stainless steel, the machine-ability of brass is good, and it also has good soldering properties.

Brass is very heavy due to its high density so it is ideal for heavy parts, such as a flywheel or balance weight for model engines.

Brass is prized for the highly polished finish it can produce however, since brass surface will oxidise when exposed to the elements, it preferable to apply a clear lacquer protective coating.

Brass is very expensive when compared to other materials so it is used very selectively.

Fig. 1.4 Brass (JIS C2800)

## 3 Material Identification

Usually, a billet (column) of material is sold in unit lengths of 1 to 2 meters (or more). These billets typically carry the material identification written on the end of the billet as seen in the photos on the right, as shown in Fig. 1.5. As the billet is usually cut to provide the work piece, take care to cut from the end opposite the markings so as to leave the markings for subsequent identification.

Fig. 1.5 Material Indication

**Vacabulary**

metal ['metəl]   n. 金属

construction [kən'strʌkʃən]   n. 结构

combine ... with 把……和……结合(起来)
iron ['aiən] n. 铁
carbon ['kɑːbən] n. 碳；石墨
ferrous ['ferəs] adj. 亚铁的；铁的，含铁的
ferrous metals 黑色金属
non-ferrous metals 有色金属
copper ['kɔpə] n. 铜
aluminum [əˈljuːminəm] n. 铝
lead [liːd] n. 铅
zinc [ziŋk] n. 锌
tin [tin] n. 锡

metallurgical [ˌmetəˈlɜːdʒik,-kəl] adj. 冶金的；冶金学的
strength [streŋθ] n. 强度；实力
hardness [ˈhɑːdnis] n. 硬度
plasticity [plæsˈtisiti] n. 塑性，可塑性；适应性；柔软性
ore [ɔː] n. 矿；矿沙(石)
impurity [imˈpjuərəti] n. 杂质；不纯
mineral [ˈminərəl] adj. 矿物的；矿质的 n. 矿物；(英)矿泉水；无机物
brass [brɑːs, bræs] n. 黄铜；黄铜制品；铜管乐器；厚脸皮

**Notes**

[1] About two thirds of all elements found in the earth are metals 中, found in the earth 是过去分词短语, 作 all elements 的后置定语, 可译为: 地球上发现的各种元素。而 two thirds 是指"三分之二", 故全句可译为: 在地球上发现的各种元素中大约三分之二是金属元素, 但并不是所有的金属都能够用于工业上。

[2] Metals consisting of iron combined with some other elements are known as ferrous metals 中, consisting of 是短语动词的现在分词形式, 与其后面的宾语组成现在分词短语, 作 metals 的后置定语。本句的短语动词是 are know as。因此本句可译为: 由铁跟某种其他元素相结合组成的金属称为黑色金属。

**Exercises**

1. Give an explanation of the following terms:
   oxidise    brass    mild steel    work piece
2. List the classification of materials.
3. List the types of metal.
4. What is the difference between non-ferrous metal and ferrous metal?

# Lesson 2  Mechanical Properties of Metallic Material

## 1 Kinds of Steel

There are two general kinds of steels: carbon steel and alloy steel. Carbon steel contains only iron and carbon, while alloy steel contains some other alloying elements such as nickel, chromium, manganese, molybdenum, tungsten, vanadium, etc.

(1) Carbon steels

① Low carbon steel containing from 0.05 to 0.15 percent carbon; this steel is also known as machine steel.

② Medium carbon steel containing from 0.15 to 0.60 percent carbon.

③ High carbon steel containing from 0.6 to 1.50 percent carbon, which is sometimes called "tool steel".

(2) Alloy steels

① Special alloy steel, such as nickel steel, chromium steel.

② High speed steel also known as self-hardening steel[1].

Carbon steels are the most common steels used in industry. The properties of these steels depend only on the percentage of carbon they contain. Low carbon steels are very soft and can be used for bolts and for machine parts that do not need strength.

Medium carbon steel is a better grade and stronger than low carbon steel. It is also more difficult to cut than low carbon steel.

High carbon steel may be hardened by heating it to a certain temperature and then quickly cooling in water. The more carbon the steel contains and the quicker the coolingis, the harder it becomes[2]. Because of its high strength and hardness this grade of steel may be used for tools and working parts of machines.

But for some special uses, for example, for gears, bearings, springs, shafts and wire, carbon steels cannot be always used because they have no properties needed for these parts.

# 2 Mechanical Properties of Metals

## 2.1 Introduction

Often materials are subject to forces (loads) when they are used. Mechanical engineers calculate those forces and material scientists how materials deform (elongate, compress, twist) or break as a function of applied load, time, temperature, and other conditions.

Materials scientists learn about these mechanical properties by testing materials. Results from the tests depend on the size and shape of material to be tested (specimen), how it is held, and the way of performing the test. That is why we use common procedures, or standards, which are published by the ASTM (American Society for Testing Material).

## 2.2 Concepts of Stress and Strain

To compare specimens of different sizes, the load is calculated per unit area, also called normalization to the area. Force divided by area is called stress. In tension and compression tests, the relevant area is that perpendicular to the force. In shear or torsion tests, the area is perpendicular to the axis of rotation.

$s = F/A_0$    tensile or compressive stress

$t = F/A_0$    shear stress

The unit is the Megapascal = $10^+$ Newtons/m$^2$.

There is a change in dimensions, or deformation elongation, D$L$ as a result of a tensile or compressive stress. To enable comparison with specimens of different length, the elongation is also normalized, this time to the length $L$. This is called strain, $e$.

$$e = DL/L$$

The change in dimensions is the reason we use $A_0$ to indicate the initial area since it changes during deformation. One could divide force by the actual area, this is called true stress.

For torsional or shearstress, the deformation is the angle of twist, $q$ and the shear strain is given by:

$$g = \tan q$$

## 2.3 Stress—Strain Behavior

**Elastic Deformation.** When the stress is removed, the material returns to the dimension it had before the load was applied. Valid for small strains (except the case of rubbers).

Deformation is *reversible, non permanent*.

**Plastic Deformation.** When the stress is removed, the material does not return to its previous dimension but there is a *permanent*, irreversible deformation.

In tensile tests, if the deformation is *elastic*, the stress-strain relationship is

called Hooke's law:
$$s = Ee$$
That is, $E$ is the slope of the stress-strain curve. $E$ is *Young's Modulus* or *Modulus of Elasticity*. In some cases, the relationship is not linear so that $E$ can be defined alternatively as the local slope:
$$E = ds/de$$
Shear stresses produce strains according to:
$$t = Gg$$
where $G$ is the *shear modulus*.

Elastic moduli measure the *stiffness* of the material. They are related to the second derivative of the interatomic potential, or the first derivative of the force vs. internuclear distance. By examining these curves we can tell which material has a higher modulus. Due to thermal vibrations the elastic modulus decreases with temperature. $E$ is large for ceramics (stronger ionic bond) and small for polymers (weak covalent bond). Since the interatomic distances depend on direction in the crystal, $E$ depends on direction (i. e., it is anisotropic) for single crystals. For *randomly* oriented polycrystal, $E$ is isotropic.

### 2.4 Anelasticity

Here the behavior is elastic but not the stress-strain curve, it is not immediately reversible. It takes a while for the strain to return to zero. The effect is normally small for metals but can be significant for polymers.

### 2.5 Elastic Properties of Materials

Materials subject to tension shrink laterally. Those subject to compression, bulge. The ratio of lateral and axial strains is called the *Poisson's Ratio* ($n$).
$$n = e_{lateral}/e_{axial}$$
The elastic modulus, shear modulus and Poisson's ratio are related by $E = 2G(1+n)$.

### 2.6 Tensile Properties

**Yield Point.** If the stress is too large, the strain deviates from being proportional to the stress. The point at which this happens is the *yield point* because there the material yields, deforming permanently (plastically).

**Yield Stress.** Hooke's law is not valid beyond the yield point. The stress at the yield point is called *yield stress*, and is an important measure of the mechanical properties of materials. In practice, the yield stress is chosen as that causing a permanent strain of 0.002. *The yield stress measures the resistance to plastic deformation.*

The reason for plastic deformation, in normal materials, is not that the atomic bond is stretched beyond repair, but the motion of dislocations, which involves breaking and reforming bonds.

*Plastic deformation is caused by the motion of dislocations.*

**Tensile Strength.** When stress continues in the plastic regime, the stress-strain passes through a maximum, called the *tensile strength* ($S_{TS}$), and then falls as the material starts to develop a *neck* and it finally breaks at the *fracture point*.

Note that it is called strength, not stress, but the units are the same, MPa. *For structural applications, the yield stress is usually a more important property than the tensile strength, since once it is passed, the structure has deformed beyond acceptable limits.*

**Ductility.** The ability to deform before braking. It is the opposite of brittleness. Ductility can be given either as percent maximum elongation $e_{max}$ or maximum area reduction.

$$\%EL = e_{max} \times 100\%$$
$$\%AR = (A_0 - A_f)/A_0$$

These are measured after fracture (repositioning the two pieces back together).

**Resilience.** Capacity to absorb energy *elastically*. The energy per unit volume is the *area under the strain-stress curve in the elastic region*.

**Toughness.** Ability to absorb energy up to fracture. The energy per unit volume is the *total area under the strain-stress curve*. It is measured by an impact test.

## 2.7 True Stress and Strain

When one applies a constant tensile force, the material will break after reaching the tensile strength. The material starts necking (the transverse area decreases) but the stress cannot increase beyond $S_{TS}$. The ratio of the force to the initial area, what we normally do, is called the engineering stress. If the ratio is to the actual area (that changes with stress) one obtains the *true stress*.

## 2.8 Elastic Recovery during Plastic Deformation

If a material is taken beyond the yield point (it is deformed plastically) and the stress is then released, the material ends up with a permanent strain. If the stress is reapplied, the material again responds elastically at the beginning up to a new yield point that is higher than the original yield point (strain hardening). The amount of elastic strain that it will take before reaching the yield point is called *elastic strain recover*.

## 2.9 Compressive, Shear, and Torsional Deformation

Compressive and shear stresses give similar behavior to tensile stresses, but in the case of compressive stresses there is no maximum in the s-e curve, since no necking occurs.

## 2.10 Hardness

Hardness is the resistance to plastic deformation (e. g. , a local dent or scratch). Thus, it is a measure of plastic deformation, as is the tensile strength, so they are well correlated. Historically, it was measured on an empirically scale, determined by the ability of a material to scratch another, diamond being the hardest and talc the softer. Now we use standard tests, where a ball or point is pressed into a material and the size of the dent is measured. There are a few different hardness tests: Rockwell, Brinell, Vickers, etc. They are popular because they are easy and non-destructive (except for the small dent).

## 2.11 Variability of Material Properties

Tests do not produce exactly the same result because of variations in the test equipment, procedures, operator bias, specimen fabrication, etc. But, even if all those parameters are controlled within strict limits, a variation remains in the materials, due to uncontrolled variations during fabrication, non homogenous composition and structure, etc. The measured mechanical properties will show scatter, which is often distributed in a Gaussian curve (bell-shaped), that is characterized by the mean value and the standard deviation (width).

## 2.12 Design/Safety Factors

To take into account variability of properties, designers use, instead of an average value of, say, the tensile strength, the probability that the yield strength is above the minimum value tolerable. This leads to the use of a *safety factor* $N>1$. Thus, a working value for the tensile strength would be $S_W = S_{TS}/N$.

## Vacabulary

alloy [ˈælɔi, əˈlɔi]　n. 合金　v. 熔合(结)
alloying elements　合金元素
nickel [ˈnikəl]　n. 镍;镍币;五分镍币 vt. 镀镍于
chromium [ˈkrəumjəm]　n. [化学]铬(金属元素,原子序号24,符号 Cr)
manganese [ˈmæŋgə,niːs; ˌmæŋgəˈniːz]　n. [化学]锰(金属元素,原子序号25,符号 Mn)
molybdenum [məˈlibdinəm]　n. [化学]钼(金属元素,原子序号42,符号 Mo)
characteristic [ˌkærəktəˈristik]　adj. 特有的,有特色　n. 特性,性能
response [riˈspɔns]　n. 响(反)应(曲线);特性曲线
essential [iˈsenʃəl]　adj. 本质的;重要的　n. 本质;实质

construct [kənˈstrʌkt]　vt. 构造(制,筑)
conduct [kənˈdʌkt]　v. 进行;实施
specimen [ˈspesimin, -əmən]　n. 试样(件)
tension　n. 张(拉,应)力
compression [kəmˈpreʃən]　n. 压缩,压力
shear [ʃiə]　v. 剪(切,断)　n. 剪(切)力
bending [ˈbendiŋ]　n. 弯曲(度);挠曲(度)
stiffness [ˈstifnis]　n. 刚性(度),劲性(度)
tungsten [ˈtʌŋstən]　n. [化学]钨(金属元素,原子序号74,符号 W)
vanadium [vəˈneidiəm]　n. [化学]钒(金属元素,原子序号23,符号 V)
low carbon steel　低碳钢
high speed steel　高速钢
self-hardening steel　自硬钢;风钢
high carbon steel　高碳钢
difficult [ˈdifikəlt]　adj. 困(艰)难的

## Notes

[1] high speed steel also known as self hardening steel 是一短语,并非句子;known as ……是一过去分词短语,作 high-speed steel 的后置定语。本句可译为:也叫做风钢(自硬钢)的高速钢。

[2] The more carbon the steel contains and the quicker the cooling is, the harder it becomes. 这是一种比较级的特殊用法,它属于"the＋比较级……(主句)"句式。第一部分是比较状语从句,这里并列两个比较状语从名句 the more carbon the

steel contains 和 the quicker the cooling is，其意思是"钢含碳越多……"和"冷却越快……"，而主句中 the harder it becomes 的意思是"钢就变得越硬"。词序发生改变，主句中谓语放在主语前面，进行强调。总的意义是"越……，就越……"。

**Exercises**

1. Give an explanation of the following terms:

    anelasticity        ductility              elastic deformation
    elastic recovery    engineering strain     engineering stress
    hardness            modulus of elasticity  plastic deformation
    poisson's ratio     proportional limit     shear
    tensile strength    toughness              yield strength

2. List the mechanical properties of metallic material.
3. What is the difference between carbon steels and alloy steels?

# Lesson 3   Hot working

## 1  An Introduction to Heat Treatment

Conditioning of steel by thermal or heat treatment relies on the different mechanical properties which are exhibited by the various structures present in plain carbon steels. Fig. 3.1 illustrates the equilibrium structures present at different temperatures with changing carbon content for the iron-carbon system. Fig. 3.2 demonstrates the effect of chill rate upon final structure, and is called a time-temperature-transformation or TTT diagram. Essentially, when cooling from the melt or high temperature phases, there is an incubation period below the equilibrium melting point or transformation temperature (723℃ in the case of the steel shown) before the transformation occurs. This undercooling provides the driving force for the transformation. During a furnace cool (i.e., slow cooling rate) the austenite will start to transform to ferrite and cementite after sufficient undercooling, resulting in a microstructure of coarse pearlite. With a high cooling rate such as that experienced with a water quench, it is possible to miss the "nose" of the TTT curve altogether. Martensite is produced starting at about 220℃ for the composition shown. The finish temperature of the martensite reaction for certain alloys can be below room temperature, so that at room temperature some unstable austenite is present.

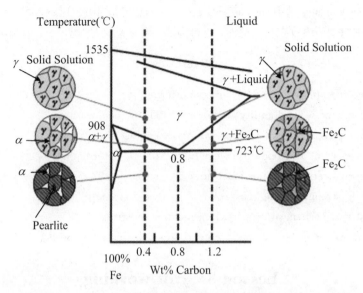

Fig. 3.1  Part of the equilibrium phase diagram for the Fe-C system

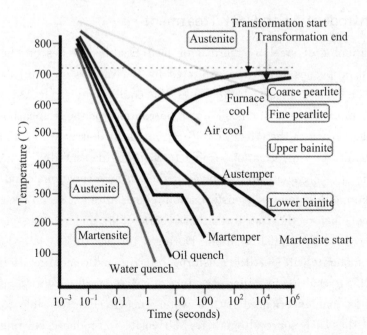

Fig. 3.2  The TTT diagram for AISI 1080 steel (0.79%C, 0.76% Mn) austenitised at 900℃

The design of steels and cooling conditions to produce required amounts of martensite has its own branch of technology, "hardenability". In plain carbon steels, the nose of the TTT curve occurs at very short times, hence fast cooling rates are required to produce martensite. In thin sections of steel, a rapid quench can produce distortion and cracking. In thick plain carbon steels, it is not possible to produce an all martensitic structure. All common alloying elements shift the nose of the TTT diagram to longer times, thus allowing the development of martensite in thick sections at slower cooling rates.

## 2  Heat Treatment Method of Metals

We can alter the characteristics of steel in various ways. In the first place, steel which contains very little carbon will be milder than steel which contains a higher percentage of carbon, up to the limit of about 1.5%. Secondly, we can heat the steel above a certain critical temperature, and then allow it to cool at different rates. At this critical temperature, changes begin to take place in the molecular structure of the metal. In the process known as annealing,[1] we heat the steel above the critical temperature and permit it to cool very slowly. This causes the metal to become softer than before, and much easier to machine. Annealing has a second advantage, it helps to relieve any internal stresses which exist in the metal. These stresses are liable to occur through hammering or working the metal, or through rapid cooling. Metal which we cause to cool rapidly contracts more rapidly on the outside than on the inside. This produces unequal contraction, which may give rise to distortion or cracking. Metal that cools slowly is less liable to have these internal stresses than metal which cools quickly.

On the other hand, we can make steel harder by rapid cooling. We heat it up beyond the critical temperature, and then quench it in water or some other liquid. The rapid temperature drop fixes the structural change in which occurred at the critical temperature, and makes it very hard. But a bar of this hardened steel is more liable to fracture than normal steel. We therefore heat it again to a temperature below the critical temperature, and cool it slowly. This treatment is called tempering. It helps to relieve the internal stresses, and makes the steel less brittle than before. The properties of tempered steel enable us to use it in the manufacture of tools which need fairly hard steel. High carbon steel is harder than tempered steel, but it is much more difficult to work[2].

These heat treatments take place during the various shaping operations. We can obtain bars and sheets of steel by rolling the metal through huge rolls in a rolling mill. The roll pressures must be much greater for cold rolling than for hot rolling, but cold rolling enables the operators to produce rolls of great accuracy and uniformity and with a better surface finish[3]. Other shaping operations include drawing into wire, casting in moulds and forging.

The mechanical working of metal is the shaping of metal in either a cold or a hot state by some mechanical means[4]. This does not include the shaping of metals by machining or grinding, in which processes metal is actually machined off, nor does it include the casting of molten metal into some form by use of molds[5]. In mechanical working processes, the metal is shaped by pressure actually forging, bending, squeezing, drawing, or shearing it to its final shape. In these processes the metal may be either cold or hot worked. Although normal room temperatures are ordinarily used for cold working of steel, temperatures up to the recrystallization range are sometimes used. Hot working of metals takes place above the recrystallization or work hardening range[6]. For steel, recrystallization starts around from 650℃ to 700℃, although most hot work on steel is done at temperatures considerably above this range. There is no tendency for hardening by mechanical work until the lower limit of the recrystalline range is reached. Some metals, such as lead and tin, have a low recrystalline range and can be hot-worked at room temperature, but most commercial metal require some heating. Alloy composition has a great influence upon the proper working range, the usual result being to raise the recrystalline range temperature. This range may also be increased by prior cold working.

## Vacabulary

molecular [məu'lekjulə]　adj. 分子的
annealing [əni:liŋ]　n. (低温)退火，焖火
relieve [ri'li:v]　v. 解除；消除
stress [stres]　n. 应力；受力(状态)
liable ['laiəbl]　adj. 易于……的，可能的
contract ['kɔntrækt, kən'trækt]　v. 收缩；缩紧

rise ['rais]　v. 上[提]升
give to　导致；产生
shaping ['ʃeipiŋ]　n. 成形；造型
mechanical means　机械设备(工具)
grinding ['graindiŋ]　n. 磨削加工
machined off　切离(金属切屑)
bend [bend]　v. 弯曲

| | |
|---|---|
| bending    n. 弯曲(度);扭曲(度) | rolls [rəul]    n. 薄板卷;泛指钢材 |
| squeeze [skwi:z]    v. 挤(压,干)压榨(缩) | draw [drɔ:]    v. 拉;拔(出) |
| prior ['praiə]    adj. 在先的;居先的 | drawing    n. 拉;冲压成形 |
| distortion [dis'tɔ:ʃən]    n. 变形;挠曲 | shear [ʃiə]    v. 剪(切);切(断) n. 剪切 |
| quench [kwentʃ]    v. & n. 把……淬火;淬硬 | recrystallization [ri:ˌkristəlai'zeiʃən] n. 重(再)结晶(作用) |
| fix ['fiks]    v. & n. (使)固定;确定 | hardening ['hɑ:dəniŋ]    n. 硬化;淬火 |
| tempering ['tempəriŋ]    n. 回火;回韧 | crystalline ['kristəlain]    adj. 结晶(质)的 n. 结晶体(质) |
| brittle ['britl]    adj. 脆(性)的;易碎的 | |

## Notes

[1] known as … 当"称做"、"叫做"讲,在这里作定语,说明其前的名词 process。

[2] High carbon steel is harder than tempered steel, but it is much more difficult to work. 句中 it 是代词,指代前面的 high carbon steel,不定式 to work 是形容词 difficult 的宾语。全句可译:高碳钢比回火钢硬,可是加工则困难得多。

[3] 介词短语 with a better surface finish 和句中另一个介词短语 of great accuracy and uniformity 是并列关系,两者都作 rolls 的定语。

[4]  The mechanical working of metal is … by some mechanical means 中,the mechanical working 指的是金属"制作加工",包括"冷作"和"热作";加工在内。而 some mechanical means 是进行冷作或热作加工的"某些机械工具或设备"。这一句是"主-系-表"结构,其中主语是动名词 working,而表语也是动名词 shaping。因此本句可译为:金属的机械加工是借助某些机械工具对冷的或热状态的金属进行成形加工。

[5] This does not … by use of molds 中,machining 是指切削加工,grinding 是磨削加工,而 … is machined off 是指从金属零件上"切离金属屑加工"。在这个长句 This does not …, not does it … 中,nor 是连词,表示"也不"或者是"而且……也不"的意思。故本句可译成:这既没有包括……也没有包括……

[6] Hot working of metals takes place … range 中,Hot working of metals 是指热作加工金属,而 takes place 在此译作"进行"、"开展"。work hardening 原意是"加工硬化"、"冷作加工",在此,从全句来看 work hardening 指的是"淬火温度区",而不是"冷作加工温度范围"。

## Exercises

1. Give an explanation of the following terms:

austenite　　pearlite　　martensite
hardenability　ferrite　　cementite
2. List the heat treatment method of metals.
3. What is the difference between annealing and tempering?

# Lesson 4　Forming Processes

## 1 Introduction

Forming processes involve shaping materials which are solid. As mentioned before, a simple example is moulding with plasticene. However, metals can be moulded using forming processes as well, as long as their yield stress is not too high and enough force is used. One way to lower a metal's yield stress is to heat it up. So we can shape metals without melting them; think of the blacksmith working on a horseshoe, heated, but still solid.

However, we have identified a key quandary in forming that actually applies to materials processing in general. The properties you want from a material during processing often conflict with the material properties you require for the product in service. If you have decided that the best route to make something is to squeeze it into shape, then the properties that are required to make the product will clearly be different from the properties required when in use. For easy forming, a material needs to be soft, with a low flow (or yield) stress. These are not properties that are generally attractive or useful in finished products. More often, high strength is required; so some way must be found to make the forming of such products easier — often through the use of high temperatures.

## 2 Properties for processing-forming

Forming processes involve applying forces to the material being shaped. A good way of telling how a given material responds to applied force is to look at diagrams representing its stress-strain behaviour. Fig. 4.1 shows the stress-strain curves, at room temperature, for two different metals. The two important things for the feasibility of squeezing-type processes are the point at which the solid starts to flow and the extent to which it can be persuaded to flow before it separates (i.e., fails). This is described by two properties, yield stress (or flow stress) and ductility. Remember that the yield stress is a good measure of the strength of a ductile material.

If you look at the curves, you can see that the one for the steel (curve A), after the elastic region, shows plastic deformation up to a strain of about 40 percent. This provides a measure of the ductility of the steel, and the extent to which it can be squeezed, stretched or bent at this temperature. Curve B (for lead) shows much higher ductility and a much lower yield stress.

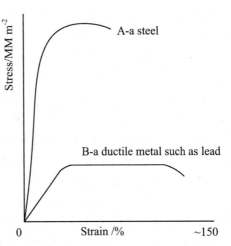

Fig.4.1  Schematic stress-strain curves

However, 40 percent is not a lot of strain for many manufacturing purposes. Being able to change a material's dimensions by only 40 percent would mean that forming would be virtually a waste of time. In addition, once the steel has been strained plastically, it has also increased in yield stress and become harder (Fig. 4.2).

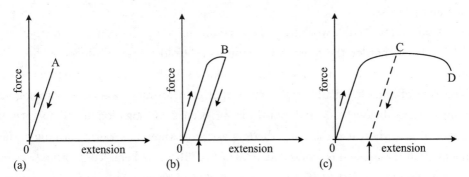

Fig.4.2  The effect of progressively straining a material

The steel can be loaded elastically up to its yield strength, point A in Fig. 4.2. Removing the load below this level leaves no permanent extension, i.e., the steel can return to its original size and shape. If the material is taken above its yield strength, say to point B, then even after unloading, the steel is permanently deformed. What's more, when the material is then reloaded, it has to be loaded to a stress equal to point B — i.e., more than its original yield point at A — before it continues to flow. This is called work hardening: the plastic deformation causes an increase in strength (and hardness). But further plasticity is then limited. If the material is loaded to point C, where about half the available plasticity has been "used up", then on reloading only the remaining plasticity from C to D is available before the material breaks.

However, all is not lost. The work hardening effect can be eliminated, and the original, softer, condition restored, by annealing the metal. This involves heating to a temperature where the atoms in the material become more mobile, so that the material softens. This type of process is widely applied in manufacturing whenever a part-formed product has been worked so much that it is in danger of cracking; and is why blacksmiths keep reheating a horseshoe during working. The precise mechanism of softening varies from material to material, but it occurs for most materials at a high homologous temperature. Homologous temperature, $T_h$, is the ratio of the operating temperature of a material to its melting point (in kelvins, K).

In the context of forming, if a metal is "hot worked", it is deformed at a temperature where there is virtually no work hardening, and this resoftening effect carries on continuously. Very high strains can be imposed during the forming process.

Conversely "cold working" does result in work hardening, so that the material gets harder the more it is deformed. "Cold working" does not literally mean cold, though — it is all measured relative to the homologous temperature. The rule of thumb usually employed is that cold forming occurs at homologous temperatures below 0.3 and hot forming occurs at homologous temperatures above 0.6. In between the two, there is a region known as warm forming. This means that if tungsten is worked at 1000℃ (1273K) it is being cold formed, as its melting point is 3410℃ (3683K). Conversely, at room temperature, solder can be hot worked! So working temperature is all about being able to deform the metal without failure.

# 3 Forming Casting

As the stresses needed to make solids flow are considerably higher than those required for liquids, forming processes normally require a lot of energy and strong, resilient tooling. This means high expenditure on capital equipment as well as tooling and energy. As a result, forming is often economically viable only for production volumes large enough to justify the high tooling costs.

So when do we use forming rather than casting? There are three reasons why, for many products, forming is preferable to casting.

**Geometry.** Products with one dimension significantly different in size from the others are most suitable for forming processes — "long" products such as rails or "thin" products such as car-body panels are usually made by a forming process. Imagine trying to cast a 50 metre length of pipe; large forces would be needed to squeeze the metal down into the mould, and it might be difficult to keep the metal liquid for long enough. There would also be a lot of scrap to discard.

**Microstructure.** As noted earlier, the microstructure of the material has a direct bearing on the properties of the final product. Controlling the microstructure is easier during forming than during casting. Also, the type of microstructures produced by forming are inherently stronger than those produced by casting, as the products of forming do not contain the dendritic structure and porosity inherent to castings. We will return to this point later.

Some materials are difficult to process as liquids, e. g. , they may have high melting points, or react with the atmosphere.

## 4 Forming Processes

Forming processes are used to convert cast ingots into basic product forms such as sheets, rods and plates, as was noted in the previous section. However, here we will concentrate on forming processes that produce end products or components. There are some basic shapes that lend themselves to manufacture by forming. Forming processes are particularly good at manufacturing "linear" objects, that is, long thin ones, where the product has a constant cross section. Forming processes involve moving the material through an opening with the desired shape. These processes are used for making components such as fibres, wires, tubes and products such as curtain rails. The plastic ink tube in your ballpoint pen was almost certainly produced by this method.

## 5 Extrusion

The principle of this process is very similar to squeezing toothpaste from a tube. Material is forced through a shaped hollow die in such a way that it is plastically deformed and takes up the shape of the die. [1] The hole in the die can have almost any shape, so if the die is circular, for example, a wire or rod is produced (Fig. 4.3).

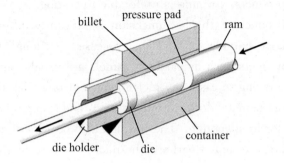

Fig.4.3  Metal extrusion

It is also possible to produce hollow sections using extrusion. In this case, the die contains a short piece (or mandrel) in the shape of the hole. This mandrel is attached to the die by one or more "bridges". As the extruded material encounters the bridges it is forced to separate, but it flows around the bridges and joins up again, much the same as water flowing around the piers of a bridge. Fig. 4.4 shows such a "bridge die". Note that in the picture the die has been split to show the material passing through it. In reality, the die and the ring fit together, with a gap for the extruded material to flow through. This works successfully even for processing of solid metals.

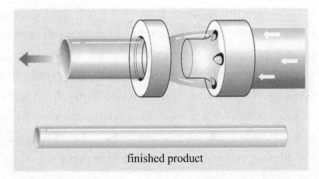

Fig.4.4  Extrusion bridge die making a hollow section product

Extrusion can be used on most materials that can plastically flow as a solid, and solid metals and alloys are frequently extruded. To reduce the stresses required, and therefore the size and cost of the extrusion machine, and also to ensure hot working conditions, a metal is usually extruded at a high homologous temperature, usually between 0.65 and 0.9. This allows large changes in the shape of the material and hence large strains without fracture. During metal extrusion the raw material in the form of a metal ingot, known as the billet, is heated and pushed through the die by a simple sliding piston or ram.

The mechanism for extruding thermoplastics is illustrated in Fig. 4.5. In this case a rotating screw is used to transfer the raw material in the form of granules through a heated cylinder to the die, just like in the case of injection moulding for polymers. The thermoplastic granules are compressed and mixed by the screw (the granules may contain a second constituent such as colouring). The material softens and melts as the temperature rises due to heating through the walls of the cylinder, and also from the heat generated within the thermoplastic as it is sheared by the screw. The thermoplastic flows through the die and emerges with a constant cross section in the shape of the die aperture. An almost infinite variety of cross-sectional shapes can be produced.

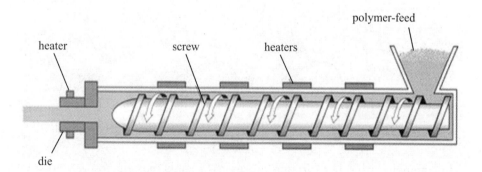

Fig.4.5  Thermoplastics extrusion

## 6  Rolling

In rolling (Fig. 4.6), material is passed through the gap between two rotating rollers that squeeze the material as it passes between them. The rolled material emerges with a thickness roughly equal to the gap between the rollers.

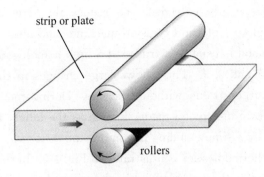

Fig.4.6  Rolling

When the rollers are cylindrical, rolling produces material in the form of plate or sheet. Sheet steel and aluminium for the bodies of cars and domestic appliances is made this way. Rolled sheet is often termed a "semifinished" product, as it requires further processing to shape it into the final product.

Rolling is not restricted to flat sheets, though. If the desired product has a contoured surface, then by using profiled rollers the contour can be rolled on. If the surface pattern needs to be deeper than is possible during one rolling pass then multiple rollers can be used; for example, railway tracks are made by rolling between pairs of progressively deeper contoured rollers. The various stages for rails are shown in Fig. 4.7.

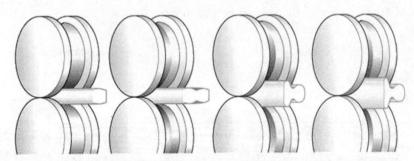

Fig.4.7  **Stages in rolling railway track**

In common with other forming processes, metals may be hot or cold rolled. The significant differences between hot and cold rolling are in the amount of energy needed to roll a given volume of material and in the resulting microstructures. The cooler the metal, the higher its yield stress and the more energy has to be supplied in order to shape it. As in extrusion, metals in large lumps are often hot rolled at homologous temperatures above 0.6. At this temperature the yield stress and work hardening are reduced. Railway lines require hot rolling in order to achieve the large change in shape from a rectangular bar. However, a major disadvantage of hot rolling is that the surface of the material becomes oxidised by the air, resulting in a poor surface finish.

If the metal is ductile then it may be cold rolled using smaller strains. This has some advantages: the work hardening at these temperatures can give the product a useful increase in strength. During cold rolling, oxidation is reduced and a good surface finish can be produced by using polished rollers. So, cold rolling is a good finishing treatment in the production of plate and sheet. The sheets of steel for car bodies are finished by cold rolling because a good surface finish is essential in this product.

## 7  Metal Forging

Forging is typified by countless generations of blacksmiths with their hammers and anvils. Besides still being used for special "hand-made" items, this type of forging is similar to that used, on a somewhat larger scale, for the initial rough shaping of hot metal ingots. Forging is particularly good at making 3D solid shapes. The basic types of forging processes are shown in Fig. 4. 8.

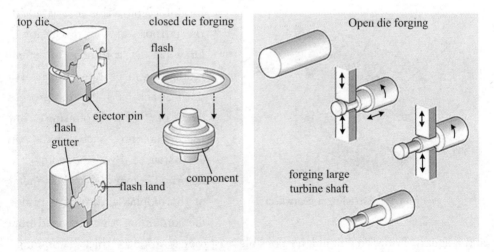

Fig. 4. 8  Forging processes

For example, the first stage in making a large roller or shaft would be to forge a large billet as sketched in Fig. 4. 8. The process consists of a large succession of bites between a pair of dies in an hydraulic press, with the ingot moved between each bite. As the ingot is moved through the dies it is reduced to a more manageable size before final shaping — this process is known as open die forging.

In closed die forging components are made in one action, being squeezed between upper and lower shaped dies as shown in Fig. 4.8. There is usually a small amount of excess material which is forced out of the die cavity as flash. This must then be removed from the component. The force needed to close the dies together is dependent both on the size of the component and the temperature, since as we noted earlier, the flow stress reduces as the forging temperature increases. The quality of the surface finish of the forging decreases with temperature, however, because of increased surface oxidation.

## 8  Forming Our Gearwheel

We have just seen that simple 2D "linear" objects can be produced by rolling, drawing or extrusion. So could our gearwheel be made using these techniques?

Because the gearwheel has a constant section it is geometrically feasible (actually the section is not quite constant because it is countersunk on one side, but let's ignore this fine detail for the purpose of this discussion). Drawing is confined to small reductions in cross-sectional area during each pass, so this process does not look promising, but there is no such limit on extrusion. By extruding a deformable material such as metal or thermoplastic through a bridge die containing a gear-shaped hole and a square bridge it should be possible to produce a very "thick" (or long, depending on how you want to describe it!) gearwheel (see Fig. 4.9). [2] This can then be cut up into identical gearwheels of the required thickness, so this might be a possibility.

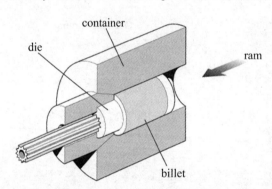

Fig.4.9  **Extruding a gearwheel**

Would rolling be an alternative manufacturing process? It would be difficult to roll the gear teeth profile, but you could use rolled steel sheet as a starting material. You could then punch out a gear-shaped blank using sheet metal forming (Fig. 4.10). This would be expensive, but is possible.

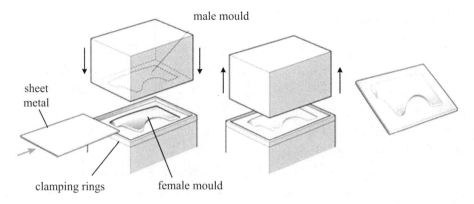

Fig. 4.10  Sheet metal forming of a car body panel

However, both extrusion and the sheet-metal route would produce flow lines not suitable for an engineering gear, as described in failure of replacement gears.

So let's go back to our gearwheel again and decide whether a gearwheel can be made by forging. The answer is yes, but only partly. Some other processing would be needed either before or after the forging process.

One approach is to start with steel bar (itself produced by rolling between contoured rolls). The bar contains longitudinal flow lines in its microstructure, produced from the rolling operation. This bar is forged into a circular, gear-sized, disc by compressing the bar parallel to its length (Fig. 4.11).

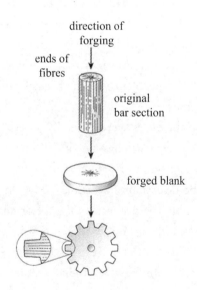

Fig. 4.11  Forging a gear

The forging "folds over" the longitudinal flow lines into the radial direction. So in this case, all the gear teeth have the optimum orientation of flow lines and the final product is stronger than that made from rolling. Failure of replacement gears describes why the microstructure of gears can be of critical important to their performance.

## 9  Failure of Replacement Gears

A heavy commercial vehicle company announced that it would no longer supply spare parts for one of its vehicles. This was a problem for customers, as the two largest gears in the gearbox tended to wear faster than the others and it became impossible to replace them even when the other parts still had a great deal of useful life. A specialist firm set out to manufacture spare parts and soon had orders for dozens of sets of these two particular gears.

This firm had measured the gears and manufactured new ones of identical dimensions, using one of the strongest steels available. It machined the gears and sent them out for heat treatment as, in addition to hardening and tempering the whole gear, the teeth had to be surface hardened to match the hardness of the originals.

All seemed to be well until a pair of gears was returned, having failed by teeth breaking off in just over three weeks' service. The failure was assumed to be due to poor driving. So another pair was put in the gearbox, but a similar failure occurred in less than one week.

The problem was then easily identified by comparing the new gears to the originals.

The gears were made of steel that started off as cast billets. In the as-cast state, the steel has no directionality to its microstructure, but as it is worked down to billet or bar, directionality appears as grains and inclusions are extended in the direction of working. The directionality is revealed as "flow lines" which resemble the grain in timber. For any given quality of steel, the strength is much better across the flow lines than in parallel with them.

Fig. 4. 12 is a view of the gear showing the inner upper ring of teeth which were breaking off. A radial section was cut from the original gear and a similar one from an unused new gear. These were polished and the flow lines revealed by etching. An unused gear (on the right) showing the ring of teeth which were breaking off — the smaller teeth at the top of the gear. The gear on the left was a used gear where the teeth have been worn away. Fig. 4. 13 shows the old gear at the left and the new gear at the right. The teeth which were breaking off were the small ones which are at the top in the sections of Fig. 4. 12. In the old gear they are worn down, which is why the gears needed replacing. The unused new gear shows the teeth in side profile. The section has been cut so as to include the full section of the large teeth around the outside.

Fig. 4.12   View of the gear showing the inner upper ring of teeth which were breaking off

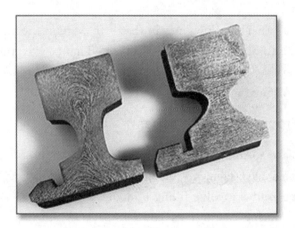

Fig. 4.13   Sections etched to reveal flow lines: (left) original gear, inner teeth worn now; (right) new gear, inner teeth full profile. The teeth are on the bottom left of the cross-sections-compare the sections to the cuts in Fig. 4.12

What difference is there in the flow lines in these two sections?

In the new gear they all run parallel to the axis, and if this were made of wood you would expect them to break off easily. In the old gear the flow lines are in a looped, radial pattern tending to run at right angles to the gear's axis. If you look carefully at the small teeth you will see that they run pretty well at right angles to the direction of the flow lines in the new gear.

The original gears had been forged before the teeth were cut, whereas the replacements had been machined directly from round bar. The flow lines tell us that the old gears had started off as a length of round bar about twice as long as the gear is thick, but of smaller diameter. This was hot forged to squash it down, causing the outside to spread out so that the shape finished up with a much larger diameter and shorter length than when it started. This was done specifically to develop the flow line pattern you can observe. When the teeth were cut, the grain flow was oriented at right angles to the applied bending stresses in service. The teeth were thus as tough as they could be for this type of steel and the flow lines were oriented in directions which imparted the maximum resistance to failure.

In contrast, the new gears had been machined from stock of the full diameter the gear required. There was no forging, so the flow lines remained parallel to the gear axis.

The result was that the flow lines in the teeth were in the most unfavourable orientation to resist fatigue and brittle fracture. This is why they broke off so quickly under service loads, despite having the same hardness (and tensile strength) as the original gears.

## 10　Powder Processing Techniques

Before we leave forming we should consider powder processing techniques, (Fig. 4.14), which have elements of both casting and forming. Essentially all powder processing routes involve filling a mould with powder (this is similar to filling the mould during casting, as powders flow as slurries), which is then compressed in between dies to begin the process of reducing the space between the powder particles. The powder compact produced is then heated to a high temperature to produce a solid component.

The process of sintering starts with the material in powder form and is used for a wide variety of materials, especially those with properties which preclude shaping by melting and casting. Examples are ceramics such as alumina and silicon nitride; brittle metals with high melting temperatures (over 2300K), such as tungsten; and the polymer PTFE (Poly tetrafluoro ethylene), which has a viscosity too high to suit other moulding methods.

The starting powder is mixed with a lubricant/binder and is then moulded to shape by compressing it in a die to form what is called a "green" compact.

Although this is highly porous, it has enough rigidity to support its own weight and permit gentle handling. The compact is then sintered — that is, heated at a high temperature and sometimes under pressure for a prolonged time. During sintering, the powder particles coalesce (small particles join together to form larger ones) and grow to fill the pore spaces. The compact shrinks correspondingly, forming a solid homogeneous (uniform) mass in the shape of the original mould. Depending on the sintering process used, the final component can have various degrees of porosity and therefore strength, as any porosity can act as defects in the form of cracks. Very high temperatures and/or pressures during sintering are used to minimise porosity.

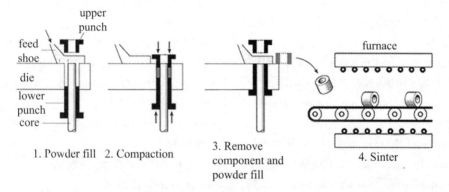

Fig. 4.14 Powder processing

In powder processing, the volume of the workpiece does not stay constant. As the powder fuses together, most of the spaces between the powder disappear and the volume of the finished component is considerably reduced.

Sintering is sometimes economically competitive with alternative methods of shaping; for volume production of complex parts it is often cheaper than machining. A wide variety of components can be manufactured using powder processing: these can range from processing domestic ceramics for applications such as bathroom sinks to the insulating sleeve in a spark plug.

So can we consider production of the gearwheel using powder processing? As you have seen powders of many materials can be used for this process and this includes metals. This would appear to be an attractive idea because the wheel can be made in one piece, with little or no waste of material and with a modest expenditure of energy and labour. The only major problem is the need for a shaped punch and die. This is expensive, but if the price of the punch and die can be spread over a long production run, the cost of the product may be quite reasonable. So as well as extrusion and forging, which we identified earlier, we can add powder processing to our list of candidate processes to make our gearwheel.

## Vacabulary

squeezing [skwiːziŋ]　adj. 挤压的；压榨的　n. 压榨；推挤
schematic [skiːˈmætik]　n. 原理图；图解视图　adj. 图解的；概要的
ductility [dʌkˈtiləti]　n. 延展性；柔软性；顺从
homologous [həˈmɒləgəs]　adj. 相应的；[生物] 同源的；类似的；一致的
resilient [riˈziliənt, -jənt]　adj. 弹回的，有弹力的
extrusion [ekˈstruːʒən]　n. 挤出；挤压
mandrel [ˈmændrəl]　n. （圆形）心轴；轴柄
thermoplastics [ˌθɜːməˈplæstiks]　n. 热塑性塑料（thermoplastic 的复数）
rolling [ˈrəuliŋ]　n. 压延加工；轧制
forging [ˈfɔːdʒiŋ]　n. 锻造；锻件；伪造　v. 锻造；打制（forge 的现在分词）

gearwheel [ˈgiəhwiːl]　n. 齿轮；大齿轮
slurries　n. 泥浆（slurry 的复数）；料浆；釉浆　v. 使成浆（slurry 的三单形式）
polymer [ˈpɒlimə]　n. [高分子] 聚合物
PTFE　abbr. 聚四氟乙烯（Polytetrafluoroethylene [ˈpɒli, tetrə-, fluərəuˈeθiliːn]）
plasticene [ˈplæstisiːn]　n. 橡皮泥
yield stress　屈服应力
dendritic [denˈdritik, -kəl]　adj. 树枝状的；树状的
fibre [ˈfaibə]　n. 纤维；纤维制品
carbon fibre　碳纤维
glass fibre　玻璃纤维
chemical fibre　化学纤维
powder processing　[材料学] 粉末加工，粉末处理

## Note

[1] Material is forced through a shaped hollow die in such a way that it is plastically deformed and takes up the shape of the die. 可译为：材料被压进一个具有一定形状的空心模具中，通过这么一种方式，材料发生塑性变形并呈现模具的形状。

[2]　By extruding a deformable material such as metal or thermoplastic through a bridge die containing a gear-shaped hole and a square bridge it should be possible to produce a very "thick" (or long, depending on how you want to describe it!) gearwheel (see Fig. 4.9). 可译为：将某变形材料（如金属或热塑性）挤压通过一个带有齿轮形状空腔的桥式拉模，就可以得到一个非常"厚"的齿轮（或者"长"的

齿轮,这取决于你想如何描述它!),如图 4.9 所示。

## Exercises

1. Why are car-body panels produced by forming and not casting? (Hint: think in terms of the shape of the final product and the form of the starting material.)

2. Could extrusion be used for the following products?

(1) The body of a food mixer

(2) Copper pipe for a central heating system

(3) The body of a pen.

3. Which of the processes (including both casting and forming) covered so far would be the most appropriate to manufacture the following products? Use the shape hierarchy for both casting and forming to help guide you through some of the options.

(1) A church bell.

(2) Aluminum foil for food use.

(3) A plastic beaker.

(4) The plastic body of a food mixer.

(5) Copper pipe for use in plumbing.

(6) A shaft for use in a car engine.

(*Hint*: the component is manufactured from solid steel. The shaft requires high strength for this application. Think about its shape-I would classify it as non-complex.)

# Unit 2  Machine Tools & Cutting Technology

## Lesson 5  Machine Tools

### 1 Introduction

Machine tools are heavy, power-driven machinery and equipment that perform specific actions on materials like metal and plastic. The most common jobs these machines are used for include material removal (turning, milling, drilling, grinding, water-jet or laser cutting); material forming (stamping, bending, joining); and "workholding" (chucks, fixtures, clamps, blocks). The majority of this equipment is technical in nature, with computer numerical control (CNC) or programmable logic control (PLC) built in.

The tooling and machining industry is critical to our country's economic health as it makes possible the existence of virtually every other manufacturing industry. Tooling is, basically, the means of production. Machining involves the use of a wide variety of machine tools to cut or form material, usually metal, to precise shapes and dimensions.

Machine tools can be considered to serve four main purpose:

(1) They hold the work or the part to be cut;

(2) They hold the cutting tool or tools;

(3) They impart to the cutting tool or work or both whatever motion is required for cutting or forming the part;

(4) They are arranged, ordinarily, for regulating the cutting speed and also the feeding movement between the tool and the work.

In the production of machine parts of various shapes and sizes, the type of machine and cutting tool used will depend upon the nature of the metal-cutting operation, the character of the work, and possibly, other factors such as the number of parts required and the degree of accuracy to which the part must be made.

Machine tools are built to produce certain shapes such as cylindrical surface, holes, plane surface, irregular contour, gear teeth, etc. Many machine, however, can produce a variety of surface. Thus, machine tools are built as general purpose machine, high production machines, and as special purpose machine.

As the name implies, general purpose of machine tools are designed to be quickly and easily adapted to a large variety of operations on many different kinds of parts. They are used extensively in jobbing shops, repair shops, and in tool and die shops.

High production machine are designed to perform an operation, or a sequence of operations, in a repetitive manner in order to achieve a rapid output of machined parts at minimum cost. They can be set up to machine a variety of different parts, however, thus operation is economical only when the quantity of parts to be machined is relatively large.

Special purpose machine tools are designed to perform one operation, or a sequence of operations repetitively on a specific part. These machines are usually automatic and are unarranged except when it is necessary to change and to adjust the cutting tools. They are used in mass-production shops such as are found in automotive industry.

## 2 Lathe

The lathe is one of the most useful and versatile machines in the workshop, and is capable of carrying out a wide variety of machining operations. The main components of the lathe are the headstock and tailstock at opposite ends of a bed, and a tool post between them which holds the cutting tool. The tool post stands on a cross slide which enables it to move sideward across the saddle or carriage as well as along it depending on the kind of job it is doing[1]. The ordinary centre lathe can accommodate only one tool at a time on the tool post, but a turret lathe is capable of holding five or more tools on the revolving turret. The lathe bed must be very solid to prevent the machine from bending or twisting under stress.

The headstock incorporates the driving and gear mechanism, and a spindle which holds the workpiece and causes it to rotate at a speed which depends largely on the diameter of the workpiece. A bar of large diameter should naturally rotate mere slowly than a very thin bar; the cutting speed of the tool is what matters[2].

(see Appendix of Lesson 30) Tapered centres in the hollow nose of the spindle and of the tail stock hold the work firmly between them [3]. A feed shaft from the headstock drives the tool post along the saddle, either forwards or backwards, at a fixed and uniform speed. This enables the operator to make accurate cuts and to give the work a good finish, gears between the spindle and the feed shaft control the speed of rotation of the shaft, and there for control the forward or backward movement of the tool post[4]. The gear which the operator will select depends on the type of metal which he is cutting and the amount of metal he has to cut off. For a deep or roughing cut the forward movement of the tool should be less than for a finishing cut.

Centres are not suitable for every job on the lathe. The operator can replace them by various types of chucks, which hold the work between jaws, or by a front plate, depending on the shape of the work and the particular cutting operation. He will use a chuck, for example, to hold a short piece of work or work for drilling, boring or screw cutting. A transverse movement of the tool post across the saddle enables the tool to cut across the face of the workpiece and give it a flat surface. For screw cutting, the operator engages the lead-screw, a long screwed shaft which runs a long in front of the bed and which rotates with the spindle. The lead-screw drives the tool post forwards along the carriage at the correct speed, and this ensures that the threads on the screw are of exactly the right pitch. The operator can select different gear speeds, and this will alter the ratio of spindle and lead-screw speeds and therefore will alter the pitch of the threads. A reversing lever on the headstock enables him to reverse the movement of the carriage and so bring the tool back to its original position.

## 3  Milling

The milling machine is a machine that removes metal from work with a revolving milling cutter as the work in fed against it.

The milling cutter is mounted on an arbor where it is held in place by spacers or bushing. The arbor is fixed in the spindle with one end, while the other end of the arbor rotates in the bearing mounted on the arbor yoke.

The most important parts of the milling machine are: ① starting levers; ② spindle; ③ column; ④ knee; ⑤ elevating screw; ⑥ table; ⑦ index head; ⑧ speed levers; ⑨ feed levers; ⑩ table movement levers; ⑪ foot stock;

⑫ arbor yoke.

The spindle of the milling machine is driven by an electric motor through a train of gears mounted in the column.

The table of the plain milling machine may travel only at right angles to the spindle while the Universal Milling Machine is provided with a table that may be swiveled on the transverse slide for milling gear teeth, threads, etc.

## 4  Shaper and Planer

The machine tools of this group are generally used for machining flat surfaces, which is usually performed by a cutter that peels the chip from the work. The main motion is reciprocating and the feed is normal (perpendicular) to the direction of the main motion.

The tool and the apron of a shaper are located on the ram. A chip is peeled off the work on the forward stroke. An adjustable table with "T"-slots holds work, vise, and other fixtures for holding the work.

The shaper has a rocker arm which drives the ram, and a mechanism for regulating the length of the stroke. The ram supports the tool head. The head carries the down feed mechanism and will swivel from side to side to permit the cutting of angles. This is generally a hand feed, but some shapers are required with a power down feed in addition to the regular hand downfeed.

The table of the shaper is of box form with "T"-slots on the top and sides for clamping the work. The cross rail is bolted directly to the frame or column of the shaper with bolts.

The automatic feed or power feed is obtained by a pawl which engages in a notched wheel or ratchet.

The main parts of the planer include the bed, the table that moves back and forth, the column, the crossrail which moves up and down on the column, and the tool heads that are fastened to the crossrail.

## 5  Grinding Machines

A grinding machine is a machine which employs a grinding wheel for producing cylindrical, conical or plane surfaces accurately and economically and to the proper shape, size, and finish. The surplus stock is removed by feeding the work against the revolving wheel or by forcing the revolving wheel against the work.

There is a great variety of grinding machines. The machines that are generally used are cutter grinder, surface grinder, centerless grinder, external grinder, internal grinder.

Principal parts of a Plain Grinding Machine:

(1) Base.

The main casting of a plain grinding machine is a base that rests on the floor.

(2) Tables.

A sliding table, which is mounted on ways at the front and top of the base, may be moved longitudinally by hand or power to feed workpieces past the face of the grinding wheel.

(3) Headstock and Tailstock.

A motor-driven headstock and a tailstock are mounted on the left and right ends, respectively, of the swivel table for holding workpieces on centers. The headstock center on a grinder is a dead center, which is both centers are "dead" to insure concentricity of the periphery of ground work with its axis.

(4) Wheel head.

A wheel head that carries a grinding wheel and its driving motor is mounted on a slide at the top and rear of the base. The wheel head may be moved perpendicularly to the table ways, by hand or power, to feed the wheel to the work.

## 6 Automatic Machine

Each machine tool discussed previously represents a basic cutting machine. Some particular cutting operation, such as turning, drilling, milling, or grinding, can be performed on each. They can be highly productive. Nevertheless each perform only a single function or at best a limited number of functions. Most parts require several different operations in their fabrication — one surface is rough machined, another superfinished, a hole drilled and a slot milled, all on the one part. Thus, the tool must be changed, the workpiece indexed and shifted from one machine to another. This results in much expenditure of labor and much nonproductive down-time.

One way of improving this situation is to design a machine tool on which more than one kind of cutting operation can be performed. Another is to enable the machine to perform its operations successively or even simultaneously on the same workpiece without any intermediate handing. A third is automatic gaging of machine features with an arrangement for ejecting the finished part and inserting another blank. A final refinement is to incorporate feedback controls that regrind and even reset tools, or make other adjustments as directed automatically by gage reading[5].

Complete automation of a machine tool includes all the above. Thus, the machine is equipped not only to perform its cutting automatically but also to "decide" what adjustments must be made to machine work according to specifications[6].

Broadly then, automatic machining comprises cutting where all tool and work-material movements are so actuated that duplicate parts may be made repeatedly without continuous attention[7]. If cutting operations are automatic but an operator is needed to remove finished parts or reload or reset the machine, semi-automatic operation is generally said to exist. In either case, machine time is reduced and dimensional precision often improved.

## Vocabulary

ordinary [ˈɔːdinəri, -neri]   adj. 普通的;通常的

accommodate [əˈkɔmədeit]   v. 调节;(使)适应;接纳;提供

cross-slide   横向拖板

saddle [ˈsædl]   n. 鞍,鞍状物;车座  vt. 承受  n. 溜板座

carriage [ˈkæridʒ]   n. 运输;运费;四轮马车  n. 溜板箱

turret [ˈtʌrit]   n. 转台,转塔;六角头

twist [twist]   v. 搓;扭转;扭变(曲,歪)

incorporate [inˈkɔːpəreit, inˈkɔːpərət]   v. (使)结合;(使)合并;组成公司

taper [ˈteipə]   n. 圆锥(形);尖锥(形);带梢的

tapered [ˈteipəd]   adj. 圆锥形(度)的

hollow [ˈhɔləu]   adj. 空心的,中空的

firmly [ˈfəːmli]   ad. 坚固地;稳固地断然

rough [rʌf]   ad. (粗,毛)糙的;简陋的

suitable [ˈsjuːtəbl]   adj. 适合的

front plate   花盘

chuck [tʃʌk]   n. 夹盘(具);卡盘;吸盘

lead-screw   导(螺)杆;丝杆

engage [inˈgeidʒ]   v. 啮(接)合

ensure [inˈʃuə]   vt. 确保;担保

lead-scerw   丝杠

feed-shaft   进给杆

thread [θred]   n. 螺纹

pitch [pitʃ]   n. 螺距

exactly the right pitch   精密准确的螺距

reverse [riˈvəːs]   v./n./adj./ad. 反向(的);相反(的)

reversing lever 反向手柄;反向操纵杆
original [ə'ridʒənəl] adj. 原始(先);最初
tool-post 刀架,刀座
mill [mil] n. 铣削
arbor ['a:bə] n. 心轴;柄轴;刀轴
spacer ['speisə] n. 垫片
bushing ['buʃiŋ] n. [电]套管;衬套
yoke [jəuk] n. 万向节叉;支座,支架
knee [ni:l] vi. 跪下,跪 n. 升降台
column ['kɔləm] n. 列;立柱
elevating screw 升降丝杠
index head 分度头
table ['teibl] 工作台
foot stock 底座
arbor yoke 刀杆支座
transverse slide 横滑板
peel [pi:l] n. 削,剥
shaper ['ʃeipə] n. 牛头刨床
planer ['pleinə] n. 龙门刨床
reciprocating [ri'siprəkeitiŋ] n. 往复 adj. 往复的;交互的;摆动的
apron ['eiprən] n. 围裙;床鞍;挡板
ram [ræm] abbr. 随机存取存储器 (random access memory 缩写);滑枕
stroke [strəuk] n. 中风;冲程;行程
vise [vais] n. 台钳,虎钳
fixture ['fikstʃə] n. 夹具
rocker ['rɔkə] n. 摇杆;摇臂
regulate ['regjuleit] n. 调节
clamp [klæmp] n. 夹钳 vt. 夹紧
pawl [pɔ:l] n. 棘爪

notch [nɔtʃ] n. 刻痕,凹口;槽口
ratchet ['rætʃit] n. 棘轮;棘齿
crossrail ['krɔ:s,reil] n. 横梁
fasten ['fa:sən, 'fæ-] vt. 使固定;锁紧
tool head 刀架
conical ['kɔnikəl] adj. 圆锥的;圆锥形的
surplus ['sə:plʌs] n. 剩余 adj. 剩余的
longitudinally [lɔ:ŋdʒi'tju:dinəli] n. 纵向地,经度地
concentricity [kɔnsen'trisiti] n. 同心;同轴度
periphery [pə'rifəri] n. 外[周]围,外缘
ground work 基准
finish ['finiʃ] n. 粗糙度
universal milling machine 万能铣床
cutter grinder 工具磨床
surface grinder 平面磨床
centerless grinder 无心磨床
external grinder 外圆磨床
internal grinder 内圆磨床
index ['indeks] n. 变位,换位
gauge [geidʒ] n. 测量
simultaneously [,siməl'teiniəs] ad. 同时;一并地
eject [i'dʒkt] vt. 推出;弹出[射]
incorporate [in'kɔ:pəreit] v. 采用;转换角度
broadly [brɔ:dli] ad. 广阔地;广泛地
duplicate ['dju:plikət, 'dju:plikeit] adj. 完全相同的 n. 复制品

## Notes

[1] ... which enables it to move sidewards across the saddle or carriage as well as along

Unit 2　Machine Tools & Cutting Technology

it. depending on the kind of job it is doing：根据加工工件的类型不同，横刀架使刀座既能在鞍架(也叫溜板)上作纵向运动，也能作横向运动。

① or 在这里的意思是"即"，不是"或"，因 saddle 和 carriage 指的是同一样东西，只是称谓不同而已。

② as well as 这个词组在这里当"既……又……"、"而且"讲，起连词作用，连接 across... 和 along... 这两个并列的介词短语，它通常强调其前面的部分，如 A as well as B，它的意思是"既 B 又 A"或"不仅 B 而且 A"，翻译时必须注意。

[2]　the cutting speed of the tool is what matters：要紧的是刀具的切削速度。what matters 是一个名词从句，在这里作表语。what＝the thing(s) which，matters 中这里是动词现在时第三人称单数形式，当"有关系"、"要紧"讲。

[3]　Tapered centers in the hollow nose of the spindle and of the tailstock...（主轴空心端内的顶类和尾架上的顶尖……）注意句中介词短语 of the tailstock 不是与 of the spindle 并列作 nose 的定语，而是与 in the hollow nose 并列作 centers 的定语。如果它是 nose 的定语，则 nose 应当是复数形式。

[4]　...and therefore forward or backward movement of the tool post，(……因而也控制刀座的前进或后退)这是省略句，在 therefore 之后省去了前一句中的动词 control，这种省略在英语是常见的，但在译成汉语时，往往必须重复动词。本课倒数第二句有类似的情况，不同的是在 therefore 后只省去了 will，保留了 alter。

[5]　A final refinement is to incorporate feed-back controls that regrind and even reset tools, or make other adjustments ad directed automatically by gage readings. 句中以 to incorporate... 不定式作表语，不定式表语中又以 that 引出定语从句去说明 feed-back controls，定语从句中有三个并列的谓语动词，regrind，reset 和 make，而 as 和 by 引出方式状语去修饰上述三个谓语动词。因此本句可译为：最后一项改进是采用反馈控制，按照测量仪表读数自动指示的情况重新刃磨刀具，甚至可重新装平刀具或进行其他方面的调整。

[6]　Thus, the machine is equipped not only to perform its cutting automatically but also to "decide" what adjustments must be made to machine work according to specifications，句中，what 引出的是宾语从句，what 在从句中作定语，说明 adjustment，意为"哪些"、"怎样的"。本句可译为：因此，(在机床上)所采用的装置不仅能使之自动进行切削，而且能"决定"必须作出怎样的调整才能按规格对工件进行加工。

[7]　Broadly then, automatic machining comprises cutting where all tool and work-material movements are so actuated that duplicate parts may be made repeatedly without continuous attention. 句中 where 引出定语从句说明 cutting，而 that 引出

状语从句,与前面的 so 相呼应,so... that 为:"这样……以致"或"使得"和"因此"。全句可译为:一般地说,自动加工指的是切削时刀具和工件材料的全部运动都是自动进行的,以使重复地生产相同类型的零件时,操作者无须一直地照管。

### Exercises

1. Give an explanation of the following terms:
   workshop  job  spindle  chuck  table  chip
   drill  bore  mill  grind  fixture  clamp
2. List the various types of the lathe chucks and their function.
3. List the types of machine tools.
4. What is the difference between a basic cutting machine and an automatic machine?

# Lesson 6  Tool Life

## 1 Introduction

A tool is any device, instrument, or machine for the performance of an operation. In the present paper only working and stamping tools will be treated. In general tools can be classified with reference to their application, operating temperature, the material they are made of, the degree of automation, etc.

The tool life depends on a number of factors, which, however, are not completely known for all tools. It often happens that tool damage occurs well before the stated and rightfully expected time. This is particularly true of pressure casting dies, working, and stamping tools. During operation, some tools are subjected to mechanical loads only, others to thermal loads, and still others to both thermal and mechanical loads. Because of the various loads, tools will become worn, will break, and get cracks which gradually propagate. How can a partially damaged tool be repaired is a very difficult question. Welding is the only technology fit for repair of tools and thus to extend their operation times. Moreover, surfacing by welding may well improve mechanical properties and extend the operation time of a brand new tool since surfacing is applied to those parts of the tool which will be subjected to the strongest loading[1].

## 2 Theoretical Background of the Problem

The paper aims to describe some measures permitting to extend tool life,

i. e. , the operating time of the tools designed for different jobs. The tool life depends on a number of factors such as the type of parent metal used, the manufacturing method employed (forging, rolling), the method of machining in tool manufacture (cutting, spark erosion), the type of heat treatment, the way the tool is used in operation, repair welding (process, filler material, measures before and after welding). Some of the factors can be influenced, but others cannot. Everyday practice shows that only some influences of these factors are known. It is quite a problem nowadays that all the influences exerted by all the factors related with the tool life are not known.

To select optimum values of the above mentioned factors, various services and experts should cooperate. It is important to engage, as early as at the stage of selection and purchase of the parent metal (chemical composition and size of a blank), experts on tools knowing which steel is to be used for a specific tool, the type of loading the tool will be subjected to in operation, and whether damaged tool can be repair welded or not.

## 3 Tool Life

The tool life is defined as the time period in which a tool will operate without any unexpected interventions. It is most often measured with the number of products manufactured by the tool. In terms of tool functions, the tool life can be divided into three separate, yet logically linked periods. The first period involves tool manufacture and the second the use of the tool. The third period starts with the occurrence of any damage to the tool which results in a tool repair. Among current technologies, welding seems to be the only technology fit for repair of damaged tools so that they may be again put into operation. The tool life after repair, however, almost entirely depends on the quality of welding performed and additional measures taken.

### 3.1 Manufacture of Tools

In the entire tool life, the phase of its manufacture plays a major role. In the manufacture, several different factors should be considered. When designing a tool, the type of material to be used shall be selected, taking into account the type of tool and the purpose of its use. As far as the steel selected is concerned, it is also important to know the orientation of its structure, the latter being dependent on the machining process used in the manufacture of the tool concerned. The tool life largely depends on the relationship between the structural orientation of the material and the location of burrs at the tool.

A majority of tools are still being manufactured by cutting-off. The various cutting processes at and below the surface produce various residual stresses. A special chapter in this context is spark erosion machining. In this case, the material is removed practically by evaporation. This means that the surface will be considerably changed after such treatment. For an optimum manufacture of tools, all the factors should be considered.

Machining is followed by heat treatment. High-quality heat treatment, however, can be performed only by using advanced devices (vacuum oven), adequate cooling media, and qualified personnel. Nowadays, a whole range of different heat-treatment processes and processes increasing hardness and wear resistance of the tool surface are known. One of the processes improving mechanical properties is surfacing by welding.

### 3.2 Use of Tools

After having been manufactured, tools are used for various processes, e. g., casting, forming, punching, and this mostly by non-qualified workers. Consequently, it is extremely important that detailed instructions for use are supplied with each tool. In addition to the instructions, which should be clear and easy to understand by a non-qualified worker, control and reliable measuring parameters should be established in the manufacturing process too.

### 3.3 Repair of Tools by Welding

Of the three functional phases mentioned, it is repair of tools by welding which has been studied least and, consequently, applied to practical cases least although the possibilities offered are numerous[2]. An appropriate welding technology, the selection of an adequate filler material and a suitable preheating temperature, forging of beads in the course of welding and an appropriate postweld heat treatment operation make it possible to repair the majority of tools and recondition them for further use, ensuring almost the same life as that of a new tool. The cost of repair can amount to only few percentages, mostly around 10%, and at maximum 50% of the cost of a new tool.

### 3.3.1 Selection of a Welding Process

There are not many welding processes from which to choose a process for repair welding of tools because it should be taken into account that the welding positions used may be different. Workpieces may have a difficult access and various shapes. Consequently, manual TIG welding seems to be the most appropriate process to be used. Plasma arc welding may be used as well. Recently manual and automatic laser welding with a filler material being a wire or a powder has been used too. The same system can be applied to repair welding of tools. Other welding processes such as MAG/MIG welding with a solid or cored wire and manual metal arc welding are applied to larger tools and in the case that a large quantity of a material shall be deposited. Submerged arc welding, electron-beam welding, electroslag welding or brazing are applied even more rarely.

### 3.3.2 Selection of a Filler Material

A filler material is mainly selected with regard to the parent metal used. Because of the burn-off of some elements (Ti, Cr, Al, Zr), slightly overalloyed filler materials should be used. In case of poorly weldable materials, it is recommended to use two different types of filler material. With root and filling beads a very tough material can be used, with final runs, i. e., with working tool surfaces, a material ensuring adequate mechanical properties should be used.

The filler materials used can have different forms, i. e., those of a rod, a wire on a spool and a powder. The form of the filler material added depends mainly on the welding process used.

### 3.3.3 Measures Taken Before Welding

Before welding, a groove should be prepared and a heated up adequate temperature. In preparing the groove care should be taken of its shape and position. The groove should not show sharp angles or sharp transitions. The root of preparation should be rounded. The location of groove should correspond, if possible, to the type of load applied to the tool during its operation. It is recommended that the groove is affected, via the weld metal, by pure compression stresses, but not by shear, tensile, or combined stresses.

### 3.3.4 Measures Taken After Welding

For a tool, postweld heat treatment is very important. It is selected in dependence of the type of tool material and the type of filler material. For example, tools made of austenitic stainless steels should be welded without preheating, with a very low energy input, the temperature of a bead being reduced below 150℃ before the next bead can be made; after welding, the tool should cool slowly, without any heat treatment being applied. In welding of tools made of martensitic stainless steels, the procedure is precisely the opposite, i. e., the tool should be preheated up to 350 ℃, the same temperature shall be maintained during welding, and the tool shall be annealed after welding. A third instance is welding of casting dies with the addition of maraging steel as a filler material. Such a tool, containing a weld, should be aged. The ageing temperature and duration of ageing affect the mechanical properties of the weld, particularly hardness and toughness.

## 4 Conclusions

The selection of a suitable parent metal, manufacturing parameters, optimum heat treatment for a tool and particularly an optimum repair of the damaged tool can extend the tool life substantially, in most favourable cases even up to 100 %. In repair welding, the decisive factors are the welding process used, the filler material added, the measures taken before, during, and after welding, and in manual welding, the ability of the welder.

### Vocabulary

stamping tool　　冲压工具
pressure casting　　压铸件
propagate ['prɔpəgeit]　vt. 繁衍；传导
welding ['weldiŋ]　n. 焊接
forging ['fɔːdʒiŋ]　n. 锻造；锻件
rolling ['rəuliŋ]　n. 滚压
spark erosion　　电火花腐蚀
burr [bəː]　n. 毛刺
residual stress　　残余应力
spark erosion machine　　电火花腐蚀机床
evaporation [i,væpəˈreiʃən]　n. 蒸发；消失
vacuum oven　　真空电炉
recondition [,riːkənˈdiʃən]　vt. 修理

plasma arc　　等离子体电弧
submerged arc welding　　潜弧焊
electron beam　　电子束
electroslag welding　　电渣焊
burn off　　蒸发
spool [spuːl]　n. 线轴
transition [trænˈsiʒən, -ˈziʃən, trɑːn-]　n. 变迁
austenitic [,ɔstiˈnitik]　adj. 奥氏体的
martensitic [,mɑːtinˈzitik]　adj. 马氏体的
stainless steel　　不锈钢
anneal [əˈniːl]　n. 退火
maraging steel　　马氏体时效钢

## Notes

[1] Moreover, surfacing by welding may well improve mechanical properties and extend the operation time of a brand new tool since surfacing is applied to those parts of the tool which will be subjected to the strongest loading. Surfacing by welding 为焊接形成的表面,improve and extend 是谓语,since 是从句,which 是定语从句修饰 tool。此句可译为:而且,焊接形成的表面可以很大的提高机械性能和延长新工具的使用寿命,这是因为焊接表面形成于工具受最大载荷的部分。

[2] Of the three functional phases mentioned, it is repair of tools by welding which has been studied least and, consequently, applied to practical cases least although the possibilities offered are numerous. it is ... which 是强调句式,although 引导状语从句,整句译为:所提及的三个功能阶段,通过焊接进行工具的修复是研究得最少的,因此,应用到实际中也是最少的,虽然可能提供的实例是很多的。

## Exercises

1. What factors affect the tool life?
2. What is tool life?
3. Which technology can extend tool life?
4. How many welding technology can repair tool?
5. Why slightly overalloyed filler materials should be used?
6. What determines the preheating temperature?

# Lesson 7   Tolerances

## 1  Why Tolerancing

(1) No component can be manufactured to an exact size, so the designer has to decide on appropriate upper and lower limits for each dimension.

(2) Parts made by different companies have to be interchangeable.

(3) Assemblies: Parts will often not fit together if their dimensions do not fall within a certain range of values.

(4) Accurately toleranced dimensioned features usually take much more time to manufacture correctly and therefore can increase production costs significantly.

(5) Good engineering practice finds the optimum balance between required accuracy

for the function of the component and minimum cost of manufacture.

## 2  Terminology

Tolerance is the technique of dimensioning parts within a desired range of variation.

Fit is the general term used to signify the range of tightness or looseness that may result from the application of a specific combination of allowances and tolerances in mating parts, as shown in Fig. 7.1.

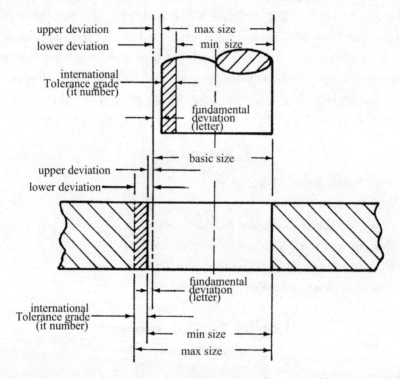

Fig. 7.1  Terms related to fit

**Basic Size or Basic dimension**: It is the theoretical size from which limits of size are derived by the application of allowances and tolerances.

**Actual Size**: is the measured size of the finished part.

**Deviation**: is the difference between the basic size and the hole or shaft size.

**Upper Deviation**: is the difference between the basic size and the permitted maximum size of the part.

**Lower Deviation**: is the difference between the basic size and the minimum permitted size of the part.

**Fundamental Deviation:** is the deviation closest to the basic size.

**Tolerance:** is the difference between the permitted minimum and maximum sizes of a part.

**Tolerance Zone:** refers to the relationship of the tolerance to basic size. It is established by a combination of the fundamental deviation indicated by a letter and the IT grade number. In the dimension 50H8, for the close running fit, the H8 specifies the tolerance zone.

## 3 Types of Fit

There are three types of fits between parts

(1) Clearance Fit: an internal member fits in an external member (as a shaft in a hole) and always leaves a space or clearance between the parts;

(2) Interference Fit: the internal member is larger than the external member such that there is always an actual interference of material;

(3) Transition Fit: may result in either a clearance or interference condition.

Of the various methods used to apply the system of fits. The principal ones are the shaft-basis system and hole-basis system. The hole-basis system of preferred fits is a system in which the basic diameter is the minimum size of the hole. For the generally preferred hole-basis system, the fundamental deviation is specified by the upper-case letter H. The shaft-basis system of preferred fits is a system in which the basic diameter is the maximum size of the shaft. The fundamental deviation is given by the lowercase letter H. Normally, it is easier to produce a shaft with a specified tolerance than a hole with the same tolerance. Consequently, in modern engineering design, the hole-basis system is most extensively used and our discussion will refer mostly to this system. However, the designer should decide on the adoption of either system to enable general interchangeability.

## 4 Symbols for Tolerances and Fits

A tolerance is designated by a letter (in some cases, two letters) a symbol, and a numerical symbol. The letter symbol denotes the deviation of actual size from the basic size. The deviation designated by the letter is also known as fundamental deviation. The letter symbol shows the closeness of the tolerance zone to the basic size. The number symbol represents the zone of tolerance with respect to the grade of manufacture. This symbol is responsible for the grade of manufacture designed by International Grade, IT, and the tolerance represented by the number symbol is known as fundamental tolerance.

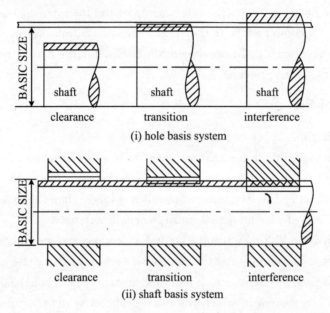

Fig. 7.2 Hole-basis and shaft-basis system

## 5 Calculation of Fundamental Tolerance

In the way of calculation of fundamental tolerance and fundamental deviation, the entire calculation is totally dependent upon the geometric mean D of the extreme diameter of each step.

It provides 18 grades of tolerance $IT01$, $IT0$, $IT1$, $IT2$, $IT3$, to $IT16$. The value of standard tolerance for grades 5 to 16 are determined from the tolerance unit "i" and formula is given below

$$i = 0.45 D^{\frac{1}{3}} + 0.001 D \text{ mm}$$

Where, $D$ is in mm.

The standard tolerance corresponding to IT01, IT0 and IT1 are calculated by formula given below

$$IT01 = 0.3 + 0.008 D$$

$$IT0 = 0.5 + 0.0012D$$
$$IT1 = 0.8 + 0.20D$$

The value of $IT2$, $IT4$ are determined between $IT1$ and $IT5$ values, geometrically.

## 6 Concept of Fundamental Deviation

The symbols of fundamental deviation for holes are A, B, C, D, E, F, G, H, J, K, L, M, N, P, R, S, T, U, V, X, Y, Z, ZA, ZB, ZC. The rest of the letters, i. e. , I, L , O, Q, and W, are not used. For shafts the same symbols are used but in lower-case letters.

For holes of symbol among A to H, the lower deviation is above zero line, with lower deviation for hole H being zero. For holes having symbol among J to ZC, it is below zero line. In simple words, we can say that the lower deviation for holes A to H is the fundamental deviation and for holes J to ZC the fundamental deviation is the upper deviation.

For shafts, the concept of fundamental deviation is opposite to holes. For shafts a to h, the upper deviation is below zero line and having the upper deviation being zero for shaft h. For shafts having symbol in between j and zc, it is above zero line, i. e. , the fundamental deviation for shafts a to h is the upper deviation and for shafts j to zc, it is lower deviation.

Let me show you a few examples of these symbols:

50H8/g7 or 50H8-g7, 40H7/G6 or 40H7-g6

In these examples, 50 and 40 are the basic sizes. The symbol represents the fundamental deviation for holes and small letter "g" represents the fundamental deviation for shaft. The numeric symbols represent the fundamental tolerance. You can get the table of ISO tolerance on the web as well as in the market and in some books, too. You just find the values of fundamental deviation and fundamental tolerance using those tables according to the symbol given. Now, we can easily calculate the actual size of shaft and hole only by small addition and subtraction.

There are a number of combinations of shafts and holes that may be used for a fit. It is better to select hole-basis fit. Because it is better as the production of shafts to the required size is easier. But, the shaft-basis system is very good for manufacturing bright drawn bars.

## 7  Surface Roughness

As it is not possible to achieve, in practice, a geometrically ideal surface of a work-piece, an engineering drawing must also contain information about the permissible surface conditions of the body. The surface condition is a function of the finishing process adopted.

Roughness is a measure of the texture of a surface. It is quantified by the vertical deviations of a real surface from its ideal form. If these deviations are large, the surface is rough; if they are small the surface is smooth. Roughness is typically considered to be the high frequency, short wavelength component of a measured surface.

Roughness plays an important role in determining how a real object will interact with its environment. Rough surfaces usually wear more quickly and have higher friction coefficients than smooth surfaces. Roughness is often a good predictor of the performance of a mechanical component, since irregularities in the surface may form nucleation sites for cracks or corrosion.

Although roughness is usually undesirable, it is difficult and expensive to control in manufacturing. Decreasing the roughness of a surface will usually increase exponentially its manufacturing costs. This often results in a trade-off between the manufacturing cost of a component and its performance in application.

A roughness value can either be calculated on a profile or on a surface. The profile roughness parameter ($R_a$, $R_q$, ...) are more common. The area roughness parameters ($S_a$, $S_q$, ...) give more significant values.

Each of the roughness parameters is calculated using a formula for describing the surface. There are many different roughness parameters in use, but $R_a$ is by far the most common. Other common parameters include $R_z$, $R_q$, and $R_{sk}$. Some parameters are used only in certain industries or within certain countries. For example, the $R_k$ family of parameters is used mainly for cylinder bore linings, and the Motif parameters are used primarily within France.

Since these parameters reduce all of the information in a profile to a single number, great care must be taken in applying and interpreting them. Small changes in how the raw profile data is filtered, how the mean line is calculated, and the physics of the measurement can greatly affect the calculated parameter.

By convention every 2D roughness parameter is a capital R followed by additional characters in the subscript. The subscript identifies the formula that was used, and the R means that the formula was applied to a 2D roughness profile. Different capital letters imply that the formula was applied to a different profile. For example, $R_a$ is the arithmetic average of the roughness profile, Pa is the arithmetic average of the unfiltered raw profile, and $S_a$ is the arithmetic average of the 3D roughness.

## Vocabulary

limit ['limit]　n. 极限
tolerance ['tɔlərəns]　n. 公差
terminology [ˌtəːmi'nɔlədʒi]　n. 术语
mating parts　配件
deviation [ˌdiːvi'eiʃən]　n. 偏差；误差
clearance fit　间隙配合
interference fit　过盈配合
transition fit　过渡配合
shaft-basis system　基轴制
hole-basis system　基孔制

interchangeability [ˌintəˌtʃeindʒə'biliti]　n. 互换性
surface roughness　表面粗糙度
texture ['tekstʃə]　n. 纹理
wear [wɛə]　n. 磨损
crack [kræk]　n. 破裂
corrosion [kə'rəuʃən]　n. 腐蚀
trade-off　平衡
profile ['prəufail]　n. 轮廓

## Notes

[1] Good engineering practice finds the optimum balance between required accuracy for the function of the component and minimum cost of manufacture. for the function of the component 修饰 required accuracy, 可表述为满足零件功能需要的合适精度；此句可译为：优良的工程实践找到了满足零件功能需求的合适精度和制作最小成本之间的最优平衡。

[2] Since these parameters reduce all of the information in a profile to a single number, great care must be taken in applying and interpreting them. Reduce ... to ... 短语表示简化为；此句可译为：由于这些参数把轮廓的所有信息简化为一个数值，因此在应用和解释这些参数时必须格外仔细。

## Exercises

1. What is tolerance?

2. Why is tolerance important in manufacturing?

3. Why is the hole-basis system used extensively in modern engineering design?

4. Describe three main types of fit in detail.

5. Why is surface roughness important?

# Lesson 8  Machining Fundamentals

## 1 Introduction

Machining as a shape-producing method is the most universally used and the most important of all manufacturing processes. Machining is a shape-producing process in which a power-driven device causes material to be removed in chip form. Most machining is done with equipment that supports both the workpiece and cutting tool although in some cases portable equipment is used with unsupported workpiece[1].

## 2 Two Applications of Machining in Manufacturing

Low setup cost for small quantities. Machining has two applications in manufacturing. For casting, forging, and press working, each specific shape to be produced, even one part, nearly always has a high tooling cost. The shapes that may be produced by welding depend to a large degree on the shapes of raw material that are available. By making use of generally high cost equipment but without special tooling, it is possible, by machining, to start with nearly any form of raw material, so long as the exterior dimensions are great enough, and produce any desired shape from any material[2]. Therefore, machining is usually the preferred method for producing one or a few parts, even when the design of the part would logically lead to casting, forging or press working if a high quantity were to be produced.

Close accuracies, good finishes. The second application for machining is based on the high accuracies and surface finishes possible. Many of the parts machined in low quantities would be produced with lower but acceptable tolerances if produced in high quantities by some other process. On the other hand, many parts are given their general shapes by some high quantity deformation process and machined only on selected surfaces where high accuracies are needed. Internal threads, for example, are seldom produced by any means other than machining and small holes in press worked parts may be machined following the press working operations.

## 3  Mechanism of Surface Finish Production

There are basically five mechanisms which contribute to the production of a surface which have been machined. These are:

(1) The basic geometry of the cutting process. In, for example, single point turning the tool will advance a constant distance axially per revolution of the workpiece and the resultant surface will have on it, when viewed perpendicularly to the direction of tool feed motion, a series of cusps which will have a basic form which replicates the shape of the tool in cut.

(2) The efficiency of the cutting operation. It has already been mentioned that cutting with unstable built-up-edges will produce a surface which contains hard built-up-edges fragments which will result in a degradation of the surface finish. It can also be demonstrated that cutting under adverse conditions such as apply when using large feeds small rake angles and low cutting speeds, besides producing conditions which lead to unstable built-up-edge production, the cutting process itself can become unstable and instead of continuous shear occurring in the shear zone tearing takes place, discontinuous chips of uneven thickness are produced, and the resultant surface is poor. This situation is particularly noticeable when machining very ductile materials such as copper and aluminum.

(3) The stability of the machine tool. Under some combinations of cutting conditions: workpiece size, method of clamping, and cutting tool rigidity relative to the machine tool structure, instability can be set up in the tool which causes it to vibrate. Under some conditions this vibration will reach and maintain a steady amplitude whilst under other conditions the vibration will built up and unless cutting is stopped considerable damage to both the cutting tool and workpiece may occur. This phenomenon is known as chatter and in axial turning is characterized by long pitch helical bands on the workpiece surface and short pitch undulations on the transient machined surface.

(4) The effectiveness of removing swart. In discontinuous chip production machining, such as milling or turning of brittle materials, it is expected that the

chip (swarf) will leave the cutting zone either under gravity or with the assistance of a jet of cutting fluid and that they will not influence the cut surface in any way. However, when continuous chip production is evident, unless steps are taken to control the swarf it is likely that it will impinge on the cut surface and mark it. Inevitably, this marking besides looking unattractive, often results in a poorer surface finishing.

(5) The effective clearance angle on the cutting tool. For certain geometries of minor cutting edge relief and clearance angles it is possible to cut on the major cutting edge and burnish on the minor cutting edge. This can produce a good surface finish but, of course, it is strictly a combination of metal cutting and metal forming and is not to be recommended as a practical cutting method. However, due to cutting tool wear, these conditions occasionally arise and lead to a marked change in the surface characteristics.

## Vocabulary

fundamental [ˌfʌndəˈmentəl] adj. 基础的;根本的 n. 基本原则;基础
machining [məˈʃiːniŋ] n. 机械加工[切削]
shape-producing 产生形状;成形
a power-driven device 驱动装置
chip [tʃip] n. 切屑
workpiece [ˈwəːkpiːs] n. 工件
portable [ˈpɔːtəbl] adj. 轻便(可移动)的
support [səˈpɔːt] vt. 支持
equipment [iˈkwipmənt] n. 装(设)备
Low setup cost for small quantities 小批量生产低费用
exterior [ikˈstiəriə] adj. 外部(表,来)的
start with 从……着手(开始)
the preferred method 所推荐的方法
logically [ˈlɔdʒikli] ad. 逻辑上;推理

lead to 导致;导向
pressure working 压力加工
close accuracy 严密的精度
good finish 合适的表面粗糙度
degradation [ˌdegrəˈdeiʃən] n. 降级
tear [tɛə, tiə] n. 裂纹
ductile [ˈdʌktail, -til] adj. 易拉长的,可延展的
clamp [klæmp] n. 夹紧
undulation [ˌʌndjuˈleiʃən] n. 波纹,振动
transient [ˈtrænziənt] adj. 瞬态的,短暂的
swarf [swɔːf, swɑːf] n. 金属屑
impinge [imˈpindʒ] v. 冲击,撞击
replicate [ˈreplikit, ˈreplikeit] v. 重复,复制
built-up-edge 切削瘤

## Notes

[1] Most machining is done with equipment that supports ... although in ... workpiece. 句中 that 引出一定语从句去修饰 equipment，意指既支承工件又支承刀具的装备。although 是连词，引导出状语从句，表示让步，意指：尽管在某些无支承工件情况下使用移动式装备来进行加工。所以全句可译为：尽管在某些场合，工件无支承情况下，使用移动式装备来实现加工，但大多数的机械加工还是通过既支承工件又支承刀具的装备来完成。

[2] By making use of ... special tooling, it is possible, by machining, to start with ... raw material, so long as ... are great enough, any material. 句中 By making use of ... 是介词＋动名词短语作方式状语，表示手段。本句的主句是 it is possible，其中 it 为形式主语，其真正主语是并列的不定式短语 to start ... and produce ... 。在并列不定式短语中又插入了 so long as ... 引导的条件状语从句，表示：只要外部尺寸是足够大的，则…；从全句来看，尚有状语 by machining 表示加工手段，即通过机械加工使得 to start ... and produce ... ，这件事情是可能的。这样全句可译为：一般来说，通过利用高价设备而又无需特种加工条件，几乎可以从任何种类原材料开始，借助机械加工把原材料加工成任意所需求的结构形状，只要外部尺寸足够大，那都是可能的。

[3] In, for example, single point turning the tool will advance a constant distance axially per revolution of the workpiece and the resultant surface will have on it. when viewed perpendicularly to the direction of tool feed motion, a series of cusps which will have a basic form which replicates the shape of the tool in cut. 本句中，for example 是插入语。advance a constant distance axially per revolution of the workpiece 可译为：工件转一周，刀具沿轴线方向进给一个固定的距离；the resultant surface will have on it 中的宾语后置，即 a series of 从句，该从句中 which will have a basic form 修饰 cusps，(尖角)．which replicates the shape of the tool in cut 修饰 form。整句可译为：例如，在单点车削时，工件每转一周，刀具就沿轴线方向进给一个固定的距离。从垂直刀具进给的方向观察，所得到的表面上有很多尖角，这些尖角的形状与切削刀具的形状相同。

[4] It can also be demonstrated that cutting under adverse conditions such as apply when using large feeds small rake angles and low cutting speeds.

beside producing conditions which lead to unstable built-up-edge production, the cutting process itself can become unstable and instead of continuous shear occurring in the shear zone. tearing takes place. discontinuous chips of uneven thickness are produced, and the resultant surface is poor. 该句为一长句,可译为:已经证明,在采用进给量大,前角小,切削速度低的不利情况下,除了产生不稳定的切削瘤外,切削过程也会不稳定,同时,在切削区里进行的也不再是切削,而是撕裂,导致厚度不均匀,不连续的切屑,加工出的表面质量差。

[5] This phenomenon is known as chatter and in axial turning is characterized by long pitch helical bands on the workpiece surface and short pitch undulations on the transient machined surface. 该句中的 chatter 译为"刀振",long pitch helical bands 译为"长间距螺旋状带"。

**Exercises**

1. Machining has some applications in manufacturing, please discuss them.
2. Which will lead to unstable built-up-edge production?
3. What is the phenomenon of chatter?

# Unit 3　Mechatronics

## Lesson 9　Expert System

### 1　Introduction

An expert system is a set of programs that manipulate encoded knowledge to solve problems in a specialized domain that normally requires human expertise. An expert system's knowledge is obtained from expert sources and coded in a form suitable for the system to use in its inference or reasoning processes. The expert knowledge must be obtained from specialists or other sources of expertise, such as texts, journal articles, and databases. Once a sufficient body of expert knowledge has been acquired, it must be encoded in some form, loaded into a knowledge base, then tested, and refined continually throughout the life of the system.

Expert systems differ from conventional computer systems in several important ways. A typical expert system is shown in Fig. 9.1.

- ◆ Expert systems use knowledge rather than data to control the solution process. This permits the incremental addition and modification (refinement) of the knowledge base without recompilation of the control programs;
- ◆ Expert systems are capable of explaining how a particular conclusion was reached, and why requested information is needed during a consultation;
- ◆ Expert systems use symbolic representations for knowledge (rules, networks, or frames) and perform their inference through symbolic computations that closely resemble manipulations of natural language.

There are in fact four essential components of fully-fledged expert systems:
- ◆ The knowledge base;
- ◆ The inference engine;

- ◆ The knowledge-acquisition module;
- ◆ The explanatory interface.

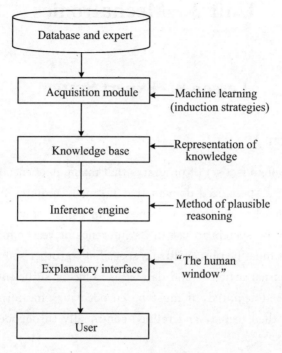

Fig. 9.1  A typical expert system

A knowledge base contains facts (or assertions) and rules. Facts are short-term information that can change rapidly, e.g., during the course of a consultation. Rules are the longer-term information about how to generate new facts or hypotheses from what is presently know. Basic ways in the inference engine, used to represent the knowledge are forward chaining and backward chaining, forward chaining involves reasoning from data to hypotheses, while backward chaining attempts to find data to prove, or disprove, a hypothesis. Up to now, the main bottleneck in the development of expert systems has been acquiring the knowledge in computer-usable form. The fourth main component of a true expert system is the explanatory interface, which can be named "the human window". It permits the users to communicate with the system in a more natural way by permitting the use of simple selection menus or the use of a restricted language, which is close to a natural language.

## 2  What is Artificial Intelligence?

An expert system is a computer program, which uses non-numerical domain — specific knowledge to solve problems with a competence comparable with that of human experts.

Artificial Intelligence (AI) is a branch of computer science concerned with the study and creation of computer systems that exhibit some form if intelligence: systems that learn new concepts and tasks, systems that can reason and draw useful conclusions about the world around us, systems that can understand a natural language or perceptive and comprehend a visual scene, and systems that perform other types of feats that require human types of intelligence.

As we had known, intelligence is referred as the ability to acquire, understand and apply knowledge, or the ability to exercise thought and reason. Of course, intelligence is more than this. It embodies all of the knowledge and feats, both conscious and unconscious, which we have acquired through study and experience, highly refined sight and sound perception thought, imagination and much more.

Intelligence is the integrated sum of those feats that gives us the ability to remember a face not seen for thirty or more years, or to build and send rockets to the moon. And, as we shall see, the food for this intelligence is knowledge.

Systems have already been developed to perform many types of intelligence tasks, and expectations are high for recent development for even more impressive systems. We now have systems that can learn examples, from being told, from past-related experiences, and through reasoning. We have systems which can solve complex problems in mathematics, in scheduling many diverse tasks, in finding optimal system configurations, in planning complex strategies for the military and for the business, in diagnosing medical diseases, to name a few. We have systems that can understand large parts of natural languages. We have systems that can see well enough to recognize objects from photographs, video cameras and other sensors. We have systems that can reason with incomplete and uncertain facts. Clearly, with these developments, much has been accomplished since the advent of the digital computers.

In spite of these impressive achievements, we still have not been able to produce coordinated, autonomous systems that possess some of the basic abilities of a three-year-old child. These include the ability to recognize and remember numerous diverse objects in a scene, to learn new sounds and associate them with objects and concepts, and to adapt readily to many diverse new situations. These are the challenges now facing researchers in AI. And they are not easy ones. They will require important breakthrough before we can expect to equal the performance of our three-year-old.

Even through one can argue that all programs exhibit some degree of intelligence, an AI program will go beyond this in demonstrating a high level of intelligence to a degree that equals or exceeds the intelligence required of a human in performing some task. AI isn't the study of the mind, nor of the body, nor of the language, as customarily found in the fields of psychology, physiology, cognitive science, or linguistics. To be sure, there is some overlap between these fields and AI. AI seeks a better understanding of the human's intelligence and sensing processes. But in AI, the goal is to develop working computer systems that are truly capable of performing tasks that require high levels of intelligence. The programs aren't necessarily meant to imitate human senses and thought processes. Indeed, in performing some tasks differently, they may actually exceed human abilities. The important point is that the systems all be capable of performing intelligence tasks effectively and efficiently.

Finally, a better understanding of AI is gained by looking at the component areas of study that make up the whole. These include of such topics as robotics, memory organization, knowledge representation, storage and recall, learning models, inference technique, commonsense reasoning, dealing with uncertainty in reasoning and decision-making, understanding natural language, pattern recognition and machine vision methods, search and matching, speech recognition and synthesis, and a variety of AI tools.

AI is coming of an age when practical commercial products are now available including a variety of robotic devices, vision systems that recognize shapes and objects, expert systems that perform many different tasks as well as or better than their human expert counterparts, intelligent instructions systems that help pace a student learning and monitor the student's progress, "intelligent" editors that assist users in building special knowledge bases, and systems which can learn to improve their performance.

There are several programming languages that are known as AI languages because they are used almost exclusively for AI applications. The two most common are LISP and Prolog.

## 3 Artificial Intelligence in Mechatronics

Recent work using artificial intelligence has attempted to integrate various control modules to increase productivity and quality in manufacturing operations. Further, the developments in expert systems, fuzzy logic, and neural networks are expected to be used at the higher level in the control hierarchy for machining processes.

A recent trend in the area of automation manufacturing is the incorporation of artificial intelligence to enhance the online process control and inspection. Intelligence online process control and inspection in modern manufacturing system have significant potential for improving production performance and product quality. Various studies suggest that incorporation of artificial neural networks results in a very promising synergy in intelligence manufacturing systems and processes. One reason for this is the dependence on knowledge-based system, which are widely used and acknowledged for their relevancy, consistency, organization, and completeness[1]. (see Appendix of Lesson 30) The problem of acquiring expert knowledge in a form usable by an expert system is known as knowledge acquisition. This has been identified as a major bottleneck to the implementation of knowledge-based system technology. However, the acquisition process ends with the implementation of a knowledge-based system that cannot adapt to change and is unable to handle situations slightly different from known prototype conditions[2]. This has paved the way for the development of brain-like computation, namely artificial neural networks that can efficiently conduct production process control and inspection with a wide range of tolerance and uncertainties [3].

The field of artificial intelligence, particularly the technologies of artificial neural networks, is very useful at higher levels in the control hierarchy of manufacturing processes. The two basic AI approaches for providing decision support have been the macro, or top-down, modeling of human intelligence and the micro, or bottom-up, modeling of human intelligence [4].

- ◆ In the macro approach, as in knowledge-based systems, the human brain is treated as a black-box, and the human reasoning process is

modeled through modeled through cognitive analysis of the decision-making tasks as described by the expert;
◆ In the micro approach, as in neural networks, the human brain is treated as a white-box, and the human reasoning process is modeled through the observation of neural connections in the brain.

On the most fundamental level, neural networks perform pattern recognition more effectively than any other technique known. Once the network has detected a pattern, the information can be used to classify, and analyze the causes of the pattern. Below are some unusual features of neural networks.
◆ Recall of information is highly resistant to hardware failure (in contrast to traditional computers, in which retrieval can fail as result of a single memory element);
◆ Positive and negative aspects of information are automatically balanced as a network reorganizes to solve a problem;
◆ Abstraction of data occurs automatically as a by-product of learning information;
◆ Pattern recognition occurs via parallel consideration of multiple constraints;
◆ Hierarchical data structures can be conveniently represented as multiple-layer networks;
◆ Networks can exhibit properties reminiscent of adaptive biological learning and can select and generate their own pattern features from exposure to stimuli[5];
◆ ANN can capture patterns occurring both in time (for example, auditory information) and space (such as visual data) and can operate in discrete or continuous representation modes.

From an engineering perspective, this new paradigm is a very powerful method for searching through solution space; however, its wide-range applications also include other fields such as business, medical, etc. ANN is best at solving problems that involve pattern recognition, adaptation, generalization, and prediction. Its implementation also offers particular advantages when solving problems that are very noisy, in which the performance of the system cannot be measured with each example, or potentially small improvements in performance can result in a substantial advantage in resource allocation and profits[6]. In the context of diagnostics, ANN is most valuable in applications that process continuous inputs, such as signal data. ANN solutions are working hard at detecting fraud (credit applications, insurance and warranty claims, and credit card fraud), in modeling and forecasting (bankruptcy prediction, credit scoring, securities trading, portfolio evaluation, mail list management, machine diagnostics, flaw detection, product development, and industrial inspection). However, for ANN to reach its maximum potential, supporting hardware is needed that will make the network faster and thus more practical.

## 4 Knowledge-Based System

Knowledge-based systems are the part of the AI field that focuses mainly on replicating cognitive human behavior. They do so by capturing problem-solving expertise of experts within a narrow problem domain and making it available for other organizational systems. The expertise is typically stored in a knowledge base in static form of If-Then-Else rules or a hierarchy of frames and objects. The knowledge base is used by an inference engine, which reasons with the knowledge in a serial manner, and applied to the different problem presented by user. Conventional knowledge-based systems are generally static, which make them inflexible in dynamic environments that require constant learning based on the action taken and feedback obtained from the action. Thus, an intelligence process control and inspection system cannot rely solely on a conventional knowledge-based system technology that uses a static knowledge base. Rather, it needs a dynamic learning mechanism that can help the system to deal with an uncertain reasoning environment with high flexibility and adaptability to the change in its condition.

Knowledge acquisition is probably the most difficult step in the development of an expert or knowledge-based system. The complexity of the problem at hand and the human factors of interacting and understanding the decision-making process of individuals combine to make the task of knowledge acquisition one that requires special tools, time, and considerable skill to perform accurately and effectively[7]. Difficulties with the expert may arise if the information provided is incorrect or is misinterpreted by the knowledge engineer. In addition, although experts may be highly skilled at solving the problem, they may be limited in their ability to describe the decision-making process in the meticulous detail required to make the expert system function properly. The expert may also provide extraneous information that can be eliminated from the knowledge base without affecting the decision-making capability.

## Vacabulary

mechattronics [ˌmekəˈtrɔniks] n. 机电一体化
encode [enˈkəud] vt. 把（电文、情报等）译成电码（或密码）编码
incremental [ˌinkriˈmentəl] adj. 增加的，增加 n. 增量
perceptive [pəˈseptiv] adj. 有理解的，有知觉的
feat [fiːt] n. 技艺，功绩，技艺表演 adj. 漂亮的，合适的
bottleneck [ˈbɔtlnek] n. 瓶颈
artificial intelligence 人工智能
autonomous [ɔːˈtɔnəməs] adj. 自治的，自主的
cognitive [ˈkɔgnitiv] adj. 认知的，认识的
counterpart [ˈkauntəˌpaːt] n. 副本，极相似的人或物，配重，配对物
allocation [æləˈkeiʃən] n. 配置
artificial neural network 人工神经网络
decision-making n. 决策
insurance and warranty claim 保险与担保索赔
expertise [ˌekspəˈtiːz] n. 专家技能
portfolio [pɔːtˈfəuljəu] n. 投资组合

## Notes

[1] One reason for this is the dependence on knowledge-based system, which are widely used and acknowledged for their relevancy, consistency, organization, and completeness. 可译为：其理由是可以可靠地利用这种基于知识的系统，这样的系统使用较广，主要是由于它们具有很好的关联性、协同性、组织性和完整性。

[2] However, the acquisition process ends with the implementation of a knowledge-based system that cannot adapt to change and is unable to handle situations slightly different from known prototype conditions. 可译为：然而，获取过程之后执行基于知识的系统，这个系统不能适应于变化，不能处理和已知原型条件有轻微变化的情况。

[3] This has paved the way for the development of brain-like computation, namely artificial neural networks that can efficiently conduct production process control and inspection with a wide range of tolerance and uncertainties. 可译为：这就为类似大脑计算的发展铺平了道路，这种计算被称为人工神经网络。人工神经网络可以有效处理具有大范围允许偏差和不确定性的生产过程控制和检测。

[4] The two basic AI approaches for providing decision support have been the macro,

or top-down, modeling of human intelligence and the micro, or bottom-up, modeling of human intelligence. 可译为：人工智能可以通过两种手段提供决策支持：一种是宏观的，即由上到下的人工智能建模；另一种是微观的，也就是自下而上的人工智能建模方式。

[5] Networks can exhibit properties reminiscent of adaptive biological learning and can select and generate their own pattern features from exposure to stimuli. 可译为：网络显示的特性可以使人联想到自适应生物学习，能够从受到的刺激中选择并产生自己的模型特性。

[6] Its implementation also offers particular advantages when solving problems that are very noisy, in which the performance of the system cannot be measured with each example, or potentially small improvements in performance can result in a substantial advantage in resource allocation and profits. 可译为：当解决含有各种干扰因素的问题时，它的执行也提供了特别的优势，在这类问题中，系统的性能不能通过一个一个的例子来检测，或者可能在性能上很小的改善都会导致资源分配和收益上很大的好处。

[7] The complexity of the problem at hand and the human factors of interacting and understanding the decision-making process of individuals combine to make the task of knowledge acquisition one that requires special tools, time, and considerable skill to perform accurately and effectively. 可译为：所遇问题的复杂性及相互影响和理解个体决策过程中人的因素结合起来，使得知识获取的任务需要专门工具、时间和相当多的技能，这样才能准确、有效地执行。

**Exercises**

1. Answer the following questions.
(1) What is an expert system?
(2) What is the difference between expert systems and conventional computer systems?
(3) Please list two basic AI approaches for providing decision support.
2. Translate the following sentences into English.
(1) 专家系统在许多方面与传统的计算机系统不同。
(2) 专家系统的五个核心组成部分是学习模式、知识库、推理机、解释界面和用户。
(3) 专家系统的主要瓶颈问题是如何以计算机可以使用的方向来获取知识。
(4) 人工神经网络可以有效处理具有大范围允许偏差和不确定的生产过程控制和检测。

# Lesson 10  Robot and Robotics

## 1  Definition of Robot

The definition developed by the robot institute of America is given by the following description:

A robot is a reprogrammable multifunctional manipulator designed to move material, parts, tools, or specialized devices through variable programmed motions for the performance of a variety of tasks[1]. In a broader context, the term robot also includes manipulators that are activated directly by an operator.

The key words are reprogrammable and multifunctional, since most single-purpose machines do not meet these two requirements.

Reprogrammable means that the machine must be capable of being reprogrammed to perform a new or different task or to be able to change significantly the motion of the arm or tooling. Multifunctional emphasizes the fact that a robot must be able to perform many different functions, depending on the program and tooling currently in use.

Despite the tremendous capability of currently available robots, even the most poorly prepared worker is better equipped than a robot to handle many of the situations which occur in the work cell. Workers, for example, realize when they have dropped a part on the floor or when a parts feeder is empty. Without a host of sensors, a robot simply does not have any of his information; and even with the most sophisticated sensor system available, a robot cannot match an experienced human operator. The design of a good automated work cell therefore requires the use of peripheral equipment interfaced to the robot controller to even imitate the sensory capability of a human operator.

## 2  Components of a Robot System

The components of a robot system could be discussed either from a physical point view or from a system point of view. Physically, we could divide the system into the robot, power system, and controller (computer). Likewise, the robot itself could be partitioned anthropomorphically into base, shoulder, elbow, wrist, gripper, and tool.

Consequently, we will describe the components of a robot system from the point of view of information transfer[2]. That is, what information or signal enters the component; what logical or arithmetic operation does the component perform; and what information or signal does the component produce? It is important to note that the same physical component many perform identical information operations (e. g., the shoulder and elbow actuators both convert signals to motion in very similar ways).

**Actuator.** Associated with each joint on the robot is an actuator which causes that joint to move. Typical actuators are electric motors and hydraulic cylinders. Typically, a robot system will contain six actuators, since six degrees of freedom are required for full control of position and orientation. Many robot applications do not require this full flexibility, and consequently, robots are often built with five or fewer actuators.

**Sensor.** To control an actuator, the computer must have information regarding the position and possibly the velocity of the actuator. In this context, the term position refers to a displacement from some arbitrary zero reference point for that actuator. For example, in the case of a rotary actuator, "position" would really the angular position and be measured in radians.

Many types of sensors can provide indications of position and velocity. The various types of sensors require different mechanism for interfacing to the computer. In addition, the industrial use of the manipulator requires that the interface be protected from the harsh electrical environment of factory. Sources of electrical noise such as arc welders and large motors can easily make a digital system useless unless care is taken in design and construction of the interface.

**Computation.** We could easily have labeled the computation module "computer", as most of the functions such as servo, kinematics, dynamics and workplace sensor analysis are typically performed by digital computers[3]. However, many of the functions may be performed in dedicated custom hardware or networks of computer. We will, thus, discuss the computational component as if it were a simple computer, recognizing that the need for real-time control may require special equipment and that some of this equipment may even be analog, although the current trend is toward fully digital systems.

In addition to these easily identified components, there are also supervisory operations such as path planning and operator interaction.

## 3 Industrial Robots

In Japan, the Japanese Industrial Robot Association (JIRA) classifies industrial robots by the method of input information and the method of teaching:

- ◆ Manual Manipulators. Manipulators directly activated by the operator;
- ◆ Fixed-sequence Robot. Robot that once programmed for a given sequence of operations is not easily changed;
- ◆ Variable-sequence Robot. Robot that can be programmed for a given sequence of operations and can easily be changed or reprogrammed;
- ◆ Playback Robot. Robot that "memorizes" work sequences taught by a human being who physically leads the device through the intended work pattern; the robot can then create this sequence repetitively from memory;
- ◆ Numerically Controlled (NC) Robot. Robot that operates from and is controlled by digital data, as in the form of punched tape, cards, or digital switches; operates like an NC machine;
- ◆ Intelligence Robot. Robot that uses sensory perception to evaluate its environment and make decisions and proceeds to operate accordingly.

Current and emerging robot applications in industry can be categorized on the complexity and requirements of the job. They range from simple, low technology such as pick-and-place operations through medium technology painting, some assembly and welding operations to high technology precision assembly and inspection operations.

### 3.1 Pike-and-place Operations

The earliest applications of robots were in machine loading-unloading, pick-and-place, and material transfer operations. Such robots typically were not servo controlled and worked with pneumatic or hydraulic power. The load-carrying requirements were high, working in dirty or hazardous factory environments. Replacing unskilled human labor often in hazardous jobs, these robots had to be robust and low in initial and maintenance costs.

### 3.2 Painting, Finishing, and Welding Operations

The next level in the sophistication of industrial robot applications was in spray painting, finishing operations, and spot and arc welding. These applications complemented or replaced certain skilled human labor. Often the justification was by eliminating dangerous environmental exposures. These applications often require tracking complex trajectories such as painting surface contours, hence servo controlled articulated or spherical robot structures were used. Lead-through teaching modes became common, and sometimes sophisticated sensors are employed to maintain process consistency [4] (e. g. , monitoring the weld weave in seam welding operations). Experience has shown that when properly selected and implemented, these robotic applications usually lead to reduced overall manufacturing costs and improved product quality compared with manual method.

### 3.3 Assembly Operations

The most advanced level of technology employing third-generation industrial robot is found in assembly. System repeatability is of utmost importance. End-of-arm tooling must be compliant, i. e. , have both force and displacement control to adjust part insertions, which require that the robot actually "feel" its way along[5]. This technology usually requires a measure of artificial intelligence. Assembly robots generally are electronically driven and operate in clean environments. Assembly robots are expected to exceed lower technology applications.

### 3.4 Other Applications

Other typical applications of robots include inspection, quality control, and repair; processing such as laser and water jet cutting and drilling, riveting, and clean-room operations; and applications in the wood, paper, and food-processing industries. As industrial robot technology and robot intelligence improve even further, additional applications may be justified effectively.

## 4 Walking Robots

There has been great effort in studying mobile robots that use legs as their locomotion system. Some developments are shown in Fig. 10. 1. The legs of walking robots are based on two or three degrees-of-freedom (DOF) manipulators.

Movement on legs confers walking robots certain advantages as opposed to other mobile robots:
- ◆ Legged robots can negotiate irregular terrain while maintaining their body always leveled without jeopardizing their stability;
- ◆ Legged robots boast mobility on stairs, over obstacles and over ditches as one of their main advantages;
- ◆ Legged robots can walk over loose and sandy terrain;
- ◆ Legged robots have inherent omni directionality;
- ◆ Legged robots inflict much less environmental damage than robots that move on wheels or tracks.

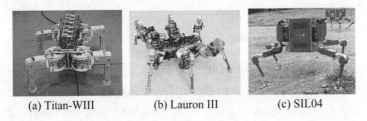

(a) Titan-WIII　　　(b) Lauron III　　　(c) SIL04

Fig. 10.1　Walking robots

## 5　Humanoid Robots

When walking about dynamically stable walking robots, humanoid robots come to mind. Actual autonomous biped robots did not appear until 1967, when Vukobratovic et al. led the first experiments with dermato-skeletons. The first controlled-based biped robot was developed at Waseda University, Tokyo, Japan, in 1972. The robot was called WL-5.

Although the first biped robots were highly simplified machines under statically stable control, later developments have yielded truly sophisticated, extremely light, skillful robots (see Fig. 10.2)[6]. These novel developments have fed a huge amount of research that can be grouped into three major research areas: gait generation, stability control, and robot design.

Research in humanoid robots is currently shifting from locomotion issues to interaction between humans and robots. The dexterity of ASIMO, HRP-2, and QRIO for moving up and down stairs, sitting down and standing up and dancing makes it difficult for biped-locomotion researchers to keep at the summit of legged-robotics research[7]. New trends in humanoid-robotics research consider the robot's ability to interact with humans safely and the robot's ability to express emotions. The final goal will be to insert humanoid robots into the human environment, to assist the elderly and the disabled, to entertain children and to communicate in a natural language.

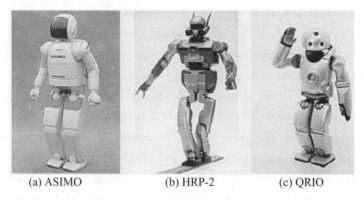

(a) ASIMO　　　　　(b) HRP-2　　　　　(c) QRIO

Fig. 10.2　Latest biped robots

# 6　Robotics

### 6.1　Introduction to Robotics

Robotics is the branch of technology that deals with the design, construction, operation, structural disposition, manufacture and application of robots. Robotics is related to the sciences of electronics, engineering, mechanics, and software.

The word robotics was derived from the word robot, which was introduced to the public by Czech writer Karel Čapek in his play R. U. R. (Rossum's Universal Robots), which premiered in 1921.

According to the Oxford English Dictionary, the word robotics was first used in print by Isaac Asimov, in his science fiction short story "Liar!", published in May 1941 in Astounding Science Fiction. Asimov was unaware that he was coining the term; since the science and technology of electrical devices is electronics, he assumed robotics already referred to the science and technology of robots. In some of Asimov's other works, he states that the first use of the word robotics was in his short story Runaround (Astounding Science Fiction, March

1942). However, the word robotics appears in "Liar!"

## 6.2 Robotics Research

Much of the research in robotics focuses not on specific industrial tasks, but on investigations into new types of robots, alternative ways to think about or design robots, and new ways to manufacture them but other investigations, such as MIT's cyberflora project, are almost wholly academic.

A first particular new innovation in robot design is the open sourcing of robot-projects. To describe the level of advancement of a robot, the term "Generation Robots" can be used. This term is coined by Professor Hans Moravec, Principal Research Scientist at the Carnegie Mellon University Robotics Institute in describing the near future evolution of robot technology. First generation robots, Moravec predicted in 1997, should have an intellectual capacity comparable to perhaps a lizard and should become available by 2010. Because the first generation robot would be incapable of learning, however, Moravec predicts that the second generation robot would be an improvement over the first and become available by 2020, with an intelligence maybe comparable to that of a mouse. The third generation robot should have an intelligence comparable to that of a monkey. Though fourth generation robots, robots with human intelligence, professor Moravec predicts, would become possible, he does not predict this happening before around 2040 or 2050.

The second is Evolutionary Robots. This is a methodology that uses evolutionary computation to help design robots, especially the body form, or motion and behavior controllers. In a similar way to natural evolution, a large population of robots is allowed to compete in some way, or their ability to perform a task is measured using a fitness function. Those that perform worst are removed from the population, and replaced by a new set, which have new behaviors based on those of the winners. Over time the population improves, and eventually a satisfactory robot may appear. This happens without any direct programming of the robots by the researchers. Researchers use this method both to create better robots, and to explore the nature of evolution. Because the process often requires many generations of robots to be simulated, this technique may be run entirely or mostly in simulation, then tested on real robots once the evolved algorithms are good enough. Currently, there are about 1 million industrial robots toiling around the world, and Japan is the top country having high density of utilizing robots in its manufacturing industry.

## Vacabulary

robot ['rəubɔt]    n. 机器人,遥控设备,自动机械;
actuator ['æktjueitə]    n. 驱动器,执行机构
anthropomorphically [ˌænθrəpəu'mɔːfikəli]    adv. 类人地,从人体结构上
articulated robot    关节型机器人
dedicated ['dedikeitid]    adj. 专用的
fixed-sequence robot    固定顺序机器人
gripper ['gripə]    夹持器,抓爪
manipulator [mə'nipjuleitə]    n. 机械手,操作器

peripheral equipment    周边设备,外围设备
playback robot    示教再现式机器人
reprogrammable    adj. 可重复编程的
trajectory ['trædʒiktəri]    n. 轨迹,路线
variable-sequence robot    可变顺序机器人
robotics [rəu'bɔtiks]    n. 机器人学,机器人技术
humanoid ['hjuːmənɔid]    adj. 类人的,有人类特点的

## Notes

[1] A robot is a reprogrammable multifunctional manipulator designed to move material, parts, tools, or specialized devices through variable programmed motions for the performance of a variety of tasks. 可译为:机器人是一种可以改编程序的多功能操纵装置,被设计用来通过可编程运动来完成多种作业,如运送材料、零件、工具或其他专用设备。

[2] Consequently, we will describe the components of a robot system from the point of view of information transfer. 可译为:因此,我们将根据信息传递的观点来描述机器人系统的组成部分。

[3] We could easily have labeled the computation module "computer," as most of the functions such as servo, kinematics, dynamics and workplace sensor analysis are typically performed by digital computers. 可译为:我们可以很容易地将计算模块称为"计算机",因为大部分功能诸如伺服控制、运动学、动力学和工作现场的传感器分析等,通常是由数字计算机来完成。

[4]  Lead-through teaching modes became common, and sometimes sophisticated sensors are employed to maintain process consistency. 可译为:示教型这种方式变得比较常见,有时还需要采用复杂的传感器来保持过程的一致性。

[5]  End-of-arm tooling must be compliant, i. e., have both force and displacement

control to adjust part insertions, which require that the robot actually "feel" its way along. 可译为:臂端工具必须具有顺应功能,也就是说,它们具有受力与位移控制功能,从而调节操作零件的介入,这就要求机器人能实际"感觉"它的运动路径。

[6] Although the first biped robots were highly simplified machines under statically stable control, later developments have yielded truly sophisticated, extremely light, skillful robots. 可译为:尽管在静态稳定控制之下,第一个双足机器人的机构得到了高度简化,但后期的发展才产生了真正精密、极度轻巧、技术熟练的机器人。

[7] The dexterity of ASIMO, HRP-2, and QRIO for moving up and down stairs, sitting down and standing up and dancing makes it difficult for biped-locomotion researchers to keep at the summit of legged-robotics research. 可译为:ASIMO,HRP-2,和QRIO 能够灵巧地上下楼,坐下与起立,还能跳舞,这对双足行走机器人的研究人员试图保持他们在有腿机器人研究方面的顶级成果提出了严峻挑战。

## Exercises

1. Answer the following questions:
(1) What is the definition of robot?
(2) What are the components of a robot system?
(3) Please discuss the attributes of playback robot.
(4) What are the basic elements of industrial robot?
(5) What is the definition of robotics?

2. Translate the following sentences into English:
(1) 可变顺序机器人。可以对这类机器人进行编程,使其按一定的顺序工作,可以很容易地改变这种顺序或者重新编程。

(2) 智能机器人。这种机器人采用感官知觉对它周围的环境进行评价和做出决定,并据此进行工作。

(3) 这些机器人通常被用来替代从事危险性工作的非技术工人,它们必须坚固耐用而且具有较低的使用费用和维修费用。

## Lesson 11    Basics of Microcomputers

### 1  Introduction to Microcomputers

A microcomputer is a computer with a microprocessor as its central processing unit. They are physically small compared to mainframe and minicomputers. Many microcomputers (when equipped with a keyboard and screen for input and output) are also personal computers (in the generic sense. It's considered a personal computer because people can use it in their homes. Microcomputers were invented in the 1970s. Before the invention of microcomputers, people used mainframes and minicomputers. They were big, bulky, expensive computers used at companies and universities. Microcomputers were smaller and cheaper than mainframes and minicomputers.

Size wasn't the only differentiator among microcomputers, minicomputers and mainframes. Minicomputers used core memory technology and a transistor, a piece of metal with wires that moved electrical currents back and forth. Mainframes used vacuum tubes that looked like light bulbs to move electrical currents. To store information, mainframes used punch cards or magnetic tape. Microcomputers use a microprocessor, which is an integrated circuit that's referred to as the central processing unit. The microprocessor is able to move information back and forth through its transistors.

In the late 1960s and early 1970s, minicomputers carried the day, being based on integrated circuits but too large to be called microcomputers. As early as 1956, Isaac Asimov wrote about the possibility of small personal computers, and by the mid-1970s, they had become technologically possible. In 1974, Intel released the Intel 8080, what has been called the first truly usable microprocessor. This microprocessor was then installed in numerous computers, such as the Altair 8800, which were the first true microcomputers. Among the early users were Bill Gates and Steve Ballmer, roommates at Harvard that would go on to found the software behemoth Microsoft. The early arcade game *Space Invaders* ran on a microcomputer powered by the 8080.

In the early and mid-1980s, microcomputers began to slowly edge out of the realm of the nerd and into the mainstream. The Apple II, which launched Apple

Computer to fame, had been released in 1977, and more and more people began to realize its utility for business and in education. Throughout the 1980s, Apple released more machines that were progressively smaller and more powerful, increasing the appeal of microcomputers. Numerous competitors emerged, running operating systems like DOS and Windows. Today, there are over a billion computers in use worldwide.

## 2  The Main Components of the Microcomputer

### 2.1  The Microprocessor

The word "microprocessor" is popularly used when "microcomputer" is meant, in much the same way that "steam engine" is used for "steam locomotive"[1]. To be exact, a microprocessor forms only part of a microcomputer. Microcomputers are based upon digital techniques, are very small and inexpensive enough to be used in limitless engineering applications.

Microcomputers have to been programmed to operate in a required sequence. The fluid power engineer is usually the one who is most familiar with the control sequence of the equipment, so the programming is best done by him.

### 2.2  The Microcomputer

The microprocessor is really quite useless on its own. It must be used with other devices. The basic elements are: microprocessor, to perform logic operation; memory, to hold programs and data; input/output device, to connect the external devices to the microcomputer; and power supply. Such a system can be on a single board which comes complete, ready made and tested. The engineer has to interface the microcomputer with the fluid power system and provide a power supply and program. Other devices added to the basic microcomputer are known as peripherals and well-known examples are printers and visual display units.

### 2.3  Made of Operation

The microprocessor is the "brain" of the microcomputer. It does its work by moving data or information between itself, the memory and the input/output device. It performs simple logical operations on data. The sequence in which it performs these operations is stored in memory in the form of a program. Data are

Unit 3  Mechatronics · 81 ·

coded in binary form or in terms of binary digits. These are expressed mathematically in either 1s or 0s and called bits. Information is handled in units of a fixed number of bits. For example, an 8-bit microprocessor moves data in "bytes" or "words" or 8 bits, whereas a 16-bit microcomputer handles 16-bit words.

The rate at which a microprocessor executes instructions is governed by a timing device. This timing device is often referred as the "clock" and is usually a quartz crystal. Typically one instruction is executed in 1 millionth of a second (1us).

### 2.4 The Bus

The interconnecting structure of the microcomputer is called the "bus". An 8-bit microprocessor will have 8 lines for transferring words of data, perhaps 16 lines for carrying a "memory address", and a few lines control and power supply.

Data are transferred though the bus system to various devices. Information on locations of addresses is transferred via the address bus.

### 2.5 Memory

The memory of a microcomputer holds the program or programs currently being used and provides storage for information such as input values, results of calculations, etc[2]. The engineer must consider two types of memory as these will invariably be present in all systems.

(1) Read Only Memory

Read only memory (ROM) comes in several types;

a. Mask programmed ROM in which the contents are "manufactured" giving a high initial cost but low unit cost. Hence it is used for volume products.

b. Programmable ROM (PROM) in which the user can determine the contents by burning our selected links in the circuit. It is used for medium volume products.

c. Erasable PROM (EPROM) in which the user inserts the contents electrically (using as EPROM programmer) and can erase the contents by means of ultraviolet light. It is used in low volume and developing application.

d. Electrically erasable PROM (EPROM). This holds its contents until erased by an electrical signal.

(2) Random Access Memory

In random access memory (RAM) of read/write memory the contents can be "written into" and "read from" by the microprocessor. It is used for temporary storage of programs and data since its contents are lost when the power supply is removed. It is known as volatile RAM. RAM can come with a battery back-up. It will keep its contents for several years and in effect behave like ROM. It is then known as non-volatile ROM. Where possible, permanent programs should be in ROM cannot be corrupt by electrical interference.

## 2.6 Other Memory Devices

Generally microcomputers used to control fluid power equipment are "dedicated" systems and will only require ROM(usually EPROM)and RAM. Other means of storage are:

Discs: These are used when a lot of memory is required. The engineer may come across them when producing programs on a "development system" with discs[3]. A development system is essentially a general purpose microcomputer with extra facilities. Disc drives are not very robust and are unsuitable for use in harsh environment.

## 2.7 Input/Output

The input/output (I/O) of a microcomputer is the part which is accessible for connecting to external devices. It will usually require an interface. There are various methods of obtaining input/output: parallel output, direct connection to the data bus, isolated input/output put, and serial input/output.

(1) Parallel Port Device

This is a component which provides ports or connections into or out of the microprocessor. Each port is usually of eight bits each in parallel; this is due to the configuration of components which make up the I/O devices. A port can be treated as a whole word or a series of single bits. In some cases, each bit can be used as either an input or an output as required. An example of input would be a signal from a limit switch, and for an output the signal to control the energizing of a solenoid on a valve. Such devices are very versatile, easy to apply and wide use in engineering applications.

(2) Direct Connecting to The Bus

The microcomputer can be expanded by connecting components to the bus. Tailor-made plug-in units, say a board to switch eight solenoids, can be obtained.

(3) Isolated Input/Output

Some microprocessors have locations reserved for I/O with a special set of instructions for fast access and simplified programming. The locations are not part of the normal memory.

(4) Serial port

Data are transmitted by a series of timed pulses rather like Morse code, but the receiving unit has a way of understanding what the pulses mean. It saves having a mass of wires as one wire will suffice. The rate at which these pulses are transmitted is called the "baud" rate. It would only be used where the fluid power system was some distance away from the microcomputer, because of the need to have devices to interpret the signals.

**2.8  DC Power Supplies**

A complete power system with microcomputer control will require various power supplied at different voltage levels. The required stability of the voltage will differ for the various elements, for example, a typical microcomputer needs a stable supply at 5V whilst a solenoid will have a moderately stable 24V DC supply or even an AC voltage supply.

Power provided by the mains needs to be converted to produce DC voltage. There are two main types of power supply which do this linear (low frequency) and switch mode (light frequency).

(1) Linear Power Supplies

The circuit has four main elements to convert alternating current into smooth DC supply:

a. transfer, which is used to convert AC AT MAINS VOLTAGE, SAY, 240V, 50Hz to the required voltage at 50 Hz;

b. Rectifier, which is used to convert the transformed voltage into a fluctuating DC voltage;

c. Capacity, which is used to remove the fluctuations in the DC voltage;

d. Zener diode, which may be added to provide a standard voltage.

A linear power supply will be:

a. inexpensive

b. easy and quick to construct using the simple components, it may be purpose-built to suit any particular requirements.

The drawbacks for such a system will be that:

a. transformer is large and heavy;

b. A large capacitor is needed;

c. The output can be affected by mains interference;

d. The low efficiency of about 30% means that a lot of energy is wasted as heat.

An example of the use for such a power supply is the powering of solenoid valves.

(2) Switch mode supplies

The total system is sophisticated. In simple terms, the method of operation is that the input power is first rectified and then switched on and off at about 20 kHz. In effect, a high frequency source is produced, which can then be harnessed in much the same way as the linear power supply.

### 2.9 Buffers

Microcomputer input/output are normally buffered. A buffer is a small amplifier which is considered as being expendable. When excessive power surges are experienced by the microcomputer, the buffer is destroyed, thus isolating and protecting the microcomputer from damage[4].

The term "buffer" is also used to describe an intermediated storage file for data in memory. This is not something with the engineer will normally be involved.

### Vacabulary

component [kəm'pəunənt]  n. 成分
locomotive ['ləukə,məutiv]  n. 机车;火车头
peripheral [pə'rifərəl]  n. 外围设备 adj. 外围的
interface ['intəfeis]  n. 分界面;接触面
sequence ['siːkwəns]  n. 顺序

binary ['bainəri]  adj. 二进制的
binary digits  二进制数字
read only memory (ROM)  只读存储器
random access memory (RAM)  读写存储器
erasable [iˈreizəbl]  adj. 可擦去的
corrupt [kəˈrʌpt]  v. 破坏;腐烂

volatile ['vɔlətail]  adj. 可丢失
configuration [kən,figju'reiʃən]  n. 结构，组态
Morse Code  莫尔斯电码
interference [,intəfiərəns]  n. 干扰
fluctuation [,flʌktju'eiʃən]  n. 脉动，波动
expendable [ik'spendəbl]  adj. 可消耗的
adaptor [ə'dæptə]  n. 转换器
transformer [træns'fɔːmə]  n. 变压器
rectifier ['rektifaiə]  n. 整流器
capacitor [kə'pæsitə]  n. 电容器
Zener diode  齐纳（稳压）二极管
buffer ['bʌfə]  n. 缓冲寄存器
Baud rate  波特率

## Notes

[1] The word "microprocessor" is popularly used when "microcomputer" is meant, in much the same way that "steam engine" is used for "steam locomotive". 可译为：当表示"微机"时，普遍使用"微处理器"这个词，这就等同于使用"蒸汽机"来指代"蒸汽机车"一样。

[2] The memory of a microcomputer holds the program or programs currently being used and provides storage for information such as input values, results of calculations, etc. 可译为：微机的内存保存有目前正在使用的程序或方案，并提供存储信息，如输入值，计算结果等等。

[3] The engineer may come across them when producing programs on a "development system" with discs. 可译为：当工程师计制作一个关于"开发系统"的方案时，可能会偶然想到使用光盘。

[4] When excessive power surges are experienced by the microcomputer, the buffer is destroyed, thus isolating and protecting the microcomputer from damage. 可译为：当微机通过过大的电涌时，缓冲区被破坏，这样可以使微机隔离以保护其免受损害。

## Exercises

1. Answer the following questions.
(1) What is a microcomputer?
(2) What are the main components of microcomputers?
2. Translate the following sentences into English.
(1) 微型计算机是指带有微处理器作为其中央处理单元的一种计算机。
(2) 微型计算机具体有五大功能部件组成，即：运算器、控制器、储存器、输入设备和输出设备。
(3) 在随机存取存储器的读/写存储器中，内容可以由微处理器"写入"和"读取"。

## Lesson 12　PLC and FMS

### 1　Introduction to PLC

A PLC (i. e. , Programmable Logic Controller) is a device that was invented to replace the necessary sequential relay circuits for machine control. The PLC works by looking at its inputs and depending upon their state, turning on/off its outputs[1]. The user enters a program, usually via software, that gives the desired results.

PLCs are used in many "real world" applications. If there is industry present, chances are good that there is a PLC present. If you are involved in machining, packing, material handling, automated assembly or countless other industries you are probably already using them. If you are not, you are wasting money and time. Almost any application that needs some type of electrical control has a need for a PLC.

For example, let's assume that when a switch turns on we want to turn a solenoid on for 5 seconds and then turn it off regardless of how long the switch is on for. We can do this with a simple external timer. But what if the process included 10 switches and solenoids? We would need 10 external timers. What if the process also needed to count how many times the switches individually turned on? We need a lot of external counters.

As you can see the bigger the process the more of a need we have for a PLC. We can simply program the PLC to count its inputs and turn the solenoids on for the specified time.

This site gives you enough information to be able to write programs far more complicated than the simple one above. We will take a look at what is considered to be the "top 20" PLC instructions. It can be safely estimated that with a firm understanding of these instructions one can solve more than 80% of the applications in existence.

In the late 1960's, PLCs were first introduced. The primary reason for designing such a device was eliminating the large cost involved in replacing the complicated relay based machine control systems. Bedford Associated (Bedford, MA) proposed something called a Modular Digital Controller (MODICON) to a major US car manufacturer. Other companies at the time proposed computer based schemes, one of which was based upon the PDP-8. The MODICON 084 brought the world's first PLC into commercial production.

When production requirements changed so did the control system. This becomes very expensive when the change is frequent. Since relays are mechanical devices they also have a limited lifetime which required strict adhesion to maintenance schedules. Troubleshooting was also quite tedious when so many relays are involved. Now picture a machine control panel that included many, possibly hundreds or thousands, of individual relays. The size could be mind boggling. How about the complicated initial wiring of so many individual devices! These relays would be individually wired together in a manner that would yield the desired outcome. Were there problems? You bet!

These "new controllers" also had to be easily programmed by maintenance and plant engineers. The lifetime had to be long and programming changes easily performed. They also had to survive the harsh industrial environment. That's a lot to ask! The answers were to use a programming technique most people were already familiar with and replace mechanical parts with solid-state ones.

## 2  History of PLC

In the middle 1970's the dominant PLC technologies were sequencer state-machines and the bit-slice based CPU. The AMD 2901 and 2903 were quite popular in Modicon and A-B PLCs. Conventional microprocessors lacked the power to quickly solve PLC logic in all but the smallest PLCs. As conventional microprocessors evolved, larger and larger PLCs were being based upon them. However, even today some are still based upon the 2903 (ref A-B's PLC-3). Modicon has yet to build a faster PLC than their 984A/B/X which was based upon the 2901.

Communications abilities began to appear in approximately 1973. The first such system was Modicon's Modbus. The PLC could now talk to other PLCs and they could be far away from the actual machine they were controlling. They could also now be used to send and receive varying voltages to allow them to enter the analog world. Unfortunately, the lack of standardization coupled continually changing technology has made PLC communications a nightmare of incompatible protocols and physical networks. Still, it was a great decade for the PLC!

The 80's saw an attempt to standardize communications with General Motor's manufacturing automation protocol (MAP). It was also a time for reducing the size of the PLC and making them software programmable terminals or handheld programmers. Today the world's smallest PLC is about the size of a single control relay!

The 90's have seen a gradual reduction in the introduction of new protocols, and the modernization of the physical layers of some of the more popular protocols that survived the 1980's. The latest standard has tried to merge PLC programming languages under one international standard. We now have PLCs that are programmable in function block diagrams, instruction lists, C and structured text all at the same time! PCs are also being used to replace PLCs in some applications. The original company who commissioned the MONICON 084 has actually switched to a PC based control system.

## 3 Introduction to Flexible Manufacturing Systems

A flexible manufacturing system (FMS) is a manufacturing system in which there is some amount of flexibility that allows the system to react in the case of changes, whether predicted or unpredicted. This flexibility is generally considered to fall into two categories, which both contain numerous subcategories.

FMS integrates all the major elements of manufacturing that have been described into a highly automated system[2]. First utilized in the late 1960s, FMS consists of a number of manufacturing cells, each containing an industrial robot serving several CNC machines and an automated material-handling system, all interfaced with a central computer. Different computer instructions for the manufacturing process can be downloaded for each successive part passing through the workstation. This system is highly automated and is capable of optimizing each step of the total manufacturing operation.

Flexible manufacturing systems represent the highest level of efficiency, sophistication, and productivity that has been achieved in manufacturing plants[3]. The flexibility of FMS is such it can handle a variety of part configurations and produce them in any order. Hence, FMS can be regarded as a system that combines the benefits of two systems: (1) the highly productive but inflexible transfer lines; (2) job-shop production, which can produce large product variety on stand-alone machines but is inefficient. Table 12.1 shows the relative characteristics of transfer lines and FMS. Note that in FMS the time required for changeover to a different part is a major attribute of FMS. A variety of FMS technologies are available from machine-tool manufacturers.

Table 12.1 Comparison of the characteristics of transfer lines and flexible manufacturing systems

| CHARACTERISTIC | TRANSFER LINE | FMS |
| --- | --- | --- |
| Types of parts made | Generally few | Infinite |
| Lot size | >100 | 1-50 |
| Part changing time | 1/2 to 8 hr | 1 min |
| Tool change | Manual | Automatic |
| Adaptive control | Difficult | Available |
| Inventory | High | Low |
| Production during breakdown | None | Partial |
| Efficiency | 60%~70% | 85% |
| Justification for capital expenditure | Simple | Difficult |

The main advantage of an FMS is its high flexibility in managing manufacturing resources like time and effort in order to manufacture a new product. The best application of an FMS is found in the production of small sets of products like those from amass production.

**Advantages**

- Preparation time for new products is shorter due to flexibility;
- Improved production quality;
- Saved labor cost;
- Productivity increment.

**Disadvantages**

- Saved labor costs must be weighed against the initial cost of FMS;
- Drawback of increased flexibility may be decreased productivity.

# 4 Elements of FMS

The basic elements of a flexible manufacturing system are workstations, automated handling land transport of materials and parts, and control systems. The types of machines in workstations depend on the type of production. For machining operations, they usually consists of a variety of three-to-five-axis machining centers, CNC lathes, milling machines drill presses, and grinders. Also included are various other pieces of equipment for automated inspection (including coordinate-measuring machines), assembly, and cleaning. Other types of operations suitable for FMS include sheet-metal forming, punching and shearing, and forging, which include heating furnaces, forging machines, trimming presses, heat-treating facilities, and cleaning equipment. The work stations in FMS are arranged to yield the greatest efficiency in production, with an orderly flow of materials, parts, and products through the system.

Because of FMS flexibility, the material-handling storage and retrieval systems are very important. Material handling is controlled by a central computer and performed by automated guided vehicles, conveyors, and various transfer mechanisms. The system is capable of transporting raw materials, blanks, and parts in various stages of completion to any machine, in random order, at any time. Prismatic parts are usually moved in specially designed pallets. Parts with rotational symmetry, such as those for turning operations, are usually moved by mechanical devices and robots.

## 5  Industrial FMS Communication

An industrial flexible manufacturing system (FMS) consists of robots, computer-controlled machines, numerical controlled machines (CNC), instrumentation devices, computers, sensors, and other stand alone systems such as inspection machines. The use of robots in the production segment of manufacturing industries promises a variety of benefits ranging from high utilization to high volume of productivity. Each Robotic cell or node will be located along a material handling system such as a conveyor or automatic guided vehicle. The production of each part or work-piece will require a different combination of manufacturing nodes. The movement of parts from one node to another is done through the material handling system. At the end of part processing, the finished parts will be routed to an automatic inspection node, and subsequently unloaded from the Flexible Manufacturing System.

The FMS data traffic consists of large files and short messages, and mostly come from nodes, devices and instruments. The message size ranges between a few bytes to several hundreds of bytes. Executive software and other data, for example, are files with a large size, while messages for machining data, instrument to instrument communications, status monitoring, and data reporting are transmitted in small size.

There is also some variation on response time. Large program files from a main computer usually take about 60 seconds to be down loaded into each instrument or node at the beginning of FMS operation. Messages for instrument data need to be sent in a periodic time with deterministic time delay. Other type of messages used for emergency reporting is quite short in size and must be transmitted and received with almost instantaneous response.

The demands for reliable FMS protocol that support all the FMS data characteristics are now urgent. The existing IEEE standard protocols do not fully satisfy the real time communication requirements in this environment. The delay of CSMA/CD is unbounded as the number of nodes increases due to the message collisions. Token Bus has a deterministic message delay, but it does not support prioritized access scheme which is needed in FMS communications. Token Ring provides prioritized access and has a low message delay, however, its data transmission is unreliable. A single node failure which may occur quite often in FMS causes transmission errors of passing message in that node. In addition, the topology of Token Ring results in high wiring installation and cost.

A design of FMS communication protocol that supports a real time communication with bounded message delay and reacts promptly to any emergency signal is needed. Because of machine failure and malfunction due to heat, dust, and electromagnetic interference is common, a prioritized mechanism and immediate transmission of emergency messages are needed so that a suitable recovery procedure can be applied. A modification of standard Token Bus to implement a prioritized access scheme was proposed to allow transmission of short and periodic messages with a low delay compared to the one for long messages.

**Vacabulary**

relay [ri'lei]　n. [电工] 继电器　　　　modular digital controller (MODICON)
　　　　　　　　　　　　　　　　　　　　模块化数字控制器

troubleshooting ['trʌbl,ʃuːiŋ] 发现并修理故障,解决纷争
panel [p'pænəl] n. 面板,嵌板,仪表板
sequencer ['siːkwənsə] n. 程序装置,定序器,序列发生器
bit-slice 位片
modbus 模块化总线(一种通信协议,即 Modbus 协议)
terminal ['təːminl] n. 终端,接线端,终点站
Flexible Manufacturing Systems (FMS) 柔性制造系统
manufacturing cell 制造单元
CNC computerized numerical control 计算机化数字控制
successive [sək'sesiv] adj. 连续的,逐步的
sophistication [sə,fistiˈkeiʃən] n. 复杂化,完善,采用先进技术
transfer line 自动生产线
retrieval [ri'triːvəl] n. 补偿,恢复
conveyor [kən'veiə] n. 传送带,传送装置
protocol ['prəutəkɔːl] n. 协议,规程,草案
collision [kə'liʒən] n. 碰撞,冲突
Token Bus 令牌总线,标记总线
Token Ring 令牌环网
topology [təu'pɔlədʒi] n. 拓扑,拓扑学
malfunction [mæl'fʌŋkʃən] n. 运转失常,出现故障

## Notes

[1] The PLC works by looking at its inputs and depending upon their state, turning on/off its outputs. 可译为:PLC 的工作原理是,通过观察其输入量并依赖于这些输入量的状态,来打开或断开其输出。

[2] FMS integrates all the major elements of manufacturing that have been described into a highly automated system. 可译为:柔性制造系统集成了一个高度自动化系统的制造业中的所有主要元素。

[3] Flexible manufacturing systems represent the highest level of efficiency, sophistication, and productivity that has been achieved in manufacturing plants. 可译为:柔性制造系统代表着在制造厂已取得的最高水平的生产效率、复杂性和生产力。

## Exercises

1. Answer the following questions.
(1) What is the meaning of PLC?
(2) What is the meaning of FMS?
(3) What are the advantages of FMS?
(4) What are the basic elements of FMS?

2. Translate the following sentences into English.

(1) 柔性制造系统由许多与中央计算机接口的制造单元组成。

(2) 柔性制造系统综合了两个系统的优点,能处理各种形状的工件,并能以任何方式进行生产。

(3) FMS 设备投资很大,因此,使用前必须对其进行包括诸如能源、物料及劳动力费用等方面的成本分析。

# Unit 4　Hydraulic Transmission

## Lesson 13　Introduction to Fluid Power

　　There are only three basic methods of transmitting power: electrical, mechanical and fluid power. Most applications actually use a combination of the three methods to obtain the most efficient overall system. To properly determine which principle method to use, it is important to know the salient features of each type. For example, fluid systems can transmit power more economically than mechanical systems over greater distances. However, fluid systems are restricted to shorter distances than electrical systems.

　　Fluid-power systems are power-transmitting assemblies employing pressurized liquid or gas to transmit energy from an energy-generating source to an energy-use area.

　　Hydraulic power transmission systems are concerned with the generation, the modulation, the control of pressure and flow and the actuators. In general such systems include:

　　(1) Pumps which convert the available power from the prime movers to the hydraulic power at the actuators.

　　(2) Valves which control the direction of pump-flow, the level of power produced, and the amount of fluid-flow to the actuators. The power level is determined by controlling both the flow and the pressure level.

　　(3) Actuators which convert hydraulic power to usable mechanical power output at the point required.

　　(4) Medium which is a liquid, provides rigid transmission and control as well as lubrication of components, sealing in valves. and cooling of the system.

　　(5) Connectors which link the various system components, provide the power conductors for the fluid under pressure, and the fluid flow return to the tank (reservoir).

　　(6) Fluid storage and conditioning equipment which ensure sufficient quality

and quantity as well as cooling of the fluid.

All hydraulic systems depend on Pascal's law, named after Blaise Pascal, who discovered the law. This law states that pressurized fluid within a closed container — such as cylinder or pipe — exerts equal force on all of the surfaces of the container[1]. (see Appendix of Lesson 30)

In actual hydraulic systems, Pascal's law defines the basis of the results which are obtained from the system. Thus, a pump moves the liquid in the system. The intake of the pump is connected to a liquid source, usually called the tank or reservoir. Atmospheric pressure, pressing on the liquid in the reservoir, forces the liquid into the pump. When the pump operates, it forces liquid from the tank into the discharge pipe at a suitable pressure.

The flow of the pressurized liquid discharged by the pump is controlled by valves. Three control functions are used in most hydraulic systems: (1) control of the liquid pressure, (2) control of the liquid flow rate, and (3) control of the direction of flow of the liquid.

The liquid discharged by the pump in a fluid-power system is directed by valves to a hydraulic motor. A hydraulic motor develops rotary force and motion, using the pressurized liquid as its energy source. Many hydraulic motors are similar to pumps, except that the motor operates in a reverse manner from a pump.

Where linear instead of rotary motion is desired, a cylindrical tube fitted with a movable piston, called a hydraulic cylinder, is often used. When the piston is moved by the pressurized fluid, the piston rod imparts a force or moves an object through a desired distance.

Restricting the movement of the piston in a hydraulic cylinder, as when the piston carries a load, creates a specific pressure relationship within the cylinder[2]. The surface area of the piston face is said to contain a specific number of square inches. The pressure of the pressurized liquid, multiplied by the piston area, produces an output force, measured in pounds, at the end of the piston rod.

The speed of movement of the piston rod depends on how fast the pressurized fluid enters the cylinder. Flow into the cylinder can be directed to either end, producing either a pushing or pulling force at the piston rod end. A seal around the rod where it passes through the cylinder end prevents leakage of the liquid.

Directional control of the piston depends on which end of the cylinder the liquid enters. As pressurized liquid enters one end of the cylinder, liquid must be drained form the other end. The drained liquid is led back to the reservoir. In a pneumatic system using air, the air in the exhausting end of the cylinder is vented to the atmosphere.

Directional-control valves, also called two-way, three-way, four-way, etc., are named in accordance with their basic function. Pressure-control and simple restrictor valves are usually two-way valves. They provide ON or OFF service. A three-way valve may perform several functions, all associated with the three-ports in the valve. For example, the power or pressurized liquid form a pump on a tractor may be sent to the hydraulic system serving the tractor's front-end loader. Or the three-way valve may send the pressurized liquid to a hydraulic motor driving a feed conveyor while the front-end loader is not being used[3].

Three-way valves may also be used to direct pressurized fluid to a single-acting (i. e., force in only one direction) hydraulic cylinder. As the three-way valve is actuated (operated) it can stop the pressurized flow to the cylinder. Further, the same valve can divert liquid from the cylinder to the reservoir, so the cylinder can retract by gravity or return springs and assume its original position.

A four-way valve has four ports or openings. The pressure port directs fluid flow to an area where pressurized liquid is desired. One of the other ports can simultaneously drain liquid from a pressurized area. The drain liquid can be directed to the reservoir.

Hydraulic systems are used in industrial applications such as stamping presses, steel mills, and general manufacturing, agricultural machines, mining industry, aviation, space technology, deep-sea exploration, transportation, marine technology, and offshore gas and petroleum exploration. In short, very few people get without somehow benefiting from the technology of hydraulics through a day of their lives[4].

The secret of hydraulic system's success and widespread use is its versatility and manageability. Fluid power is not hindered by the geometry operations when the potential difference between the tool and the work piece is sufficiently high. Also, power can be transmitted in almost limitless quantities because fluid systems are not so limited by the physical limitations of materials as the electrical systems. For example, the performance of an electromagnet is limited by the saturation limit of steel, on the other hand, the power limit of fluid systems is limited only by the strength capacity of the material[5].

Industry is going to depend more and more on automation in order to increase productivity. This includes remote and direct control of production operations, manufacturing processes and materials handling. Fluid power is the muscle of automation because of the advantages in the following four major categories:

(1) Ease and accuracy of control. By the use of simple levers and push buttons, the operator of a fluid power system can readily start, stop, speed up or slow down, provide any desired horsepower and the position forces with tolerances as precise as one ten-thousandth of an inch.

(2) Multiplication of force. A fluid power system (without using cumbersome gears, pulleys and levers) can multiply forces simply and efficiently from a fraction of an ounce to several hundred tons of output[6].

(3) Constant force or torque. Only fluid power systems are capable of providing constant force or torque regardless of speed changes. It is accomplished whether the work output moves a few inches per hour, several hundred inches per minute, a few revolutions per hour. or thousands of revolutions per minute.

(4) Simplicity, safety, economy. General, fluid power systems use fewer moving parts than the comparable mechanical or electrical systems. Thus, they are simpler to maintain and operate. This maximizes safety, compactness and reliability in turn. For example, a new power steering control designed has made all other kinds of power systems obsolete on many off-highway vehicles[7]. The steering unit consists of a manually operated directional control valve and meter in a single body[8]. Mechanical linkages, universal joints, bearings, reduction gears and so on are eliminated because the steering unit is fully fluid linked[9]. This provides a simple and compact system. In addition, very little input torque is required to produce the control force needed for the toughest applications. This is important where limitations of the control space require a small steering wheel and it becomes necessary to reduce operator fatigue[10].

Additional benefits of fluid power systems include instantly reversible motion, automatic protection against overloads and infinitely variable speed control. Fluid power systems also have the highest horsepower per weight ratio of any known power source.

You, as a student, will find the world of fluid power an interesting and challenging one. Once you master the subject, you will be able to apply the principles you have learned when you operate, maintain, design, or assemble an industrial hydraulic system.

## Vacabulary

fluid ['flu(ː)id]  adj. 流动的;流畅的;不固定的  n. 流体;液体

principle ['prinsəpl]  n. 原理,原则;本质,本义;

salient ['seiljənt, -liənt]  adj. 显著的;突出的;跳跃的  n. 凸角;突出部分

assembly [ə'sembli]  n. 装配;集会,集合

hydraulic [hai'drɔːlik]  adj. 液压的;水力的;水力学的

modulation [ˌmɔdjuˈleiʃən, -dʒu-]  n. 调制;调整

actuator ['æktjueitə]  n. 执行机构;促动器

pump [pʌmp]  vt. 打气  n. 泵,抽水机  vi. 抽水

valve [vælv]  n. 阀;真空管;活门  vt. 装阀于;以活门调节

medium ['miːdiəm, -djəm]  adj. 中间的,中等的  n. 方法;媒体;媒介;

connector [kə'nektə]  n. 连接器,连接头

tank [tæŋk]  (reservoir ['rezəvwɑː])  n. 油箱

Pascal's law  n. 帕斯卡定律

cylinder ['silində]  n. 圆筒;汽缸;圆柱状物

pipe [paip]  n. 管  vt. 用管道输送

piston ['pistən]  n. 活塞

seal [siːl]  n. 密封  vt. 密封;盖章

leakage ['liːkidʒ]  n. 泄露;渗漏物

three-way  adj. 三通的,三向的

tractor ['træktə]  n. 拖拉机;牵引机

port [pɔːt, pəut]  n. 端口,港口,接口

versatility [ˌvəːsə'tiliti]  n. 多功能性;用途广泛

manageability [ˌmænidʒə'biləti]  n. 易处理;易办

electromagnet [iˌlektrəu'mægnit]  n. 电磁体

saturation [ˌsætʃə'reiʃn]  n. 饱和;浸透;磁化饱和

lever ['liːvə, 'le-]  n. 杠杆,控制杆  v. 撬动

button ['bʌtən]  n. 按钮  vt. 扣住;扣紧

tolerance ['tɔlərəns]  n. 公差,容差

cumbersome ['kʌmbəsəm]  adj. 笨重的,累赘的

pulley ['puli]  n. 滑轮,滑车  vt. 用滑轮升起

ounce [auns]  n. 盎司,两

torque [tɔːk]  n. 转矩,扭矩

steer [stiə]  vt. 控制,引导;驾驶  vi. 驾驶,掌舵

meter ['miːtə]  n. 米;仪表  vt. 用仪表测量  vi. 用表计量

reversible [ri'vəːsəbl]  adj. 可逆的,可反转的

## Notes

[1] This law states that pressurized fluid within a closed container — such as cylinder or pipe — exerts equal force on all of the surfaces of the container. 可译为:该定律说明在密闭容器中(例如油缸或管道中)受压液体对容器的各个表面产生作用同样的力。

[2] Restricting the movement of the piston in a hydraulic cylinder, as when the piston carries a load, creates a specific pressure relationship within the cylinder. 可译为:当液压缸中活塞运动受阻时,例如当活塞携有负载时,在缸中必然产生一个比压关系。

[3] For example, the power or pressurized liquid form a pump on a tractor may be sent to the hydraulic system serving the tractor's front-end loader. Or the three-way valve may send the pressurized liquid to a hydraulic motor driving a feed conveyor while the front-end loader is not being used. 可译为:例如,从拖拉机上的泵打出的能量或压力油可以输送到为前端装载机服务的液压系统中。或者当前端装载机不使用时三通阀将压力油送到液压马达以驱动给料运输机。

[4] In short, very few people get without somehow benefiting from the technology of hydraulics through a day of their lives. 可译为:简而言之,在日常生活中很少有人不从液压技术中得到某种益处。

[5] For example, the performance of an electromagnet is limited by the saturation limit of steel, on the other hand, the power limit of fluid systems is limited only by the strength capacity of the material. 可译为:例如,一个电磁体的性能受到钢的磁饱和极限的限制,相反,液压系统的功率仅仅受材料强度的限制。

[6] A fluid power system(without using cumbersome gears, pulleys and levers) can multiply forces simply and efficiently from a fraction of an ounce to several hundred tons of output. 可译为:一个液压系统(没有使用笨重的齿轮、滑轮和杠杆)能简单有效地将不到一盎司的力放大产生几百吨力的输出。

[7] For example, a new power steering control designed has made all other kinds of power systems obsolete on many off-highway vehicles. 可译为:例如,一种用于车辆上的新型动力转向控制装置已淘汰其他类型的转向动力装置。

[8] The steering unit consists of a manually operated directional control valve and meter in a single body. 可译为:该转向部件中包含有人力操纵方向控制阀和分配器。

[9] Mechanical linkages, universal joints, bearings, reduction gears and so on are eliminated because the steering unit is fully fluid linked. 可译为:因为转向部件是

全液压的，没有万向节、轴承、减速齿轮等机械连接。

[10] This is important where limitations of the control space require a small steering wheel and it becomes necessary to reduce operator fatigue. 可译为：这对操作空间限制而需要小方向盘的场合很重要，这也是减轻司机疲劳度所必需的。

**Exercises**

1. What are the three basic methods of transmitting power?
2. What does a hydraulic power transmission system consist of?
3. What are the four major advantages of the fluid power?

# Lesson 14  Fluid Power Pumps

When a hydraulic pump operates, it performs two functions. First, its mechanical action creates a vacuum at the pump inlet which allows atmospheric pressure to force liquid from thereservoir into the inlet line to the pump. Second, its mechanical action delivers this liquid to the pump outlet and forces it into the hydraulic system.

A pump produces liquid movement or flow, but it does not generate pressure. It produces the flow necessary for the development of pressure which is a function of resistance to fluid flow in the system. For example, the pressure of the fluid at the pump outlet is zero for a pump not connected to a system (load). Further, for a pump delivering into a system, the pressure will rise only to the level necessary to overcome the resistance of the load.

## 1  Classification of Pumps

All pumps may be classified as either positive-displacement or non-positive-displacement. Most pumps used in hydraulic systems are positive-displacement.

A non-positive-displacement pump produces a continuous flow. However, because it does not provide a positive internal seal against slippage, its output varies considerably as pressure varies. Centrifugal and propeller pumps are examples of non-positive-displacement pumps.

If the output port of a non-positive-displacement pump were blocked off, the pressure would rise, and output would decrease to zero. Although the pumping element would continue moving, flow would stop because of slippage inside the pump.

In a positive-displacement pump, slippage is negligible compared to the pump's volumetric output flow. If the output port were plugged, pressure would increase instantaneously to the point that the pump's pumping element or its case would fail (probably explode, if the drive shaft did not break first), or the pump's prime mover would stall[1].

### 1.1 Positive-displacement Principle

A positive-displacement pump is one that displaces (delivers) the same amount of liquid for each rotating cycle of the pumping element. Constant delivery during each cycle is possible because of the close-tolerance fit between the pumping element and the pump case. That is, the amount of liquid that slips past the pumping element in a positive-displacement pump is minimal and negligible compared to the theoretical maximum possible delivery. The delivery per cycle remains almost constant, regardless of changes in pressure against which the pump is working. Note that if fluid slippage is substantial, the pump is not operating properly and should be repaired or replaced.

Positive-displacement pumps can be of either fixed or variable displacement. The output of a fixed displacement pump remains constant during each pumping cycle and at a given pump speed. The output of a variable displacement pump can be changed by altering the geometry of the displacement chamber.

Other names to describe these pumps are hydrostatic pumps for positive-displacement and hydrodynamic pumps for non-positive-displacement[2]. Hydrostatic means that the pump converts mechanical energy to hydraulic energy with comparatively small quantity and velocity of liquid. In a hydrodynamic pump, liquid velocity and movement are large; output pressure actually depends on the velocity at which the liquid is made to flow.

### 1.2 Gear Pumps

Gear pumps can be divided into external and internal-gear types. A typical external-gear pump is shown in Fig. 14.1. These pumps come with a straight spur, helical, or herringbone gears. Straight spur gears are easiest to cut and are the most widely used. Helical and herringbone gears run more quietly, but cost more.

A gear pump produces flow by carrying fluid in between the teeth of two

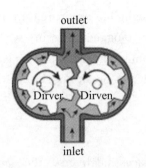

Fig. 14.1 External-gear pump

meshing gears. One gear is driven by the drive shaft and turns the idler gear. The chambers formed between adjacent gear teeth are enclosed by the pump housing and side plates (also called wear or pressure plates).

A partial vacuum is created at the pump inlet as the gear teeth unmesh. Fluid flows in to fill the space and is carried around the outside of the gears. As the teeth mesh again at the outlet end, the fluid is forced out.

Volumetric efficiencies of gear pumps run as high as 93% under optimum conditions. Running clearances between gear faces, gear tooth crests and the housing create an almost constant loss in any pumped volume at a fixed pressure[3]. This means that volumetric efficiency at low speeds and flows is poor, so that gear pumps should be run close to their maximum rated speeds.

Although the loss through the running clearances, or "slip", increases with pressure, this loss is nearly constant as speed and output change. For one pump the loss increases by about 1.5 gpm from zero to 2,000 psi regardless of speed. Change in slip with pressure change has little effect on performance when operated at higher speeds and outputs. External-gear pumps are comparatively immune to contaminants in the oil, which will increase wear rates and lower efficiency, but sudden seizure and failure are not likely to occur.

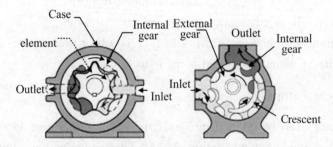

Fig. 14.2 Internal-gear pumps-gerotor and crescent

Internal-gear pumps, as shown in Fig. 14.2, have an internal gear and an external gear. Because these pumps have one or two less teeth in the inner gear than the outer, relative speeds of the inner and outer gears in these designs are low. For example, if the number of teeth in the inner and outer gears were 10 and 11 respectively, the inner gear would turn 11 revolutions, while the outer would turn 10. This low relative speed means a low wear rate. These pumps are small, compact units.

The gerotor internal-gear pump consists of a pair of gears which are always in sliding contact. The internal gear has one more tooth than the gerotor gear. Both gears rotate in the same direction. Oil is drawn into the chamber where the teeth are separating, and is ejected when the teeth start to mesh again. The seal is provided by the sliding contact.

Generally, the internal-gear pump with toothcrest pressure sealing has higher volumetric efficiency at low speeds than the crescent type[4]. Volumetric and overall efficiencies of these pumps are in the same general range as those of external-gear pumps. However, their sensitivity to dirt is somewhat higher.

The crescent seal internal-gear pump consists of an inner and outer gear separated by a crescent-shaped seal. The two gears rotate in the same direction, with the inner gear rotating faster than the outer. The hydraulic oil is drawn into the pump at the point where the gear teeth begin to separate and is carried to the outlet in the space between the crescent and the teeth of both tears. The contact point of the gear teeth forms a seal, as does the small tip clearance at the crescent. Although in the past this pump was generally used for low outputs, with pressures below 1,000-psi, a 2-stage, 4,000-psi model has recently become available.

### 1.3 Vane Pumps

In these pumps, a number of vanes slide in slots in a rotor which rotates in a housing or ring. The housing may be eccentric with the center of the rotor, or its shape may be oval. In some designs, centrifugal force holds the vanes in contact with the housing, while the vanes are forced in and out of the slots by the eccentricity of the housing. In one vane pump, light springs hold the vanes against the housing; in another pump design, pressurized pins urge the vanes outward.

During rotation, as the space or chamber enclosed by vanes, rotor and housing increases, a vacuum is created, and atmospheric pressure forces oil into this space, which is the inlet side of the pump. As the space or volume enclosed reduces, the liquid is forced out through the discharge ports.

The pump illustrated in Fig. 14.3 is unbalanced, because all of the pumping action occurs in the chambers on one side of the rotor and shaft. This design imposes a side load on the rotor and drive shaft. This type vane pump has a circular inner casing. Unbalanced vane pumps can have fixed or variable displacements. Some vane pumps provide a balanced construction in which an elliptical casing forms two separate pumping areas on opposite sides of the rotor, so that the side loads cancel out, as shown in Fig. 14.4[5]. Balanced vane pumps come only in fixed displacement designs.

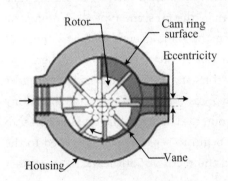    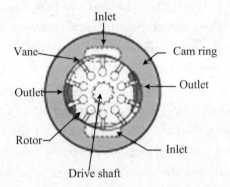

Fig.14.3  Basic (unbalanced) vane pump    Fig.14.4  Balanced vane pump

In a variable-volume unbalanced design, in Fig. 14.3, the displacement can be changed through an external control such as a handwheel or a pressure compensator. The control moves the cam ring to change the eccentricity between the ring and rotor, thereby changing the size of the pumping chamber and thus varying the displacement per revolution.

When pressure is high enough to overcome the compensator spring force, the cam ring shifts to decrease the eccentricity. Adjustment of the compensator spring determines the pressure at which the ring shifts.

Because centrifugal force is required to hold the vanes against the housing and maintain a tight seal at those points, these pumps are not suited for low-speed service. Operation at speeds below 600 rpm is not recommended. If springs or other means are used to hold vanes out against the ring, efficient operation at speeds of 100 rpm to 200 rpm is possible.

Vane pumps maintain their high efficiency for a long time, because compensation for wear of the vane ends and the housing is automatic. As these surfaces wear, the vanes move further out in their slots to maintain contact with the housing.

Vane pumps, like other types, come in double units. A double pump consists of two pumping units in the same housing. They may be of the same or different sizes. Although they are mounted and driven like single pumps, hydraulically, they are independent. Another variation is the series unit: two pumps of equal capacity are connected in series, so that the output of one feeds the other. This arrangement gives twice the pressure normally available from this pump. Vane pumps have relatively high efficiencies. Their size is small relative to output. Dirt tolerance is relatively good.

**1.4 Piston Pumps**

The piston pump is a rotary unit which uses the principle of the reciprocating pump to produce fluid flow. Instead of using a single piston, these pumps have many piston-cylinder combinations. Part of the pump mechanism rotates about a drive shaft to generate the reciprocating motions, which draw fluid into each cylinder and then expels it, producing flow. There are two basic types, axial and radial piston; both are available as fixed and variable displacement pumps. The second variety often is capable of variable reversible (overcenter) displacement.

Most axial and radial piston pumps lend themselves to variable as well as fixed displacement designs. Variable displacement pumps tend to be somewhat larger and heavier, because they have added internal controls, such as handwheel, electric motor, hydraulic cylinder, servo, and mechanical stem.

As shown in Fig. 14.5, the pistons in an axial piston pump reciprocate parallel to the centerline of the drive shaft of the piston block. That is, rotary shaft motion is converted into axial reciprocating motion. Most axial piston pumps are multi-piston and use check valves or port plates to direct liquid flow from inlet to discharge. It varies displacement by changing angle of swashplate.

As shown in Fig. 14.6, the pistons are arranged radially in a cylinder block; they move perpendicularly to the shaft centerline. Two basic types are available: one uses cylindrically shaped pistons, the other ball pistons. They may also be classified according to the porting arrangement: check valve or pintle valve. They are available in fixed and variable displacement, and variable reversible (overcenter) displacement.

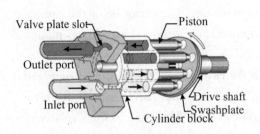
Fig. 14.5 Axial-piston pump

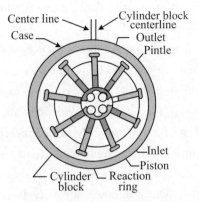
Fig. 14.6 Radial piston pump

In pintle-ported radial piston pump, the cylinder block rotates on a stationary pintle and inside a circular reacting ring or rotor[6]. As the block rotates, centrifugal force, charging pressure, or some form of mechanical action causes the pistons to follow the inner surface of the ring, which is offset from the centerline of the cylinder block. As the pistons reciprocate in their bores, porting in the pintle permits them to take in fluid as they move outward and discharge it as they move in.

The size and number of pistons and the length of their stroke determine pump displacement. Displacement can be varied by moving the reaction ring to increase or decrease piston travel, varying eccentricity. Several controls are available for this purpose.

## 2 Measuring Pump Performance

Volume of fluid pumped per revolution is calculated from the geometry of the oil-carrying chambers. A pump never quite delivers the calculated or the oretical amount of fluid. How close it comes is called volumetric efficiency. Volumetric efficiency is found by comparing the calculated delivery with actual delivery. Volumetric efficiency varies with speed, pressure, and the construction of the pump.

A pump's mechanical efficiency is also less than perfect, because some of the input energy is wasted in friction. Overall efficiency of a hydraulic pump is the product of its volumetric efficiency and the mechanical efficiency.

Pumps are generally rated by their maximum operating pressure capability and their output, in gpm, at a given drive speed, in rpm.

## 3 Matching Pump Power with the Load

Pressure compensation and load sensing are terms often used to describe pump features that improve the efficiency of pump operation. Sometimes these terms are used interchangeably, a misconception that is cleared up once you understand the differences in how the two enhancements operate[7].

To investigate these differences, consider a simple circuit using a fixed-displacement pump running at constant speed. This circuit is efficient only when the load demands maximum power because the pump puts out full pressure and flow regardless of load demand. A relief valve prevents excessive pressure buildup by routing high-pressure fluid to tank when the system reaches the relief setting. Power is wasted whenever the load requires less than full flow or full pressure. The unused fluid energy produced by the pump becomes heat that must be dissipated. Overall system efficiency may be 25% or lower.

Variable displacement pumps, equipped with displacement controls, can save most of this wasted hydraulic horsepower when moving a single load. Control variations include hand wheel, lever, cylinder, stem servo, and electrohydraulic servo controls.

While matching the exact flow and pressure needs of a single load, these controls have no inherent pressure or power-limiting capabilities[8]. And so, other provisions must be made to limit maximum system pressure, and the prime mover still must have corner horsepower capability. Moreover, when a pump supplies a circuit with multiple loads, the flow and pressure-matching characteristics are compromised.

A design approach to the system in which one pump powers multiple loads is to use a pump equipped with a proportional pressure compensator. Using a variable-displacement, pressure-compensated pump rather than a fixed-displacement pump reduces circuit horsepower requirements dramatically. Output flow of this type of pump varies according to a predetermined discharge pressure as sensed by an orifice in the pump's compensator. Because the compensator itself operates from pressurized fluid, the discharge pressure must be set higher-say, 200 psi higher-than the maximum load-pressure setting.

A two-stage pressure-compensator control, uses pilot flow at load pressure across an orifice in the main stage compensator spool to create a pressure drop of 300 psi. This over the compensator setting and shifts the main stage spool, porting pump output fluid to the stroking piston, which overcomes bias piston force and reduces pump displacement to match load requirements.

The earlier stated misconception stems from an observation that output pressure from a pressure-compensated pump can fall below the compensator setting while an actuator is moving[9]. This does not happen because the pump is sensing the load, it happens because the pump is undersized for the application. Pressure drops because the pump cannot generate enough flow to keep up with the load. When properly sized, a pressure-compensated pump should always force enough fluid through the compensator orifice to operate the compensator.

## Vacabulary

positive-displacement　adj. 容积式的
centrifugal [sen'trifjugəl]　adj. 离心的;远中的 n. 离心机;转筒
propeller pumps　n. 旋桨泵;离心泵
slippage ['slipidʒ]　n. 滑移;滑动;下降
helical ['helikəl]　adj. 螺旋形的
herringbone ['heriŋbəun]　n. 人字形图案 adj. 人字形的 vt. 在……上作人字形图案
running clearances　运行间隙;齿侧隙
contaminant [kən'tæminənt]　n. 污染物;致污物
gerotor　n. 内齿轮油泵
toothcrest [ˌtuːθkrest]　n. 齿顶
crescent ['kresənt]　n. 新月状物 adj. 新月形的;
vane [vein]　n. 叶片;[气象] 风向标;风信旗
slot [slɔt]　n. 位置;狭槽 vt. 跟踪;开槽
rotor ['rəutə]　n. 转子;旋转体

eccentricity [ˌeksen'trisəti]　n. 偏心率,偏离程度
elliptical [ˌeksen'trisəti]　adj. 椭圆的;省略的
reciprocate [ri'siprəkeit]　vt. 报答;互换 vi. 往复运动;互换;
handwheel ['hændwiːl]　n. 手轮,操纵轮;驾驶盘
servo ['səːvəu]　n. 伺服;随动系统
swashplate ['swɔʃpleit]　n. 挡板;滑盘;旋转斜盘
pintle valve　n. 针形阀;销形阀;配流轴;分流器;
bore [bɔː]　vi. 钻孔 vt. 钻孔;使烦扰 n. 孔
misconception [ˌmiskən'sepʃən]　n. 误解;错觉;错误想法
dissipate ['disipeit]　vt. 浪费;使……消散 vi. 驱散;放荡
orifice ['ɔrifis]　n. 孔口
orifice meter　孔板流量计

orifice size  喷嘴直径；节流面积
pilot ['pailət]  n. 飞行员；领航员 adj. 试点的 v. 驾驶；领航

spool spring  线性弹簧

## Notes

[1] If the output port were plugged, pressure would increase instantaneously to the point that the pump's pumping element or its case would fail (probably explode, if the drive shaft did not break first), or the pump's prime mover would stall. 可译为：如果出口被堵，压力会瞬间增加直到泵件或泵体失效（如果驱动轴不首先破坏的话就可能爆炸），或使泵的驱动电机停转。

[2] Other names to describe these pumps are hydrostatic pumps for positive-displacement and hydrodynamic pumps for non-positive-displacement. 可译为：还可以用流体静压泵来描述容积式泵，用液动力泵来描述非容积式泵。

[3] Running clearances between gear faces, gear tooth crests and the housing create an almost constant loss in any pumped volume at a fixed pressure. 可译为：在压力不变的情况下泵输出任何流量时，齿轮齿面、齿顶和容腔之间的转动间隙都产生恒定的损失。

[4] Generally, the internal-gear pump with toothcrest pressure sealing has higher volumetric efficiency at low speeds than the crescent type. 可译为：一般来说，带齿顶压力密封的内齿轮泵在低速时比新月型齿轮泵具有更高的容积效率。

[5] Some vane pumps provide a balanced construction in which an elliptical casing forms two separate pumping areas on opposite sides of the rotor, so that the side loads cancel out, as shown in Fig. 14.4. 可译为：一些叶片泵具有平衡的结构，椭圆形的容腔在转子的两侧形成两个独立的抽吸区域，使侧面负载相互抵消，如图14.4。

[6] In pintle-ported radial piston pump, the cylinder block rotates on a stationary pintle and inside a circular reacting ring or rotor. 可译为：在配流传输的径向柱塞泵中，在圆形作用环或转体的内部，缸体在静止的配流轴上旋转。

[7] Sometimes these terms are used interchangeably, a misconception that is cleared up once you understand the differences in how the two enhancements operate. 可译为：有时这些术语被互换使用，一旦你理解了这两种功能运作的区别你就会发现这是一个误解。

[8] While matching the exact flow and pressure needs of a single load, these controls have no inherent pressure or power-limiting capabilities. 可译为：当匹配单一载荷确定的流量和压力时，这些控件没有压力或功率的控制能力。

[9] The earlier stated misconception stems from an observation that output pressure from a pressure-compensated pump can fall below the compensator setting while an actuator is moving. 可译为：早期的误解源自于当执行元件动作时压力补偿泵的输出压力能够低于补偿机构设置的观察。

## Exercises

1. What is the positive-displacement principle?
2. Please describe the working principle of the gear pumps, the vane pumps and the piston pumps separately.
3. How do we measure pump performance?

## Lesson 15  Hydraulic Cylinder and Rams

The linear motion and high force produced by cylinders are big reasons why designers specify hydraulic and pneumatic systems in the first place. One of the most basic of fluid power components, cylinders have evolved into an almost endless array of configurations, sizes and special designs. This versatility not only makes more-innovative designs possible, but makes many applications a reality that would not be practical or possible without cylinders.

### 1  Cylinder Basics

The most common cylinder configuration is double acting, as shown in Fig. 15.1. Routing pressurized fluid into the rod end of a double-acting cylinder causes the piston rod to retract. Conversely, routing pressurized fluid into the cap end causes the rod to extend. Simultaneously, fluid on the opposite side of the piston flows back into the hydraulic reservoir. (If air is the fluid medium, it usually is vented to the atmosphere.)

Because the area of the rod-end piston face is smaller than the cap-end area, extension force is greater than retraction force (assuming equal fluid pressures). Because total cylinder volume is less with the cylinder fully retracted (because of rod volume) than when the cylinder is fully extended, a cylinder retracts faster than it extends (assuming equal flow rates) [1].

Single-acting cylinders, as shown in Fig. 15.2, accept pressurized fluid on only one side of the piston; volume on the other side of the piston is vented to atmosphere or returns to tank. Depending on whether it is routed to the cap end or rod end, the pressurized fluid may extend or retract the cylinder, respectively. In either case, force generated by gravity or a spring returns the piston rod to its original state. A hydraulic jack for vehicles represents a common application of a single-acting, gravity-return cylinder.

Single-acting cylinders can be spring-extend or the more common spring-return type. A spring-extend cylinder is useful for tool-holding fixtures because spring force can hold a workpiece indefinitely. The cylinder then releases the workpiece upon application of hydraulic pressure. Spring-applied/hydraulic-pressure-released (parking) brakes represent another common application of single-acting, spring-extend cylinders [2].

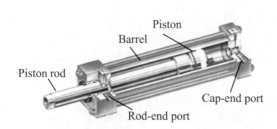 

Fig. 15.1　Double-acting cylinder　　　　Fig. 15.2　Single-acting cylinder

But the most common type of single-acting cylinder uses a return spring. In this version, pressurized fluid enters the cap end of the cylinder to extend the piston rod. When fluid is allowed to flow out of the cap end, the return spring exerts force on the piston rod to retract it. Factory automation — especially material handling — is a common application using pneumatic spring-return cylinders.

## 2　Standard Constructions

Construction variations for single- and double-acting cylinders are based primarily on how the two end caps are attached to the barrel. Additional variations include wall thickness of the barrel and end caps, and materials of construction.

Tie-rod cylinders, as shown in Fig. 15.1, have square or rectangular end caps secured to each end of the barrel by rods that pass through holes in the corners of the end caps. Nuts threaded onto the end of each tie rod secure the end caps to the barrel. Static seals in the barrel/end-cap interface prevent leakage. A number of variations to this design exist, including use of more than four tie rods on a cylinder, or long bolts that thread into tapped holes in one of the end caps.

The majority of cylinders for industrial, heavy-duty applications use tie-rod construction and usually conform to National Fluid Power Association (NFPA) standards. These standards establish dimensional uniformity so cylinders from multiple manufacturers can be interchanged. However, care should be taken when interchanging cylinders because even though it conforms to NFPA dimensional standards, a cylinder may have proprietary features from its specific manufacturer that may not be available from a different manufacturer.

Welded cylinders, as shown in Fig. 15. 3, have end flanges welded to the barrel and an end cap attached to each flange. End caps are secured in place by bolts that slip through holes in each end cap and thread into tapped holes in each end flange. This construction is lighter and more compact than the standard tie-rod configuration, which explains why welded cylinders find wide application in mobile equipment.

A variation to this construction has each end cap threaded into the end of the barrel. This construction, however, usually cannot accommodate as high a pressure rating as welded and can be more difficult to disassemble and reassemble [3].

Mill-duty cylinders, as shown in Fig. 15. 4, have flanges welded to the ends of the cylinder barrels with end caps of the same diameter as the flanges. Bolts secure the end caps to the flanges. Their construction is similar to that of welded cylinders, but mill-duty cylinders have thicker barrel walls and heavier construction in general.

Fig. 15.3  Welded cylinder

Fig. 15.4  Mill-duty cylinders

Large mill-duty cylinders often have a barrel wall thick enough for the end-cap bolts to be threaded directly into the barrel wall. As the name implies, these cylinders were originally designed for use in steel mills, foundries, and other severe-duty applications.

At the other end of the duty spectrum are non-repairable cylinders, as shown in Fig. 15.5. These cylinders are designed for economy and have end caps welded to the barrel to make them throwaway components. They cannot be disassembled for repair or seal replacement. However, this design proves very cost effective when high service life is not required. Most of these cylinders have stainless steel end caps and barrel, but because they are intended primarily for light duty cycles, many make extensive use of aluminum alloys and plastics for light weight and economy.

An alternative method of manufacture rolls the tube into a slot on the end caps to mechanically lock the three pieces together [4]. Another alternative design has the end cap welded to the barrel and a rod-end cap secured via threads or a lock ring. These modifications allow disassembling the cylinder for repair but also raise its initial cost.

Fig. 15.5  Non-repairable cylinders

Fig. 15.6  Telescoping cylinders

## 3  Common Variations

The most common type cylinder is the single-rod end, in which the rod is nearly as long as the cylinder barrel. The rod protrudes from the rod-end cap to transmit the generated force to the load. A double rod-end cylinder, as shown in Fig. 15.5, has a rod attached to both faces of the piston with each rod extending through a rod end cap. Double rod-end cylinders are useful for moving two loads simultaneously, and they also eliminate the differential area between the rod side and blank side of the piston. With equal areas (and cylinder volumes) on both sides of the piston, a given flow produces the same extension and retraction speeds.

Most telescoping cylinders, as shown in Fig. 15.6, are single acting, although double-acting versions are available. Telescoping cylinders contain five or more sets of tubing, or stages, which nest inside one another. Each stage is equipped with seals and bearing surfaces to act as both a cylinder barrel and piston rod. Available for extensions exceeding 15 ft, most are used on mobile applications where available mounting space is limited. The collapsed length of a telescoping cylinder can be as little as 15 its extended length, but the cost is several times that of a standard cylinder that can produce equivalent force. Models are available in which all stages extend simultaneously or where the largest stage extends first, followed by each successively smaller stage.

Ram cylinders are a special type of single-acting cylinders that have a rod OD the same diameter as the piston. Used mostly for jacking purposes, ram cylinders must be single acting because there is no internal cylinder volume to pressurize for retracting the rod. Ram cylinders sometimes are called plunger cylinders and are most often used for short-stroke applications. Most do not use return springs, but, rather, gravity or the load to retract the piston rod.

Short-stroke cylinders, as shown in Fig. 15.7, generally have a rod length that is less than the piston diameter. It is used where high force must be generated from a relatively low supply pressure. Short-stroke cylinders also fit into a narrow axial space but require substantial radial width. These cylinders lend themselves to air-operated, automation machinery.

Tandem cylinders, on the other hand, are designed for applications where high force must be generated within a narrow radial space where substantial axial length is available. A tandem cylinder, as shown in Fig. 15.8, functions as two single rod-end cylinders connected in line with each piston inter-connected to a common rod as well as a second rod which extends through the rod-end cap. Each piston chamber is double acting to produce much higher forces without an increase in fluid pressure or bore diameter.

Duplex cylinders also have two or more cylinders connected in line, but the pistons of a duplex cylinder, as shown in Fig. 15.9, are not physically connected; the rod of one cylinder protrudes into the non-rod end of the second, and so forth. A duplex cylinder may consist of more than two in-line cylinders and the stroke lengths of the individual cylinders may vary. This makes them useful for achieving a number of different fixed stroke lengths, depending on which individual pistons are actuated.

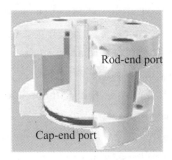

Fig. 15.7　Short-stroke cylinder　　　　Fig. 15.8　Tandem cylinder

Diaphragm cylinders, as shown in Fig. 15.10, are either of the rolling diaphragm or the short-stroke type. Both use elastomeric diaphragms to seal the barrel-piston interface. The short-stroke type uses an elastomer sheet secured between halves of the cylinder body and is commonly used for truck and bus air-brake applications. The rolling diaphragm cylinder has a hat-shaped diaphragm that rolls into the cylinder barrel as the piston advances. Both types require very low breakout forces, have zero leakage, and are single-acting, spring returned.

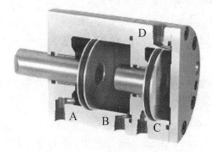
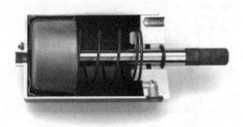

Fig. 15.9　Duplex cylinder　　　　Fig. 15.10　Diaphragm cylinder

## 4　Installation

Proper installation begins with machine layout; here are some rules:

If high shock loads are anticipated, mount the cylinder to take full advantage of its elasticity, and don't forget: the fluid lines are along for the ride, hold fixed-mounted cylinders in place by keying or pinning at one end only [5].

Use separate keys to take shear loads: at the head end if major shock loads are in thrust, at the cap end if they are in tension [6].

Locating pins may be used instead of shear keys to help take shear loads and insure cylinder alignment. Avoid pinning across corners — this can cause severe warpage when a cylinder is subjected to operating temperature and pressure. Such warpage also is imposed on fluid connectors at cylinder ports.

Pivoted mounts should have the same type of pivot as the cylinder body and the head end. Pivot axes should be parallel, never crossed.

Many fluid power cylinders incorporate cushions to absorb the energy of moving masses at the end of a stroke, including the masses of the piston and rod, the load being moved, and the fluid medium operating the cylinder. When the cushion operates, the additional thrust is imposed on the cylinder assembly and it will change length. What about the fluid conductors?

Consider protecting exposed rods from abrasion and corrosion that could destroy the rod surface and, in turn, the rod seal. In especially dirty environments, protect the rod with a cover such as a rod boot or bellows.

## Vacabulary

double-acting　adj. 双重作用的；双动的
rod-end　n. 杆端
cap-end　n. 端盖
single-acting　adj. 单作用的；单动的
jack [dʒæk]　n. 千斤顶　vt. 抬起；用千斤顶顶起某物
brake [breik]　vi. 刹车　n. 闸,刹车,阻碍　vt. 刹车
pneumatic [nju:'mætik]　adj. 气动的；充气的；有气胎的　n. 气胎
barrel ['bærəl]　vt. 把……装入桶内　n. 桶；枪管,炮管　vi. 快速移动
tie-rod　n. 连接杆,拉条
nut [nʌt]　n. 螺母,螺帽；坚果　vi. 采坚果

static seal　静态密封
bolt [bəult]　n. 螺栓；闪电
weld [weld]　vt. 焊接；使结合　vi. 焊牢　n. 焊接；焊接点
flange [flændʒ]　n. 法兰,凸缘　vt. 给……装凸缘
tapped hole　螺纹孔
pressure rating　压力等级；压力额定值
mill-duty　adj. 钢厂用的,重型的
spectrum ['spektrəm]　n. 光谱；频谱；范围
throwaway ['θrəuə,wei]　n. 废品；传单　adj. 抛弃型的
cost effective　有成本效益的；划算的
light duty　轻型的；轻负荷

Unit 4　Hydraulic Transmission

telescope ['teliskəup]　vt. 压缩；使套叠 vi. 套叠　n. 望远镜
ram [ræm]　n. 柱塞；连杆
tandem ['tændəm]　n. 串联　adj. 串联的 adv. 一前一后地
duplex cylinder　双缸
diaphragm ['daiəfræm]　n. 隔膜；隔板；光圈
locating pin　定位销

across corners　对角
key [ki:]　n. 键；关键　vt. 键入
warpage ['wɔ:peidʒ]　n. 翘曲，弯曲
overhung [,əuvə'hʌŋ, 'əuvəhʌŋ]　adj. 悬臂式的　vt. 悬于之上
skew [skju:]　n. 歪斜　adj. 歪斜的
clevis ['klevis]　n. U 形夹；连接叉
trunnion ['trʌnjən]　n. 耳轴；炮耳

## Notes

[1] Because total cylinder volume is less with the cylinder fully retracted (because of rod volume) than when the cylinder is fully extended, a cylinder retracts faster than it extends (assuming equal flow rates). 可译为：由于活塞杆的体积影响，缸全部缩进时缸内容积比缸全部伸出时要少，因此缸缩进速度会快于伸出速度（假设流动速率相等）。

[2] Spring-applied/hydraulic-pressure-released (parking) brakes represent another common application of single-acting, spring-extend cylinders. 可译为：弹簧夹紧/液压松开（停车）的刹车代表了单作用、弹簧复位缸的又一个常见应用。

[3] This construction, however, usually cannot accommodate as high a pressure rating as welded and can be more difficult to disassemble and reassemble. 可译为：然而，这种结构通常不能适应焊接缸那么高的额定压力，拆卸和重新组装也更困难。

[4] An alternative method of manufacture rolls the tube into a slot on the end caps to mechanically lock the three pieces together. 可译为：另外一个替代的制造方法是滚动管件进入端盖上的沟槽再把这三者加以机械锁定。

[5] If high shock loads are anticipated, mount the cylinder to take full advantage of its elasticity, and don't forget: the fluid lines are along for the ride, hold fixed-mounted cylinders in place by keying or pinning at one end only. 可译为：如果预计有高冲击负荷，就要充分利用弹性来安装缸，记住流体管路要随动，仅仅在缸的一端用键或销使安装缸定位。

[6] Use separate keys to take shear loads: at the head end if major shock loads are in thrust, at the cap end if they are in tension. 可译为：使用独立的键去承受剪切载荷：如果主要的冲击载荷是推力，键放置在头端，如果主要的冲击载荷是拉力，键放置在后盖。

**Exercises**

1. What is the difference between the double-acting cylinder and the single-acting cylinder?

2. Please think about the standard constructions and the common variations of cylinders.

3. What should we notice when we install and operate the cylinders?

# Lesson 16　Industrial Hydraulic Circuits

## 1　Perface

A number of circuits are used frequently in fluid power systems to perform useful functions. For example, metering circuits offer precise control of actuator speed without a lot of complicated electronics, decompression circuits reduce pressure surges within a hydraulic system by controlling the release of stored fluid energy, and pump-unloading and regenerative circuits make a system more energy efficient. Other circuits are designed for safety, sequencing of operations, and for controlling force, torque, and position. Still other circuits may enhance the application of specific components, such as pumps, motors, accumulators, filters, and airline lubricators.

The circuits appearing on the following pages are provided as a resource of general ideas. They may be used as an educational resource to aid understanding of circuits already in use, a starting point for new designs or a modification to enhance operation of existing equipment.

They certainly do not have to be implemented as shown. In fact, many of the circuits use purely mechanical components, so incorporating them into new or retrofit applications may involve integrating electronic feedback and control into the circuit as a modern alternative to mechanical control [1]. However, many existing and new applications still gain the greatest benefit from mechanical control — especially those applications where electricity could pose a threat to health and safety. However, whether using mechanical or electronic control, perhaps the greatest benefit may be gained by customizing one of these circuits to serve the specific requirements of an application [2].

## 2  Basic Circuits Used in Fluid Power Systems

### 2.1  Pump-unloading Circuits

When the open-center system is in neutral, pump output flows through the directional control valve to tank [3]. When this simple circuit handles only low flows and the directional valve spool has tapered lands, it proves to be very efficient. If several cylinders are used, the valve can be connected in series — that is, the tank port of one valve is connected to the pressure port of the next.

A pressure-compensated, variable-volume pump is controlled by system pressure. As pressure increases, displacement of the pump decreases so that pump output at the preset pressure is only sufficient to make up for leakage. Used with a closed-center valve, the pump is stroked to minimum (zero) displacement when the valve is centered, as shown in Fig. 16.1.

Many systems require a high volume at low pressure for rapid traverse of a vise or tool, and then low volume, high pressure for clamping or feeding. This can be accomplished by a hi-lo circuit using two pumps, as shown in Fig. 16.2. During rapid traverse, both pumps supply the system. When pressure rises during clamping or feed, the large-volume main pump unloads, and the small pump maintains pressure. Output flow of the small pump is low enough to prevent heating of the oil. Instead of pilot operation, the unloading valve can be solenoid controlled and actuated by a pressure switch.

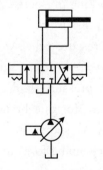
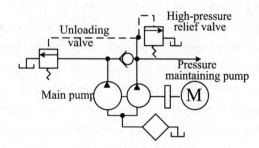

Fig. 16.1  Pressure-compensated pump circuit

Fig. 16.2  Hi-lo circuit

## 2.2 Pressure-control Circuits

When open- or tandem-center valves are used in circuits requiring pilot pressure to shift the valves, there must be a means of maintaining pressure when the valves are in neutral [4]. One method is to install a backpressure check valve in the tank line. The check valve maintains a backpressure of, say, 50 psi.

Energizing the solenoid extends the cylinder at a maximum pressure corresponding to the main system relief valve setting, as shown in Fig. 16.3. De-energizing the solenoid valve retracts the cylinder and holds it retracted at the reduced pressure setting of the pilot relief valve. The check valve prevents the pilot relief valve from operating during cylinder extension.

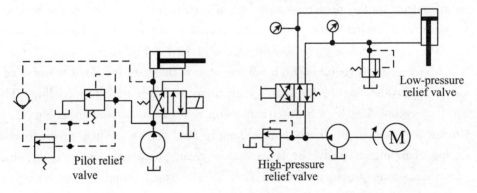

Fig. 16.3  Low-pressure retraction circuit        Fig. 16.4  Two relief valves circuit

Using two relief valves in this circuit gives two working pressures. As shown in Fig. 16.4, on the up stroke of the cylinder, the low-pressure relief valve limits system pressure. During the down stroke, the high-pressure relief valve limits maximum press tonnage for doing work. Using the low-pressure relief on the up stroke saves power by supporting the cylinder with low-pressure fluid.

In a system with only one pump, reduced pressure for one branch of the circuit can be obtained with a pressure-reducing valve. As shown in Fig. 16.5, this circuit is typical for a welder, which requires high clamping force to be set by the relief valve and reduced force on the welding gun to be set by the pressure-reducing valve. Placing the check valve in parallel with the pressure-reducing valve allows free return flow when the weld cylinder retracts.

Regulating pump pressure from a remote station can be accomplished by using small, pilot relief valves connected to the systems main pilot-operated relief valve. With the 3-way solenoid valve de-energized, system pressure is limited to 1,500 psi in this circuit as shown in Fig. 16. 6. Energizing the 3-way solenoid valve permits venting the relief valve to either 1,000 psi or 500 psi, depending on the position of the 4-way valve, which is determined by the pilot signal it receives.

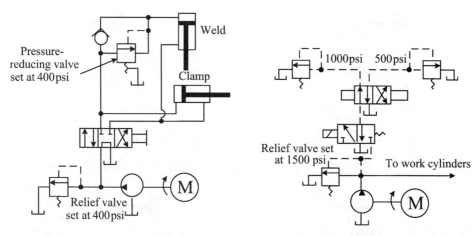

Fig. 16. 5　Reduced pressure circuit　　　　Fig. 16. 6　Remote control circuit

### 2.3　Speed-control Circuits

Speed control during a work stroke can be accomplished by regulating flow to the cylinder. A meter-in circuit normally gives finer speed control than a meter-out circuit. The check valve allows free reverse flow when the cylinder retracts.

Regulating flow from the cylinder is another way to control speed. As shown in Fig. 16. 7, this circuit maintains a constant backpressure during rod extension and prevents lunging if the load drops quickly or reverses.

As shown in Fig. 16. 8, flow to the cylinder is regulated by metering part of the pump flow to tank. This circuit is more efficient than meter-in or meter-out, as pump output is only high enough to overcome resistance. However, it does not compensate for pump slip.

Pump flow can be controlled by various means such as manual, electric motor, hydraulic, or mechanical. How closely flow output actually matches command depends on slip in part, which increases with load. As shown in

Fig. 16.9, with a pressure-compensated, variable-volume pump, output flow decreases with the increasing pressure. This type of pump can be used for traverse and clamp operations. An external relief valve is usually unnecessary when a pressure-compensated pump is used. For details on the different types of pumps, their operation, and how they vary flow, refer to the pumps section of the handbook [5].

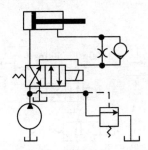

Fig. 16.7   Meter-out circuit

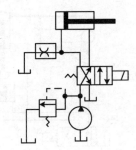

Fig. 16.8   Bleed-off circuit

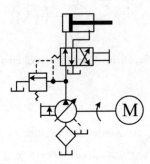

Fig. 16.9   Variable-volume pump circuit

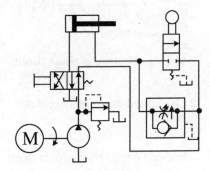

Fig. 16.10   Variable feed circuit

Many machines require intermittent fast and slow feed during their cycles. This can be accomplished by having a cam-operated 2-way valve in parallel with a meter-out flow control valve as shown in Fig. 16.10. Rapid forward movement takes place any time the 2-way valve is open. Closing off the valve slows down cylinder speed. Properly positioning the cams obtains the required speeds in sequence. The check valve in parallel with the flow control permits free return flow, allowing the cylinder rod to return rapidly.

## 2.4 Sequencing Circuits

Cylinders may be sequenced by restricting flow to one cylinder. One method of restricting flow is with backpressure check valves. They prevent flow until a set pressure is reached. In this circuit, a cylinder can extend and retract ahead of another cylinder.

Several cylinders can be connected to move in sequence on forward and return strokes. As shown in Fig. 16.11, in this circuit a clamp must close before a drill descends. On the return stroke, the drill must pull out of the work before the clamp opens. The sequence valves are arranged to cause pressure buildup when one cylinder completes its stroke, the valve opens to allow flow to the other cylinder.

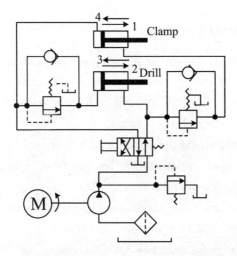

Fig. 16.11 Sequence valves circuit

Limit switches momentarily actuated by the cylinders control the solenoid valves to sequence this circuit [6]. Solenoid a is energized by a pushbutton to initiate movement 1. As shown in Fig. 16.12, at the completion of movement 1, limit switch E is actuated to energize solenoid c, initiating movement 2. At the end of movement 2, limit switch F is actuated to energize solenoid b, initiating movement 3. At the end of this movement, limit switch G is actuated to energize solenoid d, initiating movement 4. The sequence valves prevent a pressure drop in either cylinder while the other operates.

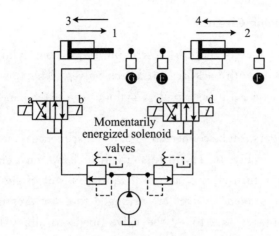

Fig. 16.12  Electrical control circuit

## 2.5  Synchronizing Circuits

An effective flow divider can be made up of two fluid motors of the same size coupled together. Both motors must rotate at the same speed and, therefore, deliver equal volumes of fluid. Variations in load or friction do not greatly affect synchronization, but motor slip is a factor.

One of the considerations in synchronizing cylinders is leakage replacement. Under normal pressure, leakage can be practically zero over one stroke. Accumulated error is the main concern. A replenishing circuit, which replaces leakage after each cylinder stroke, eliminates this trend. In the circuit of Fig. 16.13, the cylinders are connected in series and controlled by the 4-way manual valve. The cylinders actuate limit switches, which control valves A and B. On the return stroke, if cylinder 1 bottoms first, valve A is actuated to open valve C, permitting excess fluid from cylinder 2 to flow to tank. If cylinder 2's piston returns first, valve B is actuated to direct fluid to retract cylinder 1.

Mechanically tying two cylinders together by installing a rack on each piston rod and fastening the pinions to a single shaft works well when the linkage is rigid and the mesh is proper as shown in Fig. 16.14 [7]. A chain and sprocket arrangement can be used if synchronized motion is required in only one direction.

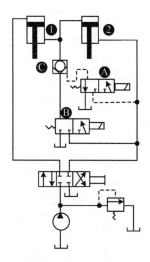
Fig. 16.13  Replenishing circuit

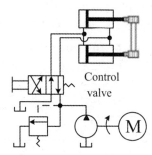
Fig. 16.14  Rack and pinion Synchronizing circuit

## 2.6  Hydraulic Motor Circuits

Driving a fluid motor at constant pressure produces a constant torque drive. When pump delivery is cut off, it continues rotating because of its inertia and that of the connected load. The motor then acts as a pump, and a source of fluid must be available to prevent cavitation. In the left-hand circuit of Fig. 16.15, the manual valve allows coasting, as well as the normal driving condition of the motor. With the valve spool up, the pump output drives the fluid motor. With the spool centered, pump output and both sides of the fluid motor are connected to tank, so the motor coasts to a stop. With the valve spool down, the pump is unloaded and the motor, acting as a pump, forces fluid through the relief valve, which brakes it to a stop. The right-hand circuit of Fig. 16.15 shows a brake valve that is a modified sequence valve. It supplies braking force as well as control of a negative work load. Under normal conditions, system pressure holds the brake valve open for free discharge from the motor. A negative load reduces pressure at the motor inlet, and the brake valve closes to throttle motor discharge and create a backpressure.

When a fluid motor and pump are connected in a closed circuit, make-up fluid to compensate for the leakage must be supplied through replenishing valves. These valves also supply fluid to the motor during braking. In the left-hand circuit of Fig. 16.16, a non-reversing variable volume pump is used and control of motor direction is by the 4-way valve. The fixed displacement pump provides supercharge pressure. The network of check and relief valves provides for replenishing and braking in either direction. Braking pressure in each direction can be set independently on the two brake valves. In the right-hand circuit, a reversing pump is used. Although the replenishing network is simpler, brake pressure must be the same in both directions.

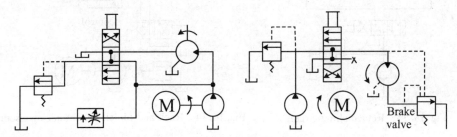

Fig. 16.15  Motor braking circuit

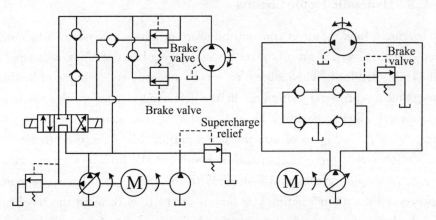

Fig. 16.16  Motor replenishing circuit

## Vacabulary

meter [mi:tə]   n. 公尺;仪表  vt. 用仪表测量

decompression [di:kəm'preʃən]   n. 降压

surge [sə:dʒ]   n. 巨涌;大浪  vi. 汹涌  vt. 使颠簸

regenerative [ri'dʒenəreitiv, -rə, ri:-]  adj. 再生的;更新的

accumulator [ə'kju:mjuleitə]   n. 蓄能器;累加器

filter [filtə]   n. 滤波器;过滤器  vt. 过滤

# Unit 4　Hydraulic Transmission

lubricator [ˈluːbrikeitə]　n. 润滑器；注油器
retrofit [ˈretrəufit]　vt. 更新；改进　n. 式样翻新
vise [vais]　n. 虎钳；夹具
solenoid [ˈsəulənɔid]　n. 电磁线圈；电磁阀
tandem-center　中位导通的
backpressure　n. 背压
check valve　单向阀
pilot relief valve　先导式溢流阀
tonnage [ˈtʌnidʒ]　n. 吨位；载重量
meter-in circuit　进口节流回路
meter-out circuit　出口节流回路
lunge [lʌndʒ]　v. 刺；扑

bleed-off circuit　旁路放油回路
synchronization [ˌsiŋkrənaiˈzeiʃən, ˌsin-, -niz-]　n. 同步；同时性
replenishing circuit　补充回路
tying [ˈtaiiŋ]　n. 结子　v. 系
rack [ræk]　n. 行李架；齿条　vt. 折磨
pinion [ˈpinjən]　n. 小齿轮；翅膀　vt. 束缚
sprocket [ˈsprɔkit]　n. 链轮齿；扣链齿轮
inertia [iˈnəːʃiə]　n. 惯性；惰性
cavitation [ˌkæviˈteiʃən]　n. 气穴现象；空穴作用
throttle [ˈθrɔtl]　n. 节流阀　vt. 使……节流；压制　vi. 节流，减速
valve spool　滑阀；阀槽

## Notes

[1]　In fact, many of the circuits use purely mechanical components, so incorporating them into new or retrofit applications may involve integrating electronic feedback and control into the circuit as a modern alternative to mechanical control. 可译为：事实上，许多回路使用纯机械部件，所以合并它们进入新的或改造应用时，可能涉及到集成电反馈和控制来替代机械控制。

[2]　However, whether using mechanical or electronic control, perhaps the greatest benefit may be gained by customizing one of these circuits to serve the specific requirements of an application. 可译为：然而，无论使用机械还是电子控制，最大的收益或许是来自于按客户要求制作服务具体应用要求的回路的。

[3]　When the open-center system is in neutral, pump output flows through the directional control valve to tank. 可译为：当开心式（常开）系统处于中位时，泵输出流量通过方向控制阀流回油箱。

[4]　When open- or tandem-center valves are used in circuits requiring pilot pressure to shift the valves, there must be a means of maintaining pressure when the valves are in neutral. 可译为：当开心式（常开）或者中位导通的阀用于要求有先导驱动压力的回路中，在这些阀处于中位时必须有一种方法来保持压力。

[5]　For details on the different types of pumps, their operation, and how they vary flow, refer to the pumps section of the handbook. 可译为：需要泵的不同类型、操作及如何变量的详情，参考手册泵的部分。

[6] Limit switches momentarily actuated by the cylinders control the solenoid valves to sequence this circuit. 可译为：被缸瞬时触发的限位开关控制电磁阀使回路顺序动作。

[7] Mechanically tying two cylinders together by installing a rack on each piston rod and fastening the pinions to a single shaft works well when the linkage is rigid and the mesh is proper as shown in Fig. 16.14. 可译为：通过在每个活塞杆上安装一个齿条、相应齿轮同轴固定的方式将两个油缸机械地连接，当连接是刚性的且啮合适当时，可以很好地工作，如图 16.14。

## Exercises

1. What basic circuits are introduced in the article?
2. Please know well the function of every basic circuit in the article.
3. How do we use these basic circuits?

# Unit 5   Computerized Manufacturing

## Lesson 17   Computer Aided Design

### 1  Introduction

Computer-aided design (CAD), also known as computer-aided design and drafting (CADD), is the use of computer technology for the process of design and design-documentation. Computer aided drafting describes the process of drafting with a computer. CADD software, or environments, provides the user with input-tools for the purpose of streamlining design processes; drafting, documentation, and manufacturing processes. CADD output is often in the form of electronic files for print or machining operations. The development of CADD-based software is in direct correlation with the processes it seeks to economize; industry-based software (construction, manufacturing, etc.) typically uses vector-based (linear) environments whereas graphic-based software utilizes raster-based (pixelated) environments.

CADD environments often involve more than just shapes. As in the manual drafting of technical and engineering drawings, the output of CAD must convey information, such as materials, processes, dimensions, and tolerances, according to application-specific conventions.

CAD may be used to design curves and figures in two-dimensional (2D) space; or curves, surfaces, and solids in three-dimensional (3D) objects.[1] (see Appendix of Lesson 30)

CAD is an important industrial art extensively used in many applications, including automotive, shipbuilding, and aerospace industries, industrial and architectural design, prosthetics, and many more. CAD is also widely used to produce computer animation for special effects in movies, advertising and technical manuals. The modern ubiquity and power of computers means that even perfume bottles and shampoo dispensers are designed using techniques unheard of by engineers of the 1960s. Because of its enormous economic importance, CAD has been a major driving force for research in computational geometry, computer graphics (both hardware and software), and discrete differential geometry.[2]

The design of geometric models for object shapes, in particular, is occasionally called Computer-aided Geometric Design (CAGD).[3]

Beginning in the 1980s, Computer-aided Design programs reduced the need of draftsmen significantly, especially in small to mid-sized companies. Their affordability and ability to run on personal computers also allowed engineers to do their own drafting work, eliminating the need for entire departments. In today's world most, if not all, students in universities do not learn drafting techniques because they are not required to do so. The days of hand drawing for final drawings are all but over. Universities no longer require the use of protractors and compasses to create drawings, instead there are several classes that focus on the use of CAD software such as Pro Engineer or IEAS-MS.

Current computer-aided design software packages range from 2D vector-based drafting systems to 3D solid and surface modellers. Modern CAD packages can also frequently allow rotations in three dimensions, allowing viewing of a designed object from any desired angle, even from the inside looking out. Some CAD software is capable of dynamic mathematic modeling, in which case it may be marketed as CADD — *computer-aided design and drafting*.

CAD is used in the design of tools and machinery and in the drafting and design of all types of buildings, from small residential types (houses) to the largest commercial and industrial structures (hospitals and factories).

CAD is mainly used for detailed engineering of 3D models and/or 2D drawings of physical components, but it is also used throughout the engineering process from conceptual design and layout of products, through strength and dynamic analysis of assemblies to definition of manufacturing methods of components. It can also be used to design objects.

CAD has become an especially important technology within the scope of computer-aided technologies, with benefits such as lower product development costs and a greatly shortened design cycle. CAD enables designers to lay out and develop work on screen, print it out and save it for future editing, saving time on their drawings.

## 2  Uses

Computer-aided design is one of the many tools used by engineers and designers and is used in many ways depending on the profession of the user and the type of software in question.

CAD is one part of the whole Digital Product Development (DPD) activity within the Product Lifecycle Management (PLM) process, and as such is used together with other tools, which are either integrated modules or stand-alone products, such as:

- ◆ Computer-aided Engineering (CAE) and Finite Element Analysis (FEA);
- ◆ Computer-aided Manufacturing (CAM) including instructions to Computer Numerical Control (CNC) machines;
- ◆ Photo realistic rendering;
- ◆ Document management and revision control using Product Data Management (PDM).

CAD is also used for the accurate creation of photo simulations that are often required in the preparation of Environmental Impact Reports, in which computer-aided designs of intended buildings are superimposed into photographs of existing environments to represent what that locale will be like were the proposed facilities allowed to be built. Potential blockage of view corridors and shadow studies are also frequently analyzed through the use of CAD.

CAD has also been proven to be useful to engineers as well by using four properties which are history, features, parameterization, and high level constraints. The construction history can be used to look back into the model's personal features and work on the single area rather than the whole model. Parameters and constraints can be used to determine the size, shape, and the different modeling elements. The features in the CAD system can be used for the variety of tools for measurement such as tensile strength, yield strength, also its stress and strain and how the element gets affected in certain temperatures.

## 3  Types

There are several different types of CAD. Each of these different types of CAD systems require the operator to think differently about how he or she will use them and he or she must design their virtual components in a different manner for each.

There are many producers of the lower-end 2D systems, including a number of free and open source programs. These provide an approach to the drawing process without all the fuss over scale and placement on the drawing sheet that accompanied hand drafting, since these can be adjusted as required during the creation of the final draft.

3D wireframe is basically an extension of 2D drafting (not often used today). Each line has to be manually inserted into the drawing. The final product has no mass properties associated with it and cannot have features directly added to it, such as holes. The operator approaches these in a similar fashion to the 2D systems, although many 3D systems allow using the wireframe model to make the final engineering drawing views.

3D "dumb" *solids* are created in a way analogous to manipulations of real world objects (not often used today). Basic three-dimensional geometric forms (prisms, cylinders, spheres, and so on) have solid volumes added or subtracted from them, as if assembling or cutting real-world objects. Two-dimensional projected views can easily be generated from the models. Basic 3D solids don't usually include tools to easily allow motion of components, set limits to their motion, or identify interference between components.

3D *parametric solid modeling* requires the operator to use what is referred to as "design intent". The objects and features created are adjustable. Any future modifications will be simple, difficult, or nearly impossible, depending on how the original part was created. One must think of this as being a "perfect world" representation of the component. If a feature was intended to be located from the center of the part, the operator needs to locate it from the center of the model, not, perhaps, from a more convenient edge or an arbitrary point, as he could when using "dumb" solids. Parametric solids require the operator to consider the consequences of his actions carefully.

Some software packages provide the ability to edit parametric and non-parametric geometry without the need to understand or undo the design intent history of the geometry by use of direct modeling functionality. This ability may also include the additional ability to infer the correct relationships between selected geometry (e.g., tangency, concentricity) which makes the editing process less time and labor intensive while still freeing the engineer from the burden of understanding the model's. These kind of non history based systems are called Explicit Modellers or Direct CAD Modelers.

Top end systems offer the capabilities to incorporate more organic, aesthetics and ergonomic features into designs. Freeform surface modelling is often combined with solids to allow the designer to create products that fit the human form and visual requirements as well as they interface with the machine.

## 4 Technology

Originally software for Computer-aided Design systems was developed with computer languages such as Fortran, but with the advancement of object-oriented programming methods this has radically changed. Typical modern parametric feature based modeler and freeform surface systems are built around a number of key C modules with their own APIs. A CAD system can be seen as built up from the interaction of a graphical user interface (GUI) with NURBS geometry and/or boundary representation (B-rep) data via a geometric modeling kernel. A geometry constraint engine may also be employed to manage the associative relationships between geometry, such as wireframe geometry in a sketch or components in an assembly.

Unexpected capabilities of these associative relationships have led to a new form of prototyping called digital prototyping. In contrast to physical prototypes, which entail manufacturing time in the design? That said, CAD models can be generated by a computer after the physical prototype has been scanned using an industrial CT scanning machine. Depending on the nature of the business, digital or physical prototypes can be initially chosen according to specific needs.

Today, CAD systems exist for all the major platforms (Windows, Linux, UNIX and Mac OS X); some packages even support multiple platforms.

Right now, no special hardware is required for most CAD software. However, some CAD systems can do graphically and computationally intensive tasks, so a modern graphics card, high speed (and possibly multiple) CPUs and large amounts of RAM may be recommended.

The human-machine interface is generally via a computer mouse but can also be via a pen and digitizing graphics tablet. Manipulation of the view of the model on the screen is also sometimes done with the use of a Spacemouse/SpaceBall. Some systems also support stereoscopic glasses for viewing the 3D model.

## 5 History

Designers have long used computers for their calculations. Initial developments were carried out in the 1960s within the aircraft and automotive industries in the area of 3D surface construction and NC programming, most of it independent of one another and often not publicly published until much later. Some of the mathematical description work on curves was developed in the early 1940s by Robert Issac Newton from Pawtucket, Rhode Island. Robert A. Heinlein in his 1957 novel *The Door into Summer* suggested the possibility of a robotic *Drafting Dan*. However, probably the most important work on polynomial curves and sculptured surface was done by Pierre Bézier (Renault), Paul de Casteljau (Citroen), Steven Anson Coons (MIT, Ford), James Ferguson (Boeing), Carl de Boor (GM), Birkhoff (GM) and Garibedian (GM) in the 1960s and W. Gordon (GM) and R. Riesenfeld in the 1970s.

It is argued that a turning point was the development of the SKETCHPAD system at MIT in 1963 by Ivan Sutherland (who later created a graphics technology company with Dr. David Evans). The distinctive feature of SKETCHPAD was that it allowed the designer to interact with his computer graphically: the design can be fed into the computer by drawing on a CRT monitor with a light pen. Effectively, it was a prototype of graphical user interface, an indispensable feature of modern CAD.

The first commercial applications of CAD were in large companies in the automotive and aerospace industries, as well as in electronics. Only large corporations could afford the computers capable of performing the calculations. Notable company projects were at GM (Dr. Patrick J. Hanratty) with DAC-1 (Design Augmented by Computer) 1964; Lockheed projects; Bell GRAPHIC 1 and at Renault (Bézier)-UNISURF 1971 car body design and tooling.

One of the most influential events in the development of CAD was the founding of MCS (Manufacturing and Consulting Services Inc.) in 1971 by Dr. P. J. Hanratty, who wrote the system ADAM (Automated Drafting And Machining) but more importantly supplied code to companies such as McDonnell Douglas (Unigraphics), Computervision (CADDS), Calma, Gerber, Autotrol and Control Data.

As computers became more affordable, the application areas have gradually expanded. The development of CAD software for personal desktop computers was the impetus for almost universal application in all areas of construction.

Other key points in the 1960s and 1970s would be the foundation of CAD systems United Computing, Intergraph, IBM, Intergraph IGDS in 1974 (which led to Bentley Systems Microstation in 1984).

CAD implementations have evolved dramatically since then. Initially, with 3D in the 1970s, it was typically limited to producing drawings similar to hand-drafted drawings. Advances in programming and computer hardware, notably solid modeling in the 1980s, have allowed more versatile applications of computers in design activities.

Key products for 1981 were the solid modelling packages — Romulus (Shape Data) and Uni-Solid (Unigraphics) based on PADL-2 and the release of the surface modeler CATIA (Dassault Systemes). Autodesk was founded 1982 by John Walker, which led to the 2D system AutoCAD. The next milestone was the release of Pro/ENGINEER in 1988, which heralded greater usage of feature-based modeling methods and parametric linking of the parameters of features. Also of importance to the development of CAD was the development of the B-rcp solid modeling kernels (engines for manipulating geometrically and topologically consistent 3D objects) Parasolid (Shape Data) and ACIS (Spatial Technology Inc.) at the end of the 1980s and beginning of the 1990s, both inspired by the work of Ian Braid. This led to the release of mid-range packages such as Solid Works in 1995, Solid Edge (then Intergraph) in 1996 and Autodesk Inventor in 1999.

## Vacabulary

pixelate ['piksəleit]    n. 像素化；视频滤镜效果
ubiquity [juːˈbikwəti]    n. 普遍存在；到处存在
perfume [pəˈfjuːm]    n. 香水；香味
dispenser [disˈpensə]    n. 药剂师；施与者；分配器
affordability [əˌfɔːdəˈbiləti]    n. 支付能力；负担能力；买得起
lay out    展示；安排；花钱；为……划样；提议
DPD    abbr. Digital Product Development 数字化产品开发
PLM    abbr. Product Lifecycle Management 产品生命周期管理
wireframe ['waiəfreim]    n. 线框（模型）
dumb [dʌm]    adj. 哑的；无声音的
analogous [əˈnæləgəs]    adj. 类似的；模拟的；基本的
prisms    n. 棱镜（prism[prizm]的复数）

tangency ['tændʒənsi]　n. 相切，接触
NURBS [nə:bz]　abbr. 曲线曲面的非均匀有理 B 样条（Non-Uniform Rational B-Spline）
B-rep　abbr. boundary representation 边界表示法
CT　abbr. 断层扫描（Computed Tomography）
independent [ˌindi'pendənt]　adj. 独立的；单独的
Pawtucket [pɔː'tʌkit]　n. 波塔基特（美国一城市）
Rhode [rəud]　n. 罗德岛
polynomial [ˌpɔli'nəumiəl]　n. [数] 多项式；adj. 多项式的
sculptured ['skʌlptʃəd]　adj. 用刻纹装饰的；具刻纹的
Renault [rə'nəu]　n. 法国雷诺公司；雷诺（姓氏）
Citroen　n. （法国）雪铁龙（汽车）
Gerber [gɛbə]　n. 美国格柏公司（刀具生产商）；戈伯（男子名）
Parasolid　n. 参数化实体（实体建模模块）

## Notes

[1] CAD may be used to design curves and figures in two-dimensional (2D) space; or curves, surfaces, and solids in three-dimensional (3D) objects. 可译为：CAD 软件可用来设计二维空间曲线和图形，或可用来设计三维空间曲线、表面和实体。

[2] Because of its enormous economic importance, CAD has been a major driving force for research in computational geometry, computer graphics (both hardware and software), and discrete differential geometry. 可译为：由于 CAD 技术的巨大经济价值，它已经成为研究计算几何、计算机图形学（包括硬件和软件）以及离散微分几何的主要驱动力。

[3] The design of geometric models for object shapes, in particular, is occasionally called computer-aided geometric design (CAGD). 可译为：特别的，物体形状的几何模型设计有时也称作计算机辅助几何设计。

## Exercises

1. What is the meaning of CAD and CADD?
2. There are several different types of CAD, please list them.
3. What is the meaning of PDM / PLM?

# Lesson 18　Computer Aided Engineering

## 1  Introduction

　　With the improvement of graphics displays, engineering workstations, and graphics standards, Computer-aided Engineering (CAE) has come to mean the computer solution of engineering problems with the assistance of interactive computer graphics.

　　CAE software is used on various types of computers, such as mainframes and superminis, engineering workstations, and even personal computers. The choice of a computer system is frequently dictated by the computing power required for the CAE application or the level (and speed) of graphics interaction desired. The trend is toward more use of engineering workstations, especially a new type known as supergraphics workstations.

　　Design engineers use a variety of CAE tools, including large, general-purpose commercial programs and many specialized programs written in-house or elsewhere in the industry. Solution of a single engineering problem frequently requires the application of several CAE tools. Communication of data between these software tools presents a challenge for most applications. Data are usually passed through proprietary neutral file formats, data interchange standards, or a system database.

　　A typical CAE program is made up of a number of mathematical models encoded by algorithms written in a programming language. The natural phenomena being analyzed are represented by an engineering model. The physical configuration is described by a geometric model. The results, together with the geometry, are made visible via a user interface on the display device and a rendering model (graphics image).

　　Computer-aided Design and Manufacturing (CAD/CAM) systems were created by the aerospace industry in the early 1960s to assist with the massive design and documentation tasks associated with producing airplanes. CAD/CAM systems have been used primarily for detail design and drafting along with the generation of numerical control instructions for manufacturing. Gradually, more CAE functions are being added to CAD/CAM systems. Modeling with CAD/

CAM systems has become fairly sophisticated. Most popular commercial systems support 2D and 3D wireframe, surface models and solid models. Rendered surface models differ from solid models in that the latter have full information about the interior of the object. For solid models a combination of three types of representation is commonly used: constructive solid geometry, boundary representation, and sweep representation.

The CAE methods for electrical and electronics engineering are well developed. The geometry is generally two-dimensional, and the problems are primarily linear or can be linearized with sufficient accuracy. Chemical engineering makes extensive use of CAE with process simulation and control software. The fields of civil, architectural, and construction engineering have CAE interests similar to mechanical CAE with emphasis on structures. Aerospace, mechanical, industrial, and manufacturing engineering all make use of mechanical CAE software together with specialized software.

## 2　CAE Tools

Software tools that have been developed to support these activities are considered CAE tools. CAE tools are being used, for example, to analyze the robustness and performance of components and assemblies. The term encompasses simulation, validation and optimization of products and manufacturing tools. In the future, CAE systems will be major providers of information to help support design teams in decision making.

In regard to information networks, CAE systems are individually considered a single node on a total information network and each node may interact with other nodes on the network[1].

CAE systems can provide support to businesses. This is achieved by the use of reference architectures and their ability to place information views on the business process. Reference architecture is the basis from which information model, especially product and manufacturing models.

CAE tools are very widely used in the automotive industry. In fact, their use has enabled the automakers to reduce product development cost and time while improving the safety, comfort, and durability of the vehicles they produce. The predictive capability of CAE tools has progressed to the point where much of the design verification is now done using computer simulations rather than physical prototype testing[2]. CAE dependability is based upon all proper assumptions as inputs and must identify critical inputs (BJ). Even though there have been many advances in CAE, and it is widely used in the engineering field, physical testing is still used as a final confirmation for subsystems due to the fact that CAE cannot predict all variables in complex assemblies (i. e. , metal stretch, thinning).

## 3  CAE Fields and Phases

CAE areas covered include:
- Stress analysis on components and assemblies using FEA (Finite Element Analysis);
- Thermal and fluid flow analysis Computational Fluid Dynamics (CFD);
- Kinematics;
- Mechanical Event Simulation (MES);
- Analysis tools for process simulation for operations such as casting, molding, and die press forming.
- Optimization of the product or process.

In general, there are three phases in any computer-aided engineering task:

Pre-processing-defining the model and environmental factors to be applied to it. (Typically a finite element model, but facet, voxel and thin sheet methods are also used)

Analysis solver (usually performed on high powered computers)

Post-processing of results (using visualization tools)

This cycle is iterated, often many times, either manually or with the use of commercial optimization software.

## 4  Optimization & Parametrics

The ultimate use of any design tool is to improve a design by minimizing cost, maximizing reliability and optimizing parameters, such as force or weight. The key to any simulation software is the ability to change a parameter and find its effect on the model.

Integrated's design software allows users to change parameters, such as dimensions and materials, and determine how they will affect the ultimate performance of the model[3]. Easily, the user can modify the design by stretching, transforming or rotating parts of the geometry, among other functions. Built in parametric features, as found in Integrated's CAE software, allow the user to change models parametrically without learning a complicated scripting language.

Through Integrated's software, simulations that may require hundreds of solutions to find the optimal design can be achieved with a very small learning curve; geometric and physical parameters are readily changed through an intuitive interface which makes the old style of scripting obsolete.

This is an important feature for designers who may not use the simulation tool daily, as no relearning is required every time a solution to a new problem is needed.

◆ Very short learning curve; no scripting required;
◆ Design optimization by parametric analysis.

## 5 Multiphysics

Many engineering design problems often involve multiphysics simulation: electromagnetic, thermal and structural combined modeling require CAE software that gives accurate answers when the various disciplines are interacting. Engineers and physicists need fast, accurate solutions when more than one physical phenomenon is involved.

For many electromechanical systems it is important for the various solvers to be combined. For example, for induction heating the induced eddy currents are used for heating up a component. This magnetic analysis is affected by the thermal analysis and vice versa[4]. Thus, the electromagnetic solvers need to be combined with the thermal solvers.

In terms of particle trajectory calculations, the path of the particle may be determined by a DC magnetic and electric field as well as a time harmonic high frequency field. In such cases all three fields need to be coupled to determine the path of the particle.

Other systems can be coupled as determined by the physics of the problem.

Integrated develops comprehensive solutions for scientists modeling prototypes that require multiphysics analysis. Integrated also includes the Boundary Element Method (BEM), Finite Element Method (FEM), and Hybrid solvers in the same package to give designers a greater choice and use the best method for any problem.

No scripting is required, therefore professionals can quickly learn how to use the software and start using it right away. The design optimization through parametric analysis, included in the software package, allows review of prototypes until the desired result is reached, thereby cutting hours of design time, especially when various disciplines interact closely.

## 6 Finite Element Method (FEM)

Finite elements solve by breaking up a problem into small regions and solutions are found for each region taking into account only the regions that are right next to the one being solved. In the case of magnetic fields where FEM is often used, the vector potential is what is solved for in these regions.

Magnetic field solutions are derived from the vector potential through differentiating the solution. This can cause problems in smoothness of field solutions. Theoretically, any partial differential equation class of problem can be solved using FEM (although some types will do better than others).

The Finite Element Method (FEM) is a numerical technique for solving models in differential form. For a given design, the FEM requires the entire design, including the surrounding region, to be modeled with finite elements. A system of linear equations is generated to calculate the potential (scalar or vector) at the nodes of each element. Therefore, the basic difference between these two techniques is the fact that BEM only needs to solve the unknowns on the boundaries, whereas FEM solves for a chosen region of space and requires a boundary condition bounding that region.

While BEM can solve nonlinear problems, the nonlinear contribution requires a volume mesh. Putting a volume mesh in begins to diminish the benefits of BEM listed above. In fact, for a saturating nonlinear magnetic problem, the saturatation characteristic is best solved with FEM.

### Vacabulary

trend [trend]　n. 趋势,倾向;走向　vt. 使趋向

supergraphics ['sju:pə'græfiks]　n. [用作单数或复数]超大图形(显示)

proprietary [prəu'praiətəri]　adj. 所有的;专利的;专有

rendering ['rendəriŋ]　n. 渲染;效果图
rendered adj. 已渲染的

interior [in'tiəriə]　adj. 内部的;国内的;本质的 n. 内部;本质

linearize ['liniəraiz]　vt. 使线性化

dependability [di,pendə'biləti]　n. 可靠性；可信任

FEA　abbr. 有限元分析（Finite Element Analysis）

facet ['fæsit]　n. 面；方面；小平面

voxel [vɔk'səl]　n. 体元，体素；立体像素

iterate ['itəreit, -rət]　vt. 迭代；重复；反复说；重做

ultimate ['ʌltimət]　adj. 最终的；极限的；根本的　n. 终极；根本

intuitive [in'tju:itiv]　adj. 直觉的；凭直觉获知的

Multiphysics ['mʌlti'fiziks]　n. 多重物理量；多物理场

vice versa　反之亦然

BEM　abbr. 边界元法（Boundary Element Method）

diminish [di'miniʃ]　vt./vi. 使减少；使变小

saturating ['sætʃəreitiŋ]　adj. 饱和的；浸透的

saturatation　n. 饱和；浸透

## Notes

[1]　In regard to information networks, CAE systems are individually considered a single node on a total information network and each node may interact with other nodes on the network. 可译为：至于信息网络，CAE 系统被认为是总体信息网络中的一个独特的节点，每个节点可以和网络中的其他节点进行交互。

[2]　The predictive capability of CAE tools has progressed to the point where much of the design verification is now done using computer simulations rather than physical prototype testing. 可译为：CAE 工具的预测能力已经发展到如此地步，即现在大多数的设计验证多采用计算机模拟而非物理原型试验。

[3]　Integrated's design software allows users to change parameters, such as dimensions and materials, and determine how they will affect the ultimate performance of the model. 可译为：集成的设计软件允许用户改变参数，如尺寸、材料，并且确定它们会怎样影响模型的最终性能。

[4]　This magnetic analysis is affected by the thermal analysis and vice versa. 可译为：这种磁性分析受热分析影响，反之亦然。

## Exercises

1. What is the meaning of CAE?
2. There are several steps of CAE, please list them.
3. There are many CAE areas, please list them.
4. What is the meaning of BEM?

# Lesson 19　Computer Aided Process Planning

## 1　Introduction

Computer-aided Process Planning (CAPP) is the use of computer technology to aid in the process planning of a part or product, in manufacturing. CAPP is the link between CAD and CAM in that it provides for the planning of the process to be used in producing a designed part. [1]

Process planning translates design information into the process steps and instructions to efficiently and effectively manufacture products. As the design process is supported by many computer-aided tools, Computer-aided Process Planning (CAPP) has evolved to simplify and improve process planning and achieve more effective use of manufacturing resources.

## 2　Process Planning

Process planning encompasses the activities and functions to prepare a detailed set of plans and instructions to produce a part. The planning begins with engineering drawings, specifications, parts or material lists and a forecast of demand. The results of the planning are:

- ◆ Routings which specify operations, operation sequences, work centers, standards, tooling and fixtures. This routing becomes a major input to the manufacturing resource planning system to define operations for production activity control purposes and define required resources for capacity requirements planning purposes;
- ◆ Process plans which typically provide more detailed, step-by-step work instructions including dimensions related to individual operations, machining parameters, set-up instructions, and quality assurance checkpoints;
- ◆ Fabrication and assembly drawings to support manufacture (as opposed to engineering drawings to define the part).

Manual process planning is based on a manufacturing engineer's experience and knowledge of production facilities, equipment, their capabilities, processes, and tooling. Process planning is very time-consuming and the results vary based on the person doing the planning.

## 3  Computer-Aided Process Planning

Manufacturers have been pursuing an evolutionary path to improve and computerize process planning in the following five stages:

Stage I — Manual classification; standardized process plans

Stage II — Computer maintained process plans

Stage III — Variant CAPP

Stage IV — Generative CAPP

Stage V — Dynamic, generative CAPP

Prior to CAPP, manufacturers attempted to overcome the problems of manual process planning by basic classification of parts into families and developing somewhat standardized process plans for parts families (Stage I). When a new part was introduced, the process plan for that family would be manually retrieved, marked-up and retyped. While this improved productivity, it did not improve the quality of the planning of processes and it did not easily take into account the differences between parts in a family nor improvements in production processes.

Computer-aided process planning initially evolved as a means to electronically store a process plan once it was created, retrieve it, modify it for a new part and print the plan (Stage II). Other capabilities of this stage are table-driven cost and standard estimating systems.

This initial computer-aided approach evolved into what is now known as "variant" CAPP. However, variant CAPP is based on a Group Technology (GT) coding and classification approach to identify a larger number of part attributes or parameters. These attributes allow the system to select a baseline process plan for the part family and accomplish about ninety percent of the planning work. The planner will add the remaining ten percent of the effort modifying or fine-tuning the process plan. The baseline process plans stored in the computer are manually entered using a super planner concept, that is, developing standardized plans based on the accumulated experience and knowledge of multiple planners and manufacturing engineers (Stage III).

The next stage of evolution is toward generative CAPP (Stage IV). At this stage, process planning decision rules are built into the system. These decision rules will operate based on a part's group technology or features technology coding to produce a process plan that will require minimal manual interaction and modification (e. g. , entry of dimensions).

While CAPP systems are moving more and more towards being generative, a pure generative system that can produce a complete process plan from part classification and other design data is a goal of the future. This type of purely generative system (in Stage V) will involve the use of artificial intelligence type capabilities to produce process plans as well as be fully integrated in a CIM environment. A further step in this stage is dynamic, generative CAPP which would consider plant and machine capacities, tooling availability, work center and equipment loads, and equipment status (e. g. , maintenance downtime) in developing process plans.

The process plan developed with a CAPP system at Stage V would vary over time depending on the resources and workload in the factory. For example, if a primary work center for an operation(s) was overloaded, the generative planning process would evaluate work to be released involving that work center, alternate processes and the related routings. The decision rules would result in process plans that would reduce the overloading on the primary work center by using an alternate routing that would have the least cost impact. Since finite scheduling systems are still in their infancy, this additional dimension to production scheduling is still a long way off.

Dynamic, generative CAPP also implies the need for online display of the process plan on a workorder oriented basis to insure that the appropriate process plan was provided to the floor. Tight integration with a manufacturing resource planning system is needed to track shop floor status and load data and assess alternate routings vis-a-vis the schedule. Finally, this stage of CAPP would directly feed shop floor equipment controllers or, in a less automated environment, display assembly drawings online in conjunction with process plans.

## 4  CAPP Planning Process

The system logic involved in establishing a variant process planning system is relatively straight forward — it is one of matching a code with a pre-established process plan maintained in the system. The initial challenge is in developing the

GT classification and coding structure for the part families and in manually developing a standard baseline process plan for each part family. [2]

The first key to implementing a generative system is the development of decision rules appropriate for the items to be processed. These decision rules are specified using decision trees, computer languages involving logical "if-then" type statements, or artificial intelligence approaches with object-oriented programming.

The nature of the parts will affect the complexity of the decision rules for generative planning and ultimately the degree of success in implementing the generative CAPP system. The majority of generative CAPP systems implemented to date have focused on process planning for fabrication of sheet metal parts and less complex machined parts. In addition, there has been significant recent effort with generative process planning for assembly operations, including PCB assembly.

A second key to generative process planning is the available data related to the part to drive the planning. Simple forms of generative planning systems may be driven by GT codes. Group technology or Features Technology (FT) type classification without a numeric code may be used to drive CAPP. This approach would involve a user responding to a series of questions about a part that in essence capture the same information as in a GT or FT code. Eventually when features-oriented data is captured in a CAD system during the design process, this data can directly drive CAPP.

## 5 CAD/CAM Integration and CAPP Features

A frequently overlooked step in the integration of CAD/CAM is the process planning that must occur. CAD systems generate graphically oriented data and may go so far as graphically identifying metal, etc. to be removed during processing. [3] In order to produce such things as NC instructions for CAM equipment, basic decisions regarding equipment to be used, tooling and operation sequence need to be made. This is the function of CAPP. Without some element of CAPP, there would not be such a thing as CAD/CAM integration. Thus CAD/CAM systems that generate tool paths and NC programs include limited CAPP capabilities or imply a certain approach to processing.

CAD systems also provide graphically-oriented data to CAPP systems to use to produce assembly drawings, etc. Further, this graphically-oriented data can then be provided to manufacturing in the form of hardcopy drawings or work instruction displays. This type of system uses work instruction displays at factory workstations to display process plans graphically and guide employees through assembly step by step. The assembly is shown on the screen and as an employee steps through the assembly process with a footswitch, the components to be inserted or assembled are shown on the CRT graphically along with text instructions and warnings for each step.

If NC machining processes are involved, CAPP software exists which will select tools, feeds, and speeds, and prepare NC programs.

## 6  CAPP Benefits

Significant benefits can result from the implementation of CAPP. In a detailed survey of twenty-two large and small companies using generative-type CAPP systems, the following estimated cost savings were achieved:

- 58% reduction in process planning effort;
- 10% saving in direct labor;
- 4% saving in material;
- 10% saving in scrap;
- 12% saving in tooling;
- 6% reduction in work-in-process.

In addition, there are intangible benefits as follows:

- Reduced process planning and production leadtime; faster response to engineering changes;
- Greater process plan consistency; access to up-to-date information in a central database;
- Improved cost estimating procedures and fewer calculation errors;
- More complete and detailed process plans;
- Improved production scheduling and capacity utilization;
- Improved ability to introduce new manufacturing technology and rapidly update process plans to utilize the improved technology.

## 7  Summary

CAPP is a highly effective technology for discrete manufacturers with a significant number of products and process steps. Rapid strides are being made to develop generative planning capabilities and incorporate CAPP into a computer-integrated manufacturing architecture. The first step is the implementation of GT or FT classification and coding. Commercially-available software tools currently exist to support both GT and CAPP. As a result, many companies can achieve the benefits of GT and CAPP with minimal cost and risk. Effective use of these tools can improve a manufacturer's competitive advantage.

## Vacabulary

routings [´ru:tiŋs] n. 工艺路线；路线安排(routing 的复数形式)
step-by-step [´stepbai´step] adj. 按部就班的，逐步
retrieve [ri´tri:v] vt. /n. [计] 检索；恢复
GT [dʒi:´ti:] abbr. 成组技术 (Group Technology)
workorder 工作定单
vis-a-vis [vi:za:´vi:] prep. 关于；和面对面 adv. 相向着；相对着
conjunction [kən´dʒʌŋkʃən] n. 结合；[语] 连接词；同时发生
implementing [´implimənting] n. 实施，执行；实现 v. 贯彻，执行(implement 的现在分词)

PCB [,pi: si: ´bi:] abbr. 印刷电路板 (Printed circuit board)
footswitch n. 脚踏开关
scrap [skræp] n. 废料
up-to-date [´ʌptə´deit] adj. 最新的，最近的；现代的，新式的
graphically [´græfikəli] adv. 生动地；用图解法
go so far as 甚至(做出某事)；竟然到(做出)的地步

## Notes

[1] CAPP is the link between CAD and CAM in that it provides for the planning of the process to be used in producing a designed part. 可译为：CAPP 是连接 CAD 和 CAM 之间的纽带，它提供工艺规划，用于加工所设计的零件。

[2] The initial challenge is in developing the GT classification and coding structure for the part families and in manually developing a standard baseline process plan for each part family. 可译为：最初的挑战是为每个零件族研发出成组分类及其编码结构，并开发出一套标准的基准工艺规程。

[3] CAD systems generate graphically oriented data and may go so far as graphically

identifying metal, etc. to be removed during processing. 可译为：CAD 系统生成面向数据的图形，甚至可以用图解识别加工过程中需被切除的金属(量)等。

**Exercises**

1. What is the meaning of CAPP?
2. Please list five development stages of CAPP.
3. Please list the benefits resulted from the implementation of CAPP.

# Lesson 20  Computer-aided Manufacturing

## 1 Introduction

Computer-aided Manufacturing (CAM) is the use of computer software and hardware in the translation of computer-aided design models into manufacturing instructions for numerical controlled machine tools. This is not the only definition for CAM, but it is the most common; CAM may also refer to the use of a computer to assist in all operations of a manufacturing plant, including planning, management, transportation and storage. Its primary purpose is to create a faster production process and components and tooling with more precise dimensions and material consistency, which in some cases, uses only the required amount of raw material (thus minimizing waste), while simultaneously reducing energy consumption. CAM is a subsequent Computer-aided process after Computer-aided Design (CAD) and sometimes Computer-aided Engineering (CAE), as the model generated in CAD and verified in CAE can be input into CAM software, which then controls the machine tool.

Traditionally, CAM has been considered as a numerical control (NC) programming tool, wherein Two-dimensional (2D) or Three-dimensional (3D) models of components generated in CAD software are used to generate G-code to drive Computer Numerically Controlled (CNC) machine tools.[1] Simple designs such as bolt circles or basic contours do not necessitate importing a CAD file.

As with other "Computer-aided" technologies, CAM does not eliminate the need for skilled professionals such as manufacturing engineers, NC programmers, or machinists. CAM, in fact, leverages both the value of the most skilled manufacturing professionals through advanced productivity tools, while building the skills of new professionals through visualization, simulation and optimization tools.

## 2 History

The first commercial applications of CAM were in large companies in the automotive and aerospace industries, such as UNISURF in 1971 at Renault for car body design and tooling.

Historically, CAM software was seen to have several shortcomings that necessitated an overly high level of involvement by skilled CNC machinists. CAM software would output code for the least capable machine, as each machine tool control added on to the standard G-code set for increased flexibility. In some cases, such as improperly set up CAM software or specific tools, the CNC machine required manual editing before the program will run properly. None of these issues were so insurmountable that a thoughtful engineer or skilled machine operator could not overcome for prototyping or small production runs; G-code is a simple language. In high production or high precision shops, a different set of problems were encountered where an experienced CNC machinist must both hand-code programs and run CAM software.

Integration of CAD with other components of CAD/CAM/CAE Product Lifecycle Management (PLM) environment requires an effective CAD data exchange. Usually it had been necessary to force the CAD operator to export the data in one of the common data formats, such as IGES or STL, that are supported by a wide variety of software. [2] The output from the CAM software is usually a simple text file of G-code, sometimes many thousands of commands long, that is then transferred to a machine tool using a Direct Numerical Control (DNC) program.

CAM packages could not, and still cannot, reason as a machinist can. They could not optimize tool paths to the extent required of mass production. Users would select the type of tool, machining process and paths to be used. While an engineer may have a working knowledge of G-code programming, small optimization and wear issues compound over time. Mass-produced items that require machining are often initially created through casting or some other non-machine method. This enables hand-written, short, and highly optimized G-code that could not be produced in a CAM package.

At least in the United States, there is a shortage of young, skilled machinists entering the workforce able to perform at the extremes of manufacturing; high precision and mass production. As CAM software and machines become more complicated, the skills required of a machinist or machine operator advance to approach that of a computer programmer and engineer rather than eliminating the CNC machinist from the workforce.

Typical areas of concern:
- High speed Machining, including streamlining of tool paths;
- Multi-function Machining;
- 5 Axis Machining;
- Feature recognition and machining;
- Automation of Machining processes;
- Ease of use.

## 3  Applications of Computer-aided Manufacturing

The field of Computer-aided Design has steadily advanced over the past four decades to the stage at which conceptual designs for new products can be made entirely within the framework of CAD software. From the development of the basic design to the Bill of Materials necessary to manufacture the product there is no requirement at any stage of the process to build physical prototypes. [3]

Computer-aided Manufacturing takes this one step further by bridging the gap between the conceptual design and the manufacturing of the finished product. [4] Whereas in the past it would be necessary for design developed using CAD software to be manually converted into a drafted paper drawing detailing instructions for its manufacture, Computer-aided Manufacturing software allows data from CAD software to be converted directly into a set of manufacturing instructions.

CAM software converts 3D models generated in CAD into a set of basic operating instructions written in G-code. G-code is a programming language that can be understood by numerical controlled machine tools — essentially industrial robots and the G-code can instruct the machine tool to manufacture a large number of items with perfect precision and faith to the CAD design.

Modern numerical controlled machine tools can be linked into a "cell", a collection of tools that each performs a specified task in the manufacture of a product. The product is passed along the cell in the manner of a production line, with each machine tool (i. e. , welding and milling machines, drills, lathes etc. ) performing a single step of the process.

For the sake of convenience, a single computer "controller" can drive all of the tools in a single cell. G-code instructions can be fed to this controller and then left to run the cell with minimal input from human supervisors.

## 4  Benefits of Computer-aided Manufacturing

While undesirable for factory workers, the ideal state of affairs for manufacturers is an entirely automated manufacturing process. In conjunction with Computer-aided Design, Computer-aided Manufacturing enables manufacturers to reduce the costs of producing goods by minimizing the involvement of human operators.

In addition to lower running costs, there are several additional benefits to using CAM software. By removing the need to translate CAD models into manufacturing instructions through paper drafts, it enables manufactures to make quick alterations to the product design, feeding updated instructions to the machine tools and seeing instant results.

In addition, many CAM software packages have the ability to manage simple tasks such as the re-ordering of parts, further minimizing human involvement. Though all numerical controlled machine tools have the ability to sense errors and automatically shut down, many can actually send a message to their human operators via mobile phones or e-mail, informing them of the problem and awaiting further instructions.

All in all, CAM software represents a continuation of the trend to make manufacturing entirely automated. While CAD removed the need to retain a team of drafters to design new products, CAM removes the need for skilled and unskilled factory workers. All of these developments result in lower operational costs, lower end product prices and increased profits for manufacturers.

## 5  Problems with Computer-aided Manufacturing

Unfortunately, there are several limitations of Computer-aided Manufacturing. Obviously, setting up the infrastructure to begin with can be extremely expensive. Computer-aided Manufacturing requires not only the numerical controlled machine tools themselves but also an extensive suite of

Unit 5  Computerized Manufacturing

CAD/CAM software and hardware to develop the design models and convert them into manufacturing instructions — as well as trained operatives to run them.

Additionally, the field of computer-aided management is fraught with inconsistency. While all numerical controlled machine tools operate using G-code, there is no universally used standard for the code itself. Since there is such a wide variety of machine tools that use the code, it tends to be the case that manufacturers create their own bespoke codes to operate their machinery.

While this lack of standardization may not be a problem in itself, it can become a problem when the time comes to convert 3D CAD designs into G-code. CAD systems tend to store data in their own proprietary format (in the same way that word processor applications do), so it can often be a challenge to transfer data from CAD to CAM software and then into whatever form of G-code the manufacturer employs.

## Vacabulary

necessitate [ni'sesi,teit, nə-]  vt. 使成为必需,需要;迫使
machinist [mə'ʃiːnist]  n. 机械工;机械师
Renault [rə'nəu]  n. 法国雷诺公司;雷诺(姓氏)
overly ['əuvəli]  adv. 过度地;极度地
involvement [in'vɔlvmənt]  n. 牵连;包含;投入
flexibility [,fleksi'biliti]  n. 灵活性;弹性;适应性
IGES  abbr. 起始图形交换规格(The Initial Graphics Exchange Specification)
STL  abbr. 标准模板库(Standard Template Library)

BOM  abbr. Bill of Materials 物料清单
workforce ['wəːkfɔːs]  n. 劳动力;工人总数,职工总数
infrastructure ['infrə,strʌktʃə]  n. 基础设施;公共建设;下部构造
additionally [ə'diʃənli]  adv. 此外;又,加之
fraught [frɔːt]  adj. 担心的,忧虑的;充满的
inconsistency [,inkən'sistənsi,-təns]  n. 不一致;易变
bespoke [bi'spəuk]  adj. 定做的;预定的

## Notes

[1] Traditionally, CAM has been considered as a Numerical Control (NC) programming tool, wherein Two-dimensional (2D) or Three-dimensional (3D) models of components generated in CAD software are used to generate G-code to

drive Computer Numerically Controlled (CNC) machine tools. 可译为:传统上，CAM 被认为是一个数控编程工具，它将 CAD 软件生成的二维或三维部件模型产生 G 代码以驱动 CNC 数控机床。

[2] Usually it had been necessary to force the CAD operator to export the data in one of the common data formats, such as IGES or STL, that are supported by a wide variety of software. 可译为:通常它(指集成)要求 CAD 操作员要以通用的数据格式输出数据，如 IGES 起始图形交换规范或 STL 标准模板库格式，它们支持各种各样的软件。

[3] From the development of the basic design to the Bill of Materials necessary to manufacture the product there is no requirement at any stage of the process to build physical prototypes. 可译为:从基本设计开发到制造产品所需的物料清单，在加工过程的任何阶段无需建立物理原型。

[4] Computer-aided manufacturing takes this one step further by bridging the gap between the conceptual design and the manufacturing of the finished product. 可译为:计算机辅助制造采用这一步骤进一步缩小了概念设计与成品制造之间的差距。

## Exercises

1. What is the meaning of CAM?

2. There are several limitations of Computer-aided Manufacturing, please list them.

3. Please list the benefits resulted from the implementation of CAM.

# Unit 6  Advance Manufacturing Technology

## Lesson 21  Agile Manufacturing

### 1 Introduction

Manufacturing industry may well be on the verge of a major paradigm shift. This shift is likely to take us away from mass production, way beyond lean manufacturing, into a world of Agile Manufacturing. Agile Manufacturing, however, is a relatively new term, one which was first introduced with the publication of the Iacocca Institute report 21st Century Manufacturing Enterprise Strategy[1]. Furthermore, at this point in time, Agile Manufacturing is not well understood and the conceptual aspects are still being defined. However, there is a tendency to view Agile Manufacturing as another programme of the month, and to use the term Agile Manufacturing as just another way of describing lean production, flexible manufacturing or CIM.

Many of our corporations today are under going massive transformations — reengineering business processes, flattening hierarchies, empowering people, implementing lean production concepts, etc. The list is almost endless. But none of these massive transformations, on their own or taken collectively, constitutes the implementation of Agile Manufacturing. What Agile Manufacturing really represents is the potential for a quantum leap forward in manufacturing. Instead of just chasing after the Japanese by copying their techniques in a prescriptive fashion, or implementing our own prescriptions such as CIM, in Agile Manufacturing we should be trying to achieve a competitive lead by doing something that our competitors are not doing.

Agile Manufacturing is something that many of our corporations have yet to fully comprehend, never mind implement. Agile Manufacturing is likely to be the way business will be conducted in the next century. It is not yet a reality. Our challenge is to make it a reality, first by more fully defining the conceptual aspects, and secondly by venturing into the frontier of implementation.

In this paper, we will examine some of the key issues relevant to the development of Agile Manufacturing. Owing to space limitations we will only provide a very brief overview of Agile Manufacturing. The reader is referred to 21st Century Manufacturing Enterprise Strategy and Agile Manufacturing: Forging New Frontiers for more detailed information.

## 2 Definition and Concepts

The problem with a new idea such as Agile Manufacturing is the lack of a good sound definition and a set of concepts that most people would agree upon.

Agile Manufacturing should primarily be seen as a business concept. Its aim is quite simple — to put our enterprises way out in front of our primary competitors. In Agile Manufacturing our aim is to develop agile properties. We will then use this agility for competitive advantage, by being able to rapidly respond to changes occurring in the market environment and through our ability to use and exploit a fundamental resource -knowledge.

One fundamental idea in the exploitation of this resource is the idea of using technologies to lever the skills and knowledge of our people. We need to bring our people together, in dynamic teams formed around clearly identified market opportunities, so that it becomes possible to lever one another's knowledge. Through these processes we should seek to achieve the transformation of knowledge and ideas into new products and services, as well as improvements to our existing products and services.

The concept of Agile Manufacturing is also built around the synthesis of a number of enterprises that each have some core skills or competencies which they bring to a joint venturing operation, which is based on using each partners facilities and resources[2]. For this reason, these joint venture enterprises are called virtual corporations, because they do not own significant capital resources of their own. This, it is believed, will help them to be agile, as they can be formed and changed very rapidly.

Central to the ability to form these joint ventures is the deployment of advanced information technologies and the development of highly nimble organisational structures to support highly skilled, knowledgeable and empowered people.

Agile Manufacturing enterprises are expected to be capable of rapidly responding to changes in customer demand. They should be able to take advantage of the windows of opportunities that, from time to time, appear in the market place. With Agile Manufacturing we should also develop new ways of interacting with our customers and suppliers. Our customers will not only be able to gain access to our products and services, but will also be able to easily assess and exploit our competencies, so enabling them to use these competencies to achieve the things that they are seeking.

## 3  Some Key Issues on Agile Manufacturing

### 3.1  The "I am a Horse" Syndrome

There is an old saying that hanging a sign on a cow that says "I am a horse" does not make it a horse. There is a real danger that Agile Manufacturing will fall prey to the unfortunate tendency in manufacturing circles to follow fashion and to relabel everything with a new fashionable label. The dangers in this are two fold. First, it will give Agile Manufacturing a bad reputation. Second, instead of getting to grips with the profound implications and issues raised by Agile Manufacturing, management will only acquire a superficial understanding, which leaves them vulnerable to those competitors that take Agile Manufacturing seriously. Of course this is good news for the competitors!

One sure way to fail with Agile Manufacturing is to hang a new sign up. Get smart, resist the temptation, and put the paint brush away.

### 3.2  The Existing Culture of Manufacturing

One of the important things that is likely to hold us back from making a quantum leap forward and exploring this new frontier of Agile Manufacturing, is the baggage of our traditions, conventions and our accepted values and beliefs. A key success factor is, without any doubt, the ability to master both the soft and hard issues in change management. However, if we are to achieve agility in our manufacturing enterprises, we should first try to fully understand the nature of our existing cultures, values, and traditions. We need to achieve this understanding, because we need to begin to recognise and come to terms with the fact that much of what we have taken for granted, probably no longer applies in the world of Agile Manufacturing. Achieving this understanding is the first step in facing up to the pain of consigning our existing culture to the garbage can of historically redundant ideas.

### 3.3 Understanding Agility

Agility is defined in dictionaries as quick moving, nimble and active. This is clearly not the same as flexibility which implies adaptability and versatility. Agility and flexibility are therefore different things.

Leanness (lean manufacturing) is also a different concept to agility. Sometimes the terms lean and agile are used interchangeably, but this is not appropriate. The term lean is used because lean manufacturing is concerned with doing everything with less. In other words, the excess of wasteful activities, unnecessary inventory, long lead times, etc. are cut away through the application of just-in-time manufacturing, concurrent engineering, overhead cost reduction, improved supplier and customer relationships, total quality management, etc.

We can also consider CIM in the same light. When we link computers across applications, across functions and across enterprises we do not achieve agility. We might achieve a necessary condition for agility, that is, rapid communications and the exchange and reuse of data, but we do not achieve agility.

Thus agility is not the same as flexibility, leanness or CIM. Understanding this point is very important. But if agility is none of these things, then what is it? This is a good question, and not one easily answered. Yet most of us would recognise agility if we saw it.

For example, we would not say the a Sumo wrestler was agile. Nor would we think that 50 Sumo wrestlers, tied together by a complex web of chains and ropes, all pulling in different directions, as agile. Quite the contrary. We would see them as lumbering, slow and unresponsive. However, we would all recognise a ballet dancer as agile. We would also think of a stage full of ballet dancers as agile, because what binds them together is something quite different.

This analogy between Sumo wrestlers and ballet dancers is very relevant to understanding the property of agility[3]. (see Appendix Lesson 30) Many of our corporations, to varying degrees, resemble Sumo wrestlers, tied together, but all pulling in different directions. If we want to develop agile properties, we need to understand what causes agility and what hinders agility. Only when we have developed this understanding can we begin to think about designing an agile enterprise. For, when we have such an understanding of the causes of agility, we can start to audit out current situation, and identify what needs to be changed.

## 4  Concluding Remarks

We have spent much time copying the Japanese. Now we may be about to teach the Japanese something. For a change, US manufacturing industry is realising that it has very little to gain, in the long term, by copying what other people are doing. There is now a growing realisation that global preeminence in manufacturing can only be achieved through innovation. We can learn from others, but in a highly competitive world we can only become world leaders if we develop new ideas that take us beyond the state-of-the-art. Basically, the issue is, should we adopt lean manufacturing in our own enterprises, i. e., should we mimic the Japanese, or should we do something different and better?

Without doubt there are a significant number of people who believe that we have to adopt lean manufacturing. But in adopting this approach we run the risk of forever chasing after a moving target. The Japanese will keep innovating. Thus, adopting lean manufacturing can only be a short term measure aimed doing something to close the competitive gap. In the longer term, if we want to catch up with and overtake the Japanese, lean manufacturing is not the answer. What we need to do is something which the Japanese cannot do. That something may well be Agile Manufacturing.

**Vacabulary**

paradigm [ˈpærədim]　n. 范例；词形变化表
Agile Manufacturing　敏捷制造
massive [ˈmæsiv]　adj. 大量的；巨大的，厚重的；魁伟的
CIM　abbr. computer-integrated manufacturing 计算机集成化制造技术
implementation [ˌimplimenˈteiʃən]　n.［计］实现；履行；安装启用
nimble [ˈnimbl]　adj. 敏捷的；聪明的

lean manufacturing　精益生产
conceptual [kənˈseptjuəl]　adj. 概念上的；概念的；概念性
saying [ˈseiiŋ]　n. 话；谚语；言论 v. 说（say 的 ing 形式）
syndrome [ˈsindrəum, -drəm-]　n.［临床］综合征；综合症状
temptation [tempˈteiʃən]　n. 引诱；诱惑物
redundant [riˈdʌndənt]　adj. 多余的，过剩的；失业的；冗长的，累赘的

agility [əˈdʒiləti] n. 敏捷;灵活;机敏
interchangeably [ˌintəˈtʃeindʒəbli]
    adv. [数]可交换地
leanness [ˈliːnnis] n. 瘦;贫瘠;缺乏
state-of-the-art [ˈsteitəvðiˈaːt] adj. 最先进的;已经发展的;达到最高水准的
innovating n. 创新 v. 革新（innovate [ˈinəuveit]的现在分词）;创立
chasing [ˈtʃeisiŋ] v. 追赶(chase 的 ing 形式) n. [建]雕镂术;车螺丝雕镂
Sumo [ˈsjuːməu] n. 相扑(日)
wrestler [ˈreslə] n. 摔跤选手,搏斗者

**Notes**

[1]　Agile Manufacturing, however, is a relatively new term, one which was first introduced with the publication of the Iacocca Institute report 21*st Century Manufacturing Enterprise Strategy*. 可译为:无论如何,敏捷制造是一个相对新的术语,它是随着艾柯卡研究院的二十一世纪制造企业战略报告的出版而首次介绍的。

[2]　The concept of Agile Manufacturing is also built around the synthesis of a number of enterprises that each have some core skills or competencies which they bring to a joint venturing operation, which is based on using each partners facilities and resources. 可译为:敏捷制造的概念,也是围绕许多企业的综合体而建立起来的,每个合作伙伴都具有一些核心技能或能力,基于利用它们的设施和资源进行合作经营。

[3]　This analogy between Sumo wrestlers and ballet dancers is very relevant to understanding the property of agility. 可译为:相扑运动员和芭蕾舞演员之间的类比对理解敏捷的特性很重要。

**Exercises**

1. Please describe the definition of Agile Manufacturing.
2. What is Agility ?
3. Please list some key issues about Agile Manufacturing discussed in this paper ?

## Lesson 22　Rapid Prototyping Technologies

### 1　Introduction

　　Rapid prototyping processes are a relatively recent development. The first machine was released onto the market in late 1987. While rapid prototyping is the term commonly applied to these technologies the terminology is now a little dated, reflecting the purpose to which the early machines were applied. A more accurate description would be layer manufacturing processes. An alternative term is free-form fabrication processes.

These processes work by building up a component layer by layer, with one thin layer of material bonded to the previous thin layer. There are several different processes. The main ones are:

- Stereolithography;
- Laser sintering;
- Fused deposition modelling;
- Solid ground curing;
- Laminated object manufacturing.

In addition, there are a number of newer processes, such as ballistic particle manufacturing and three-dimensional printing, which have appeared on the market.

All these processes essentially start with nothing and end with a completed part. This is in contrast to conventional manufacturing processes such as milling machines that start from a solid block of a substance and cut material away to form the finished part.

Rapid prototyping processes are driven by instructions which are derived from three-dimensional Computer-aided Design (CAD) models. CAD technologies are therefore an essential enabling system for rapid prototyping.

The processes use different physical principles, but essentially they work either by using lasers to cut, cure or sinter material into a layer, or involve ejecting material from a nozzle to create a layer. Many different materials are used, depending upon the particular process. Materials include thermo polymers, photopolymers, other plastics, paper, wax, metallic powder, etc.

The application of these processes is not restricted to supporting new product development activities. They can therefore be used to support one-off or small batch production runs. Thus the processes can be used to create models, tooling, prototypes, and even in some cases to directly produce metal components.

Many rapid prototyping technologies actually produce physical models. These models are then used to produce tooling using an indirect secondary process such as investment casting. The resulting tool is then used to manufacture a component. However, new processes are beginning to appear that allow the tooling to be manufactured directly from the computer model, thus eliminating the physical model production stage. In the future it is likely to be possible to manufacture components directly from the computer model, eliminating the need to produce physical models and tooling first, although these may still be required for other purposes.

The important point to understand is that, while rapid prototyping started out as an expensive tool for producing physical models for design engineers to visualise their component designs, this is now no longer an accurate description of the technologies or their application potential.[1]

The potential different applications of rapid prototyping technologies span the complete product life cycle from concept generation, through preparation of specifications and detailed design, to manufacture.

Two further points. First, rapid prototyping technologies address the area of prototyping mechanical devices, components, housings, etc. and not software or electronic components. Second, rapid prototyping technologies are often used instead of conventional manufacturing processes such as five axis milling machines. However, there are situations when the two are used in combination to produce prototypes. Sometimes, however, components are simple enough to be quickly and cost-effectively prototyped using conventional methods. In other words there are situations in which rapid prototyping processes offer no time or cost advantages over conventional technologies.

## 2　Strategic Importance of Rapid Prototyping Technologies

Increasingly companies are attaching greater importance to the need to differentiate their product and service offerings in order to remain competitive. Typically, firms are:
- ◆ Adding new technologies to their products to differentiate;
- ◆ Forming alliances with their customers;
- ◆ Adding service features to their manufactured product offerings;
- ◆ Reducing time to market for new products;
- ◆ Reducing the number of suppliers and forming longer-term relationships and alliances with those that remain;
- ◆ Expanding their product range;

- Reducing their cost base to become the lowest cost producer.

Rapid prototyping technologies have the potential to contribute something to the achievement of most, if not all these actions.

When addressing rapid prototyping technologies, seven major strategic issues need to be explored:

- The strategic nature of the technologies-aspects of rapid prototyping which take investment decisions beyond the realm of short-term return on investment calculations;
- The technologies as enablers of new strategies — the new business and marketing strategies that can be pursued as a result of using these technologies;
- The impact of rapid prototyping on the achievement of business objectives — the specific business objectives that can be directly affected by applying the technologies;
- Strategic aspects of organisational and cultural changes — what organisational and culture changes does the business strategy itself demand;
- Development of change competencies — applying rapid prototyping technologies to achieve operational change competency, and developing tactical and strategic change competencies to enable continuing developments in rapid prototyping to be deployed to satisfy existing business objectives and to develop new strategies; [2]
- Development and exploitation of knowledge — using existing knowledge and developing new knowledge for competitive advantage.

## 3  Rapid Prototyping and Manufacturing Strategy

The manufacturing business objectives potentially affected by rapid prototyping technologies are:

- Throughput time: for example, by helping to eliminate or speed up bottleneck processes;
- Flexibility to support product development: for example, by being quickly able to develop models, prototypes and tooling;
- Unit costs: for example, by reducing the costs traditionally associated with customising products;

- ◆ Delivery to schedule: for example, by exploiting time savings to manufacture products faster to meet due date promises;
- ◆ Labour productivity: for example, by eliminating time-consuming processes involved in making models and tooling;
- ◆ Flexibility to introduce new products: for example, by being able to quickly create new tooling for new products;
- ◆ Flexibility to customise products: for example, by developing specific tooling for each customer;
- ◆ Flexibility to change product specification: for example, by being able to quickly modify or create new tooling in response to specification changes;
- ◆ Flexibility to change production volumes: for example, by being able to quickly create additional tooling in response to increased demand.

## 4  The Benefits of Rapid Prototyping Technologies

Rapid prototyping is being used in just about all industrial sectors, although there are probably more applications in the automotive industry than any other. This is not surprising, however, given the intense global competitive pressures that are being experienced by automotive firms.

The application at Rockwell Automotive is a typical example of what many companies using this new technology are achieving. In Rockwell's case the technology was used to:

- ◆ Increase visualisation capability during the early phases of design by using rapid physical models;
- ◆ Detect design flaws before the manufacture of tooling;
- ◆ Rapidly create tooling to manufacture physical prototypes.

Rockwell claim that this allowed them to reduce by seven months the time taken to develop a prototype engine. They also claimed that cost savings were achieved on the development project.

## 5  Time and Cost Savings

The applications show firms using rapid prototyping technologies to achieve both cost and time savings in the process of new product development. This is to be expected given the high emphasis that is being given in most industries to reducing both the cost of new product development and time to market.

In most cases, firms using rapid prototyping have gained time reductions in the production of prototype tooling and parts, which is mostly how these time savings have been specified.

The figures for time reductions on prototyping vary greatly, ranging from 60% to 90%. On the whole, this range is likely to be realistic given that the estimation of time savings, when compared to the conventional methods of prototyping, is a fairly straightforward matter.

Little information is provided in the public domain about cost savings. Clearly there is a potential for cost reduction. For example, if mistakes can be identified before commitments are made to expensive tooling, then the costs associated with modifying such tools can be avoided. However, the information on cost reductions should be treated with some caution. The cases where cost reductions are claimed do not provide sufficient details of the basis for the calculations or the assumptions that have been made.

## 6 Innovation

Whilst pursuit of time and cost reductions are necessary business objectives, it is evident from studying the application examples, that some firms are using rapid prototyping in more innovative ways than others. Included in these innovative applications are:

- ◆ The development of new analysis and testing procedures
- ◆ Manufacture of production tooling
- ◆ Improving communications across product divisions
- ◆ Supporting customised manufacturing

Given the high capital costs of some rapid prototyping machines, especially the larger ones, these innovative applications are probably the key to the successful and cost-effective use of the technologies. It may be the case that rapid prototyping will only be seen as financially viable when these wider potential benefits are taken into account.

**Vacabulary**

Rapid Prototyping　快速原型　　　free-form ['fri:fɔ:m]　adj. 自由形态的

stereolithography 立体平版印刷；立体光刻；格式
LOM-Laminated Object Manufacturing 分层实体制造
SGC（Solid Ground Curing） 复印固化成形
Fused Deposition Modeling 融合沉积造型
eliminate [iˈlimineit] vt. 消除；排除
photopolymer [ˌfəutəuˈpɔlimə] n. [高分子]光聚合物，光敏聚合物；感光性树脂（尤用于印刷制版的）
thermopolymers [ˈθəːməuˈpɔliməs] n. 热聚合物
innovative [ˈinəuveitiv] adj. 革新的，创新的

**Notes**

[1] The important point to understand is that, while rapid prototyping started out as an expensive tool for producing physical models for design engineers to visualise their component designs, this is now no longer an accurate description of the technologies or their application potential. 可译为：重要的一点是要了解：快速成型刚开始被认为是一种生产物理模型的昂贵工具，由设计工程师用来可视化其部件设计，现在它已经不再用来精确描述有关技术或应用价值了。

[2] Development of change competencies-applying rapid prototyping technologies to achieve operational change competency, and developing tactical and strategic change competencies to enable continuing developments in rapid prototyping to be deployed to satisfy existing business objectives and to develop new strategies; 可译为：开发应变能力——应用快速成型技术以达到经营的应变能力，发展战术和战略转变能力，使持续发展的快速原型部署满足现有的商业目标，并致力于发展新的策略。

**Exercises**

1. Please describe the Rapid Prototyping Processes.
2. Why CAD technologies are an essential enabling system for rapid prototyping?
3. Please list the benefits of rapid prototyping discussed in this paper ?

# Lesson 23  E-manufacturing

## 1 Introduction

E-manufacturing is concerned with the use of the Internet and e-business technologies in manufacturing industries. It covers all aspects of manufacturing-sales, marketing, customer service, new product development, procurement, supplier relationships, logistics, manufacturing, strategy development and so on[1]. The Internet also affects products as well since it is possible to use Interent technologies to add new product functions and to provide new services.

Manufacturing companies are using the Internet successfully for many different purposes. The scope of applications is large. Certain applications such as supply chain management, procurement, trade exchanges, and of course on-line sales have attracted a lot of attention in the press. However, this should not blind people to the fact that the Internet and e-business technologies can be used to support all aspects of manufacturing enterprises' activities. The challenge is to find the right application at the right time.

Application of the Internet is not a one-off project, but a journey that involves dealing with technologies, strategies, business processes, organisation and people. Success will come to those firms adopting an integrated approach driven by business needs and opportunities.

## 2  E-Manufacturing Benefits

Top concerns for CEO's in today's manufacturing business environment are:
- ◆ The threat posed by competitors;
- ◆ Controlling costs;
- ◆ Finding new opportunities;
- ◆ Improving responsiveness;
- ◆ Better customer focus and service.

E-manufacturing is capable of delivering these benefits.

Manufacturing business of all sizes in all sectors are using the Internet in many different ways — to work with partners and suppliers, for procurement, for internal activities such as knowledge sharing and new product development, and much more.

Companies such as United Technologies, General Electric and many others are reporting benefits from the use of the Internet. These benefits include:
- ◆ Improved speed of response;
- ◆ Cost savings;
- ◆ Improved communications, information and knowledge sharing;

- ◆ Reductions in inventory;
- ◆ Improved efficiency and productivity;
- ◆ Harmonisation and standardisation of procedures;
- ◆ Better transfer of best practices;
- ◆ Acquisition of new customers and increased sales;
- ◆ Improved customer service.

However, the benefits are achieved not by technology (which is an enabler) but by addressing strategy, technology, organisation, people and business processes as an integrated whole and making changes in all these dimensions[2]. The Internet is just like other information technologies — change management, good implementation practices and clear business objectives are required in order to reap the full benefits.

Executives and managers can learn more by reading our e-business publications.

- ◆ "Electronic Business: the Executive Guide" provides an introduction to the Internet and its potential. It is written for the benefit of non-specialists and avoids the use of jargon. No prior knowledge of the Internet is assumed;
- ◆ "E-business Strategy: Case Studies, Benefits and Implementation" is a much more detailed publication which is focused on both understanding and development of an e-business strategy;
- ◆ "E-business Strategy Tools: Practical Help for Executives" is a publication that provides a number of practical tools to help formulate an e-business strategy or to check/verify an existing strategy.
- ◆ "E-business Technical Change: A Manager's Guide" is a publication that provides assistance to managers wishing to manage the organisational and people changes associated with the introduction of e-business technologies — includes guidance, checklists and analysis tools.

## 3  Case Examples of E-manufacturing Benefits

United Technologies is a large US manufacturing company operating in several areas, including elevators and aerospace. United is using electronic auctions to buy from its suppliers component such as electronic circuit boards. The company uses the Internet to request suppliers to make bids for the supply of a component. Selected suppliers submit bids during a predefined time interval, say one hour, and the winner is the one that comes up with the lowest price. The bidding process has been in operation since 1997 and is used with pre-qualified suppliers for commodity products, including motors, wire, plastic fabrications and electronic parts. Typically purchases of such items account for about one quarter of the amount United Technologies spends each year on all bought — in goods and services.

Over several years, United has made savings of $181 million through on-line auctions, achieving 25% price reductions on average.

General Electric (GE) is another example of an industrial company reporting benefits from use of the Internet. GE expects savings from its efforts to total $1.6 billion pre-tax in 2001. Savings will come from conducting nearly $14 billion in web-based auctions and from digitising GE work processes. In addition to these cost savings, GE expects sales over the Internet to accelerate to more than $15 billion in 2001. GE has identified 20 to 30 per cent cost-out opportunities by e-enabling its manufacturing operations.

GE expects e-business to contribute 10 cents in earnings-per-share growth in 2001. In 2001, GE also expects to realise $1 billion in operating margin as a result of its e-business efforts.

The above demonstrate that tangible benefits can be derived from application of e-business technologies, but the key issue is identifying the areas where benefits can be achieved. As with all investments, this means undertaking a cost-benefit analysis and preparing a business case for investment. This matter is addressed in the publication "E-business Strategy: Case Studies, Benefits and Implementation".

## 4  E-manufacturing Case Examples

### 4.1  Agilent Technologies

**Application:** Agilent Technologies was formed in 1999 from the former Hewlett-Packard test and measurement, chemical analysis, semiconductor components and medical products businesses. Agilent Technologies uses an Intranet and the Internet to support its product development teams. Teams located in different parts of the world share data and information and practice design reuse to save development time. The collaborative environment is also used to help achieve a cross-functional perspective, with marketing, design and manufacturing sharing data and information. The application helps to save time and money as a result of less travel and improved communications leading to fewer misunderstandings and the resulting rework.

**Illustrates**: The use if the Internet and an Intranet to improve communications between geographically distributed teams engaged in product development, and also to improve cross-functional working.

## 4.2 Clyde Blowers

**Application**: Clyde Blowers, an engineering company, manufactures products such as the tools used to clean the insides of coal-fired power station boilers. It has manufacturing plants in Europe, the US, China and India. The company has been using the Internet for a number of purposes. Document exchange and e-mail are used based on Lotus Notes (a widely used group working software tool) and video conferencing software is used to enable face to face meetings, thus helping to reduce travel costs. Also, the firm uses Lotus Notes to track customer enquires, so that firms throughout the group can see what is going on thus helping to avoid the situation where firms within the group are competing with each other for the same business.

**Illustrates**: The use of the Internet to improve communications between geographically distributed parts of the firm and to increase coordination of activities.

## 4.3 Frigomechanica

**Application**: Frigomeccanica is a small Italian company that designs, assembles, installs and maintains freezing and defrosting machines, drying cells and other in-process and post-process treatment cells for the food industry (ham, salami, meat, cheese, etc.). Frigomeccanica's markets, clients and network of sales agents are geographically distributed all over the world. It is common for clients to demand customised machines as well as continuous, cost-effective and efficient support during the entire working life of the machine, from pre-sales assistance, to installation and post-sales support. Frigomeccanica's equipment is always tailor-made to meet the needs of each individual customer. Many unforeseen problems have to be faced at the machine installation stage and during the initial period of use at the customer sites. Huge costs are usually incurred to assist customers on-site during these phases. Here, the problem solving process is based heavily on the skills and knowledge of a small number of very experienced technicians, who are forced to rush around the world in order to ensure the necessary customer support, and their expertise represents a scarce and critical resource. Hence, modern communication technologies such as desk-top video conferencing operating over the Internet are being investigated and piloted to support pre-and post-sales support without increasing the price to the customer.

**Illustrates**: Using the Internet to increase the productivity of skilled employees by making their expertise more accessible without the need for expensive and time consuming journeys.

### 4.4 GKN

**Application**: GKN, a British engineering company that manufactures among other things automotive components, is using its Intranet as a knowledge management tool. The objective is to enable knowledge about manufacturing techniques, normally communicated within a single plant, to be made available throughout the group, thus reducing duplication of problem solving and also unnecessary capital expenditure on eliminating problems that may have a simpler solution discovered elsewhere but not communicated company wide. In addition to sharing explicit knowledge such new ideas generated at each of its plants, GKN is also expecting that tacit knowledge will be shared.

**Illustrates**: Knowledge sharing between geographically separated parts of a large firm using the Internet as the prime means of communication.

Other manufacturing examples are included in our publication "Electronic Business: the Executive Guide".

- ◆ Dell Computers;
- ◆ Electrolux;
- ◆ Ford;
- ◆ General Electric;
- ◆ Intel;
- ◆ Rolls-Royce;

- ◆ Rover Group;
- ◆ Styles Precision Components;
- ◆ Unipart;
- ◆ United Technologies.

There are also a number of non-manufacturing examples in the Executive Guide:
- ◆ British Airways;
- ◆ J. Sainsbury.

More detailed information on two of the manufacturing examples, General Electric and Styles Precision Components, can be found in our publication "E-business Strategy: Case Studies, Benefits and Implementation", along with a detailed case study from the retail sector.

Executives and managers can learn more by reading our e-business publications. "Electronic Business: the Executive Guide" provides an introduction to the Internet and its potential. It is written for the benefit of non-specialists and avoids the use of jargon. No prior knowledge of the Internet is assumed. "E-business Strategy: Case Studies, Benefits and Implementation" is a much more detailed publication which is focused on both understanding and development of an e-business strategy. "E-business Strategy Tools: Practical Help for Executives" is a publication that provides a number of practical tools to help formulate an e-business strategy or to check/verify an existing strategy. "E-business Technical Change: A Manager's Guide" is a publication that provides assistance to managers wishing to manage the organisational and people changes associated with the introduction of e-business technologies — includes guidance, checklists and analysis tools.

## Vacabulary

E-Manufacturing [iːˌmænjuˈfæktʃəriŋ] 电子化制造;企业信息化

e-business [ˈiːbiznis] n. 电子商务

logistics [ləuˈdʒistiks] n. [军]后勤;后勤学;物流

CEO abbr. 首席执行官;执行总裁(chief executive officer)

one-off [ˈwʌnɔf, -ɔːf] adj. 一次性的 n. 一次性事物

collaborative [kəˈlæbərətiv] adj. 合作的,协作的

cross-functional [krɔs ˈfʌkʃənəl] n. 跨功能;跨职能员工

defrosting [diːˈfrɔstiŋ] v. 除霜,[制冷]

融霜;解冻(deforst 的现在分词);溶解
pre-sales   adj. 售前的
desk-top   adj. 台式的;桌面上的
GKN   吉凯恩(总部位于英国的跨国工业公司集团,业务领域涉及汽车,飞机和工作车辆)
Electrolux   n. 伊莱克斯(财富 500 强公司之一)
Rolls-Royce ['rəulz'rɔis]   n. 劳斯莱斯,劳斯莱斯汽车
rover ['rəuvə]   n. 漫游者;流浪者;漂泊者
Rover Group   罗孚公司
Unipart   优尼派特集团

## Notes

[1] E-manufacturing is concerned with the use of the Internet and e-business technologies in manufacturing industries. It covers all aspects of manufacturing — sales, marketing, customer service, new product development, procurement, supplier relationships, logistics, manufacturing, strategy development and so on. 可译为:E-制造关心的是在制造业中利用互联网、电子商务技术。它涵盖制造的各方面——销售、市场、客户服务、新产品开发、采购、供应商的关系、物流、制造、战略发展等。

[2] However, the benefits are achieved not by technology (which is an enabler) but by addressing strategy, technology, organisation, people and business processes as an integrated whole and making changes in all these dimensions. 可译为:然而,这些好处不是靠技术(这是一个使能器)实现的,而是通过寻求战略、技术、组织、人与业务流程作为一个整体,并使这些方面都发生了巨大的变化来实现的。

## Exercises

1. Please describe the definition of Agile Manufacturing?
2. Please describe the benefits of E-manufacturing.
3. Please list some manufacturing examples included in this paper?

## Lesson 24   Concurrent Engineering

### 1 Introduction

Concurrent Engineering is a method by which several teams within an organization work simultaneously to develop new products and services. By engaging in multiple aspects of development concurrently, the amount of time involved in getting a new product to the market is decreased significantly. In markets where customers value time compression, fast-cycle developers have a distinct advantage. Additionally, in many high-technology areas such as electronics and telecommunications, product-technology performance is continuously increasing and price levels are dropping almost daily. In such areas, a firm's ability to sustain its competitive edge largely depends on the timely introduction of new or improved products and technologies. More and more, the time parameter makes the difference between mere survival and substantial profit generation. Concurrent engineering is a key method for meeting this need of shortening a new product's time-to-market.

## 2 Sequential New Product Development

In the past, commercial success was practically guaranteed for companies that could design, develop, and manufacture high-quality products that satisfied real needs at competitive prices. However, beginning in the early 1990s this traditional formula radically changed as time-to-market became a vital component of commercial success. Studies have demonstrated that being a few months late to market is much worse than having a 50 percent cost overrun when these overruns are related to financial performance over the lifecycle of a new product or service. In other words, time has become a key driver of competitive success, from design and development to the actual launch of a new product or service.

Traditional project planning and execution has been marked by the definition of objectives and mile-stones. These goals are met through a progression of networked activities, some of which must be performed sequentially, others of which may be conducted in parallel. Planning techniques such as Program Evaluation and Review Technique (PERT), Graphical Evaluation and Review Technique (GERT), and Critical Path Method (CPM) have been used to support this sequencing of tasks and activities[1]. However, until the beginning of the 1990s time compression was not a major issue in the new product development environment. In the planning and scheduling of tasks and activities, any time compression concerns were only implicitly present.

## 3 Concurrent New Product Development

Because time has become a competitive weapon, time pressures have become central to the project-based new product development organization. These pressures have led to the explicit understanding that time compression is a driver of project (and subsequent business) performance. As a consequence, methods, techniques, and organizational approaches have been designed and developed that allow for time compression needs to be handled in a proper manner. All time-centered approaches have one principle in common: they attempt to maximize the number of major design or development tasks that are performed concurrently, thus the concept of concurrent engineering.

In a concurrent engineering environment, even if certain tasks cannot be completely executed at the same time, designers and developers are encouraged to achieve maximum overlap between otherwise sequential activities. In other words, concurrent engineering aims at achieving throughput time reductions by planning and executing design and development activities in parallel, or by striving for maximum overlap between activities that cannot be completely executed in parallel (for example, when one of the tasks or activities requires information to be partially generated during a previous task or activity)[2].

Therefore, concurrent engineering is based on the premise that the parallel execution of major design components will decrease the throughput time of projects, thus reducing the time-to-market for new products and services. For example, applying concepts of parallelism during the Boeing 777 transport design resulted in a time compression of 1.5 years as compared to its predecessor, the Boeing 767. Concurrent engineering allowed the Boeing Company to introduce the new airplane in time to limit the advantage of its competitor, Airbus Industrie.

Many companies have benefited from this same approach. Firms like Intel and Canon have been among the leaders in shortening their product development cycles through the implementation of concurrent engineering. However, this trend has not been limited to individual companies; complete industry sectors also have implemented concurrent engineering principles. At the beginning of the 1990s, the automotive industry pioneered many of the concurrent engineering concepts and their implementation. By early 2000s, many industries, including electronics and pharmaceuticals, were behaving in much the same manner.

## 4　Implementing Concurrent Engineering

In a concurrent engineering environment, teams of experts from different disciplines are formally encouraged to work together to ensure that design progresses smoothly and that all participants share the same, current information. The project and problem-solving methods and the technologies utilized make up the essential elements through which parallelism in new product design and development can be achieved. Following is a discussion of how each of these elements contributes to concurrent engineering implementation.

### 4.1　Project Methods

Project methods based on team-work, milestone management, and target-oriented work definition and follow-up are paramount. These methods also must be supported by appropriate senior management commitment and incentive systems. Each team is granted a large degree of autonomy to solve design problems where and when they occur, without much hierarchical intervention. However, management must ensure that the transfer of information between different activities or tasks is smooth and transparent. Also, the means of experimentation must allow the experts involved to rule out differences in interpretation on the functional and technical design parameters. In other words, for concurrent engineering to be successful, information and interpretation asymmetries between the experts involved must be avoided whenever possible.

### 4.2　Problem-solving Methods

During design and development projects, methods are utilized that foster and support smooth interdisciplinary problem definition and problem solving. Methodologies such as brainstorming open the boundaries of the team to allow for wider ranges of alternative design definitions and solutions to be considered. The use of methodologies like Quality Function Deployment (QFD) further aids experts from different disciplinary backgrounds to jointly define a product's functional and technical requirements. Activity flow chart methods such as IDEF3 allow detailed planning and monitoring of the different parallel and overlapping activities involved in project execution. Failure Mode and Effects Analysis (FMEA) allows a systematic investigation of the occurrence and impact of possible flaws in the new product design. The use of Design of Experiments (DOE) enables the systematic identification of critical product/process parameters that influence performance. These are just a few of the many supportive methods that can be used in a concurrent engineering environment. The sources listed at the end of this essay provide more detailed and exhaustive overviews on these and other methodologies supporting concurrent engineering.

## 5 Technologies

In concurrent engineering, design technologies are utilized that foster efficient cross-disciplinary analysis, experimentation, and representation of new product designs. Some examples of these technologies include Three-dimensional (3D) Computer-aided Design (CAD) systems, Rapid Prototyping Techniques, Rapid Tooling and Rapid Testing Techniques, as well as techniques that enable the representation of product designs in a virtual context. These design technologies are important because of the key information they convey: their 3D character allows the expert to interpret design features in a more effective and efficient way.

All of these technologies contribute to the reduction of interpretation asymmetries between the experts involved, as well as to fast-cycle design and development, because they allow for high-speed iterations of analysis and experimentation on both concepts and models of the product. Thus, they modify traditional project management approaches by allowing for more systematic and flexible experimentation and iteration to be included throughout the project's design and development process. In fact, the time and cost incurred by the development and construction of prototypes generally are reduced by factors of 2 to 5 when using digital (e. g., 3D CAD) and physical (e. g., Rapid Prototyping) technologies. These tools have become an important enabling factor in the concurrent engineering environment. Without their implementation and further upgrading, concurrent engineering might never be able to realize its full potential in terms of design cost and lead-time optimization.

This brief overview has provided a summary of the why, the what, and the how involved in implementing a concurrent engineering philosophy for the development of new products, services, and processes. It has outlined how introducing overlap during the execution of innovation project tasks and activities has become vital because of competitive pressures that force new product developers to be more time-conscious.

However, a final caveat is warranted. Although concurrent engineering is an important method for handling the time pressures that occur during new product development, rushing products to the market can sometimes be a mistake. First, markets need time to develop. Numerous examples exist where a new product was too early for the market to absorb it or where product variety has reached limits beyond which the product choice decision becomes too complicated for customers. Second, more revolutionary new product development, which often is based on significant technological advances, typically requires longer time horizons to reach completion. Putting too much emphasis on time compression may blind an organization to this basic fact. Third, the conceptual development of new product ideas requires time or "slack". In a high-speed development organization, time-compression imperatives may undermine this need. Therefore, both managers and new product developers need to find a balance between the paradoxical needs for speed and slack in their organizations. Despite its efficiency, concurrent engineering will only prove to be effective when this balance is achieved through the experience and leadership of an organization's senior management.

## Vacabulary

Concurrent Engineering 并行工程

overrun [ˌəuvəˈrʌn, ˈəuvərʌn] n. 泛滥成灾;超出限度 vt. 泛滥;超过;蹂躏

PERT [pəːt] abbr. (Program Evaluation and Review Technique)计划评价与审查技术

CPM abbr. (Critical Path Method)关键路径法

GERT abbr. (Graphical Evaluation and Review Technique) 图形评审技术

implicitly [imˈplisitli] adv. 含蓄地;暗中地

overlap [ˌəuvəˈlæp, ˈəuvəlæp] n. 重叠;重复 vi. 部分重叠;部分的同时发生

QFD abbr. (Quality Function Deployment)质量功能展开

IDEF Integration Definition Method 集成定义方法

FMEA abbr. 故障类型与理象分析 (Failure Mode and Effects Analysis)

DOE abbr. (Design Of Experiment)实验设计

slack [slæk] n. 煤末;峡谷 adv. 马虎地;缓慢地 adj. 松弛的;疏忽的;不流畅的 vt. 放松;使缓慢 vi. 松懈;减弱

## Notes

[1] Planning techniques such as Program Evaluation and Review Technique (PERT), Graphical Evaluation and Review Technique (GERT), and Critical Path Method (CPM) have been used to support this sequencing of tasks and activities. 可译为：规划技术，如项目评估和审查技术(PERT)、图形评审技术(GERT)以及关键路径法(CPM)已被用来支持任务和活动的排序。

[2] In other words, concurrent engineering aims at achieving throughput time reductions by planning and executing design and development activities in parallel, or by striving for maximum overlap between activities that cannot be completely executed in parallel (for example, when one of the tasks or activities requires information to be partially generated during a previous task or activity). 可译为：换句话说，并行工程旨在实现制造周期的缩减，它并行地编制计划和实施设计与开发活动，或对不能完全并行执行的活动(例如，当某一个任务或活动需要前一项任务或活动所产生的部分信息时)，争取活动之间的最大重叠。

## Exercises

1. Please describe the definition of Concurrent Engineering.
2. Please list the benefits of Concurrent Engineering discussed in this paper?
3. What is CPM?

# Unit 7    Extracurricular Reading

## Lesson 25    Nanotechnology

### 1 Introduction

Defense programs in many countries are now concentrating on nanotechnology research that will facilitate advances in such technology used to create secure but small messaging equipment, allow the development of smart weapons, improvestealth capabilities, aid in developing specialized sensors (including bio-inclusive sensors), help to create self-repairing military equipment, and improve the development and delivery mechanisms for medicines and vaccines.

Nanotechnology builds on advances inmicroelectronics during the last decades of the 20th century. The miniaturization of electrical components greatly increased the utility and portability of computers, imaging equipment, microphones, and other electronics. Indeed, the production and wide use of such commonplace devices such as personal computers and cell phones was absolutely dependent on advances in microtechnology.

Despite these fundamental advances there remain real physical constraints (e. g. , microchip design limitations) to further miniaturization based upon conventional engineering principles. Nanotechnologies intend to revolutionize components and manufacturing techniques to overcome these fundamental limitations. In addition, there are classes of biosensors and feedback control devices that require nanotechnology because — despite advances in microtechnology — present components remain too large or slow.

### 2 Advances in Nanotechnology

Nanotechnology advances affect all branches of engineering and science that deal directly with device components ranging in size between 1/10,000,000 (one ten millionth of a millimeter) and 1/100,000 millimeter. At these scales, even the most sophisticated microtechnology-based instrumentation is useless. Engineers anticipate that advances in nanotechnology will allow the direct manipulation of molecules in biological samples (e. g. , proteins or nucleic acids) paving the way for the development of new materials that have a biological component or that can provide a biological interface.

In addition to new tools, nanotechnology programs advance practical understanding of quantum physics. The internalization of quantum concepts is a necessary component of nanotechnology research programs because the laws of classical physics (e. g. , classical mechanics or generalized gas laws) do not always apply to the atomic and near-atomic level.

**Nanotechnology and Quantum Physics.** Quantum theory and mechanics describe the relationship between energy and matter on the atomic and subatomic scale. At the beginning of the 20th century, German physicist Maxwell Planck (1858~1947) proposed that atoms absorb or emit electromagnetic radiation in bundles of energy termed quanta. This quantum concept seemed counter-intuitive to well-established Newtonian physics. Advancements associated with quantum mechanics (e. g. , the uncertainty principle) also had profound implications with regard to the philosophical scientific arguments regarding the limitations of human knowledge.

Planck's quantum theory, which also asserted that the energy of light (a photon) was directly proportional to its frequency, proved a powerful concept that accounted for a wide range of physical phenomena. Planck's constant relates the energy of a photon with the frequency of light. Along with the constant for the speed of light, Planck's constant ($h = 6.626 \times 10^{-34}$ Joule-second) is a fundamental constant of nature.

Prior to Planck's work, electromagnetic radiation (light) was thought to travel in waves with an infinite number of available frequencies and wavelengths. Planck's work focused on attempting to explain the limited spectrum of light emitted by hot objects. Danish physicist Niels Bohr (1885 ~ 1962) studied Planck's quantum theory of radiation and worked in England with physicists J. J. Thomson (1856~1940), and Ernest Rutherford (1871~1937) to improve their classical models of the atom by incorporating quantum theory. During this time, Bohr developed his model of atomic structure. According to the Bohr model, when an electron is excited by energy, it jumps from its ground state to an excited state (i.e., a higher energy orbital). The excited atom can then emit energy only in certain (quantized) amounts as its electrons jump back to lower energy orbits located closer to the nucleus. This excess energy is emitted in quanta of electromagnetic radiation (photons of light) that have exactly the same energy as the difference in energy between the orbits jumped by the electron.

The electron quantum leaps between orbits proposed by the Bohr model accounted for Plank's observations that atoms emit or absorb electromagnetic radiation in quanta. Bohr's model also explained many important properties of the photoelectric effect described by Albert Einstein (1879~1955). Einstein assumed that light was transmitted as a stream of particles termed photons. By extending the well-known wave properties of light to include a treatment of light as a stream of photons, Einstein was able to explain the photoelectric effect. Photoelectric properties are key to the regulation of many microtechnology and proposed nanotechnology level systems.

Quantum mechanics ultimately replaced electron "orbitals" of earlier atomic models with allowable values for angular momentum (angular velocity multiplied by mass) and depicted electron positions in terms of probability "clouds" and regions.

In the 1920s, the concept of quantization and its application to physical phenomena was further advanced by more mathematically complex models based on the work of the French physicist Louis Victor de Broglie (1892~1987) and Austrian physicist Erwin Schrödinger (1887~1961) that depicted the particle and wave nature of electrons. De Broglie showed that the electron was not merely a particle but a waveform. This proposal led Schrödinger to publish his wave equation in 1926. Schrödinger's work described electrons as a "standing wave" surrounding the nucleus, and his system of quantum mechanics is called wave mechanics. German physicist Max Born (1882~1970) and English physicist P. A. M. Dirac (1902~1984) made further advances in defining the subatomic particles (principally the electron) as a wave rather than as a particle and in reconciling portions of quantum theory with relativity theory.

Working at about the same time, German physicist Werner Heisenberg (1901~1976) formulated the first complete and self-consistent theory of quantum mechanics. Matrix mathematics was well established by the 1920s, and

Heisenberg applied this powerful tool to quantum mechanics. In 1926, Heisenberg put forward his uncertainty principle which states that two complementary properties of a system, such as position and momentum, can never both be known exactly. This proposition helped cement the dual nature of particles (e. g., light can be described as having both wave and particle characteristics). Electromagnetic radiation (one region of the spectrum that comprises visible light) is now understood to have both particle and wave like properties.

In 1925, Austrian-born physicist Wolfgang Pauli (1900～1958) published the Pauli exclusion principle states that no two electrons in an atom can simultaneously occupy the same quantum state (i. e., energy state). Pauli's specification of spin ($+1/2$ or $-1/2$) on an electron gave the two electrons in any suborbital differing quantum numbers (a system used to describe the quantum state) and made completely understandable the structure of the periodic table in terms of electron configurations (i. e., the energy-related arrangement of electrons in energy shells and suborbitals).

In 1931, American chemist Linus Pauling published a paper that used quantum mechanics to explain how two electrons, from two different atoms, are shared to make a covalent bond between the two atoms. Pauling's work provided the connection needed in order to fully apply the new quantum theory to chemical reactions.

Advances in nanotechnology depend upon an understanding and application of these fundamental quantum principles. At the quantum level the smoothness of classical physics disappears and nanotechnologies are predicated on exploiting this quantum roughness.

## 3 Applications

The development of devices that are small, light, self-contained, use little energy and that will replace larger microelectronic equipment is one of the first goals of the anticipated nanotechnology revolution. The second phase will be marked by the introduction of materials not feasible at larger than nanotechnology levels. Given the nature of quantum variance, scientists theorize that single molecule sensors can be developed and that sophisticated memory storage and neural-like networks can be achieved with a very small number of molecules.

Traditional engineering concepts undergo radical transformation at the atomic level. For example, nanotechnology motors may drive gears, the cogs of which are composed of the atoms attached to a carbon ring. Nanomotors may themselves be driven by oscillating magnetic fields or high precision oscillating lasers.

Perhaps the greatest promise for nanotechnology lies in potential biotechnology advances. Potential nano-level manipulation of DNA offers the opportunity to radically expand the horizons of genomic medicine and immunology. Tissue-based biosensors may unobtrusively be able to monitor and regulate site-specific medicine delivery or regulate physiological processes. Nanosystems might serve as highly sensitive detectors of toxic substances or used by inspectors to detect traces of biological or chemical weapons.

In electronics and computer science, scientists assert that nanotechnologies will be the next major advance in computing and information processing science. Microelectronic devices rely on recognition and flips in electron gating [e. g., where differential states are ultimately represented by a series of binary numbers ("0" or "1") that depict voltage states]. In contrast, future quantum processing will utilize the identity of quantum states as set forth by quantum numbers. In quantum cryptography systems with the ability to decipher encrypted information will rely on precise knowledge of manipulations used to achieve various atomic states.

Nanoscale devices are constructed using a combination of fabrication steps. In the initial growth stage, layers of semiconductor materials are grown on a dimension limiting substrate. Layer composition can be altered to control electrical and/or optical characteristics. Techniques such as Molecular Beam Epitaxy (MBE) and Metallo-organic Chemical Vapor Deposition (MOCVD) are capable of producing layers of a few atoms thickness. The developed pattern is then imposed on successive layers (the pattern transfer stage) to develop desired three dimensional structural characteristics.

# 4  Nanotechnology Research

In the United States, expenditures on nanotechnology development tops $500 million per year and is largely coordinated by the National Science Foundation and Department of Defense Advanced Research Projects Agency (DARPA) under the umbrella of the National Nanotechnology Initiative. Other institutions with dedicated funding for nanotechnology include the Department of Energy (DOE) and National Institutes of Health (NIH).

Research interests. Current research interests in nanotechnology include programs to develop and exploit nanotubes for their ability to provide extremely strong bonds. Nanotubes can be flexed and woven into fibers for use in ultrastrong — but also ultralight — bulletproof vests. Nanotubes are also excellent conductors that can be used to develop precise electronic circuitry.

Other interests include the development of nanotechnology-based sensors that allow smarter autonomous weapons capable of a greater range of adaptations enroute to a target; materials that offer stealth characteristics across a broader span of the electromagnetic spectrum; self-repairing structures; and nanotechnology-based weapons to disrupt — but not destroy — electrical system infrastructure.

## 5  Further Reading

**Books**

　　Mulhall, Douglas. *Our Molecular Future: How Nanotechnology, Robotics, Genetics, and Artificial Intelligence Will Change Our World* [M]. Amherst, NY: Prometheus Books, 2002.

**Periodicals**

　　Bennewitz, R., et al., "Atomic scale memory at a silicon surface." [J]. *Nanotechnology*, 2000, 13: 499-502.

**Electronic**

　　National Science and Technology Council. "National Nano-technology Initiative." <http://www.nano.gov/start.htm> (March 19, 2003).

# Lesson 26　Reaching for a Smarter Factory

## 1  Introduction

　　Machine tools not only think but readily communicate. Those are the ambitious goals of research initiatives that not only promise a smarter factory, but are already delivering smart maintenance.

　　September 1st, 2007 — "Intelligent" and "smart" are words that machine tool makers increasingly use at product introduction time. These days, builders also seem to refer to "smart" features as routinely as their traditional claims of machine tool speed, accuracy and productivity.

So has the age of smart machines truly arrived? "Not yet," says John Kohls, executive vice president of Cincinnati's TechSolve Inc., and one of the driving forces behind the industry consortium known as the Smart Machine Platform Initiative (SMPI). Instead he describes the industry's piecemeal progress, smart characteristic by smart characteristic, towards that goal. As SMPI director his mission is to help coordinate and accelerate the evolution toward a new generation of machine tools. "While individual characteristics of the smart machine tool of the future are here now, the goal is to put the pieces together into equipment that can think," he says.

Kohls' definition of machine thinking is more complex than simple sensor reaction to a machine condition. He adheres to the original parameters outlined by the National Institute of Science and Technology (NIST), an early SMPI program participant.

In NIST's vision, a smart machine:
- Knows its capabilities and condition with the ability to be interrogated;
- Knows how to machine a part in an optimal manner;
- Makes the first part (and every subsequent part) right;
- Monitors, diagnoses and optimizes itself;
- Knows the quality of its work;
- Learns and improves over time.

Now in the second year of government funding, SMPI grew out of a series of workshops by NIST and the National Science Foundation — a smart machine workshop in 2000 and a first-part-correct workshop in 2002. The targets: gains in productivity, declines in inventory requirements and manufacturing-related product improvements impacting price, quality and energy efficiency.

In outlining the SMPI's goals, NIST reports that annual US expenses on machining operations total more than \$200 billion, about 2% of the US Gross Domestic Product (GDP). NIST's vision is for smart systems to complement and enhance the skills of machine operators, process planners and design engineers. By eliminating trial and error-based prototype development and reducing time to market, NIST sees US builds a competitive proficiency in mass customization.

Kohls says total funding for the four-year program is $12.5 million. The funding source: US Army Research Laboratory with its Benét Laboratories in Watervliet, NY., serving as the program office.

The program is now in its technology evaluation phase. The test-bed: a four-axis horizontal machining center from Waconia, Minn-based Milltronics Manufacturing Co. Kohls describes the evaluation platform as a standard machine tool with a GE Fanuc control: "What will make it smart are the technologies we are putting on it. Our intent is to use technologies that will enhance the ability to produce the first part correct."

## 2  Not Just Smart, But Also Good Listeners

Kohls expects some technologies to demonstrate synergistic benefits. "Combining feed and speed optimization with CAD/CAM, for instance, could result in a more beneficial depth of cut," he points out. "Machine intelligence could also help match tool life to the job. For example, machine operators could be forewarned if the remaining tool life would be shorter than the time needed on an upcoming cut. Machine intelligence can provide the ability to look ahead and prevent being caught with a failure-prone tool in the middle of a machining sequence."

Kohls says the goal is for machines that can predict and warn of conditions having the potential of affecting productivity, accuracy and quality. "Smart machine tools will be good listeners, too," adds Kohls. "They will react to abnormal process sound as experienced human operators would. The machine would communicate a warning and suggest ways of correcting the problem." For less critical situations detection and correction could be automatic, he notes. In addition to sound, intelligent machines could be made sensitive to force, vibration and temperature.

Thus, far SMPI has not looked at vision from an in-process standpoint. "One difficulty with vision is the inability to see the cutter interface in action," Kohls says. Among the possibilities: inspecting tools and parts before and after a cut as well as visually inspecting chips.

"The biggest change that might occur would be the advent of model-based control where a model of the process drives the controller of the machine. We are planning a thorough investigation of that possibility," he adds.

## 3  Smarter and Communicative

The next step is leveraging smart machines with a communication standard that will enable a smarter factory. Kohls sees SMPI's communication solution in MTConnect, the machine tool interoperability initiative announced in February by the Association for Manufacturing Technology (AMT), the machine tool trade group. Kohls already refers to AMT's initiative as the foundation for SMPI.

MTConnect's focus, says AMT's Paul Warndorf, vice president, technology, is on providing a uniform, easy-to-implement way of confronting the typical production floor multi-vendor mix of equipment and software. "Instead of people spending all of their money on trying to figure out how to move the data, they can now pay attention to where their core competency is — namely, how you use the data in the applications. What we want to do is move more toward the plug-and-play conventions of computer usage."

Adds Doug Wood, past AMT chairman and president of Parlec International Inc., "With computer equipment, multi-vendor implementations pose few if any connectivity or interoperability problems. However, anyone trying to install a multi-vendor implementation of production equipment and machine tools will find that it's very difficult to get them to communicate and exchange information."

Wood says it's time for the makers of machine tools and other production equipment to emulate the ability of computer equipment to be easily, quickly and seamlessly integrated. "The intent of MTConnect is to emulate that computer industry model. We want to remove the operator difficulties common to multi-vendor production environments." He notes that while the problem is minimized in single vendor environments, that approach has limited applicability.

"Unfortunately," notes Wood, "there is a tendency (for machine tool makers) to emphasize product differentiation in areas that jeopardize connectivity. Equipment users are then challenged to integrate multi-vendor environments." Even so, he does not see MTConnect removing the ability to differentiate via proprietary mechanical, electrical and hardware product approaches.

To resolve those difficulties, AMT's board of directors authorized beginning MTConnect as a two-year $1 million effort. Initial work is being performed at the University of California at Berkeley. Warndorf says the goal is to develop a standard and demonstrate it at the International Manufacturing Technology Show

(IMTS) in Chicago in September 2008.

## 4  Predict-and-prevent

The concept of the smart factory may be most advanced in — surprise — maintenance. The evidence starts with the Center for Intelligent Maintenance Systems (IMS), a National Science Foundation, multi-campus university and industry initiative led by Jay Lee, a professor in Advanced Manufacturing at the University of Cincinnati. As director of the Center, Lee's focus is on advanced prognostics and predictive maintenance technologies designed to achieve zero-breakdown productivity.

Lee says the challenge for reliability is in dealing with data from the past. "Failure is modeled, analyzed and — to some extent — predicted. Unfortunately, the prediction doesn't take into account users or working environment-related constraints, and often the results aren't that useful," says Lee.

"Condition-based Maintenance (CBM) deals with online data. Machine conditions are constantly monitored and their signatures evaluated. However, this is done at the machine level — one machine at a time. This is what we call the 'Fail-and-fix' (FAF) mode." Lee says the challenge is to transfer to a "Predict-and-prevent" (PAP) methodology.

"Today, CBM focuses on sensors and communications. All products and machines are networked by some means." Lee says that it is difficult to know, though, what to do with the data. "We need to turn data into information by using computational tools to process data locally," he adds.

The Center's development of a Watchdog Agent is Lee's solution for a more realistic, knowledge-based alternative to traditional practice of scheduled maintenance. Mounted on machine tools, the computer platform is a toolbox of more than 18 algorithms that translate sensor data, historical data and operating conditions into predictive data.

In addition to monitoring machine performance and health, the Watchdog Agent predicts the likelihood of process failure. Prognostics is the label Lee applies to this type of predictive maintenance. He describes prognostics as a paradigm shift to tomorrow's predict-and-prevent maintenance thinking.

What distinguishes Lee's characterization of prognostics is how maintenance intelligence is integrated at the machine, operations and enterprise levels. He notes that while the OnStar type of machine level data collection is now emerging in both production equipment and automobiles, degradation assessment using historical data is typically missing in both. That jeopardizes maintenance analysis. For example, Lee says the rate of change can be more significant than the degree of change.

Lee feels operations intelligence also needs further consideration. He's referring to how the maintenance function should relate individual machine problems to overall production goals. "That involves how responses to problems are prioritized, optimized and scheduled."

The Center is also focusing attention on connecting the enterprise with synchronization intelligence. The idea, says Lee, is to facilitate the automatic conversion of data to information between the machine and business systems.

Lee says the Watchdog Agent has already been tested and installed at IMS partners General Motors, Harley-Davidson, TechSolve and Toyota's Georgetown, Ky. plant. At Toyota, the Watchdog Agent was implemented in a compressor project, adds Lee. "The projects are demonstrating how the hardware and software platform can eliminate surprise shutdowns."

"The maintenance world of tomorrow is an information world for feature-based monitoring," says Lee. Intelligent sensor networks could let production equipment notice maintenance problems before they happen. "Information should represent a trend, not just a status. It should offer priorities, not just show "how much." If we do that, then our productivity can be focused on asset-level utilization, not just production rates."

The Center consists of research sites at the University of Cincinnati, the University of Michigan and the University of Missouri-Rolla, as well as two international sites and involves partnerships with over 40 global companies.

## Lesson 27  Basics of Computer Numerical Control

### 1 Introduction

Today, Computer Numerical Control (CNC) machines are found almost everywhere, from small job shops in rural communities to Fortune 500 companies in large urban areas. Truly, there is hardly a facet of manufacturing that is not in some way touched by what these innovative machine tools can do.

Everyone involved in the manufacturing environment should be well aware of what is possible with these sophisticated machine tools. The design engineer, for example, must possess enough knowledge of CNC to perfect dimensioning and tolerancing techniques for workpieces to be machined on CNC machines. The tool engineer must understand CNC in order to design fixtures and cutting tools for use with CNC machines. Quality control people should understand the CNC machine tools used within their company in order to plan quality control and statistical process control accordingly. Production control personnel should be abreast of their company's CNC technology in order to make realistic production schedules. Managers, foremen, and team leaders should understand CNC well enough to communicate intelligently with fellow workers. And, it goes without saying that CNC programmers, setup people, operators, and others working directly with the CNC equipment must have an extremely good understanding of CNC.

In this presentation, we will explore the basics of CNC, showing you much of what is involved with using these sophisticated machine tools. Our primary goal will be to teach you how to learn about CNC. For readers who will eventually be working directly with CNC machine tools, we will show you the basics of each major CNC function. Additionally, we will make suggestions as to how you can learn more about each CNC function as it applies to your particular CNC machine(s). At the completion of this presentation, you should have a good understanding of how and why CNC functions as it does and know those things you must learn more about in order to work with any style of CNC machine tool.

For readers who are not going to be working directly with CNC equipment in the near future, our secondary goal will be to give you a good working knowledge of CNC technology. At the completion of this presentation, you should be quite comfortable with the fundamentals of CNC and be able to communicate intelligently with others in your company about your CNC machine tools.

To proceed in an organized manner, we will be using a key concepts approach to all presentations. All important functions of CNC are organized into ten key concepts (We'll show five of the ten key concepts in this presentation. All five are related to programming). Think of it this way. If you can understand ten basic principles, you are well on your way to becoming proficient with CNC.

While our main focus will be for the two most popular forms of CNC machine tools (machining centers and turning centers), these ten key concepts can be applied to virtually any kind of CNC machine, making it easy to adapt to any form of CNC equipment. With so many types of CNC machine tools in existence, it is next to impossible for this presentation to be extremely specific about any one particular type. The key concepts allow us to view the main features of CNC in more general terms, stressing why things are handled the way they are even more than the specific techniques used with any one particular CNC machine tool.

With the broad background we take above, you should be able to easily zero in on any kind of CNC machine tool you will be working with. As yet a third goal, this presentation should help instructors of CNC. The key concepts approach we show has been proven time and time again during live presentations in CNC courses. This method of presentation will help instructors organize CNC into extremely logical and easy to understand lessons.

## 2  Fundamentals of CNC

While the specific intention and application for CNC machines vary from one machine type to another, all forms of CNC have common benefits. Though the thrust of this presentation is to teach you CNC usage, it helps to understand why these sophisticated machines have become so popular. Here are but a few of the more important benefits offered by CNC equipment.

The first benefit offered by all forms of CNC machine tools is improved automation. The operator intervention related to producing workpieces can be reduced or eliminated. Many CNC machines can run unattended during their entire machining cycle, freeing the operator to do other tasks. This gives the CNC user several side benefits including reduced operator fatigue, fewer mistakes caused by human error, and consistent and predictable machining time for each workpiece. Since the machine will be running under program control, the skill level required of the CNC operator (related to basic machining practice) is also reduced as compared to a machinist producing workpieces with conventional machine tools.

The second major benefit of CNC technology is consistent and accurate workpieces. Today's CNC machines boast almost unbelievable accuracy and repeatability specifications. This means that once a program is verified, two, ten, or one thousand identical workpieces can be easily produced with precision and consistency.

A third benefit offered by most forms of CNC machine tools is flexibility. Since these machines are run from programs, running a different workpiece is almost as easy as loading a different program. Once a program has been verified and executed for one production run, it can be easily recalled the next time the workpiece is to be run. This leads to yet another benefit, fast change-overs. Since these machines are very easy to setup and run, and since programs can be easily loaded, they allow very short setup time. This is imperative with today's Just-in-Time product requirements.

## 3  Motion Control-the Heart of CNC

The most basic function of any CNC machine is automatic, precise, and consistent motion control. Rather than applying completely mechanical devices to cause motion as is required on most conventional machine tools, CNC machines allow motion control in a revolutionary manner. All forms of CNC equipment have two or more directions of motion, called axes. These axes can be precisely and automatically positioned along their lengths of travel. The two most common axis types are linear (driven along a straight path) and rotary (driven along a circular path).

Instead of causing motion by turning cranks and handwheels as is required on conventional machine tools, CNC machines allow motions to be commanded through programmed commands. Generally speaking, the motion type (rapid, linear, and circular), the axes to move, the amount of motion and the motion rate (feedrate) are programmable with almost all CNC machine tools.

Accurate positioning is accomplished by the operator counting the number of revolutions made on the handwheel plus the graduations on the dial. The drive motor is rotated a corresponding amount, which in turn drives the ball screw, causing linear motion of the axis. A feedback device confirms that the proper amounts of ball screw revolutions have occurred.

A CNC command executed within the control (commonly through a program) tells the drive motor to rotate a precise number of times. The rotation of the drive motor in turn rotates the ball screw. And the ball screw causes drives the linear axis. A feedback device at the opposite end of the ball screw allows the control to confirm that the commanded number of rotations has taken place.

Though a rather crude analogy, the same basic linear motion can be found on a common table vise. As you rotate the vise crank, you rotate a lead screw that, in turn, drives the movable jaw on the vise. By comparison, a linear axis on a CNC machine tool is extremely precise. The number of revolutions of the axis drive motor precisely controls the amount of linear motion along the axis.

How axis motion is commanded-understanding coordinate systems? It would be infeasible for the CNC user to cause axis motion by trying to tell each axis drive motor how many times to rotate in order to command a given linear motion amount. (This would be like having to figure out how many turns of the handle on a table vise will cause the movable jaw to move exactly one inch!) Instead, all CNC controls allow axis motion to be commanded in a much simpler and more logical way by utilizing some form of coordinate system. The two most popular coordinate systems used with CNC machines are the rectangular coordinate system and the polar coordinate system. By far, the most popular of these two is the rectangular coordinate system, and we'll use it for all discussions made during this presentation.

One very common application for the rectangular coordinate system is graphing. Almost everyone has had to make or interpret a graph. Since the need to utilize graphs is so commonplace, and since it closely resembles what is required to cause axis motion on a CNC machine, let's review the basics of graphing.

As with any two dimensional graph, this graph has two base lines. Each base line is used to represent something. What the base line represents is broken into increments. Also, each base line has limits. In our productivity example, the horizontal base line is being used to represent time. For this base line, the time increment is in months. Remember this base line has limits — it starts at January and end with December. The vertical base line is representing productivity. Productivity is broken into ten percent increments and starts at zero percent productivity and ends with one hundred percent productivity.

The person making the graph would look up the company's productivity for January of last year and at the productivity position on the graph for January, a point is plotted. This would then be repeated for February, March, and each month of the year. Once all points are plotted, a line or curve can be drawn through each of the points to make it more clear as to how the company did last year.

Let's take what we now know about graphs and relate it to CNC axis motion. Instead of plotting theoretical points to represent conceptual ideas, the CNC programmer is going to be plotting physical end points for axis motions. Each linear axis of the machine tool can be thought of as like a base line of the graph. Like graph base lines, axes are broken into increments. But instead of being broken into increments of conceptual ideas like time and productivity, each linear axis of a CNC machine's rectangular coordinate system is broken into increments of measurement. In the inch mode, the smallest increment is usually 0.0001 inch. In the metric mode, the smallest increment is 0.001 millimeter. (By the way, for rotary axes the increment is 0.001 degrees.)

Just like the graph, each axis within the CNC machine's coordinate system must start somewhere. With the graph, the horizontal baseline started at January and the vertical base line started at zero percent productivity. This place where the vertical and horizontal base lines come together is called the origin point of the graph. For CNC purposes, this origin point is commonly called the program zero point (also called work zero, part zero, and program origin).

For this example, the two axes we happen to be showing are labeled as X and Y but keep in mine that program zero can be applied to any axis. Though the names of each axes will change from one CNC machine type to another (other common names include Z, A, B, C, U, V, and W), this example should work nicely to show you how axis motion can be commanded.

The program zero point establishes the point of reference for motion commands in a CNC program. This allows the programmer to specify movements from a common location. If program zero is chosen wisely, usually coordinates needed for the program can be taken directly from the print.

With this technique, if the programmer wishes the tool to be sent to a position one inch to the right of the program zero point, X1.0 is commanded. If the programmer wishes the tool to move to a position one inch above the program zero point, Y1.0 is commanded. The control will automatically determine how many times to rotate each axis drive motor and ball screw to make the axis reach the commanded destination point. This lets the programmer command axis motion in a very logical manner.

With the examples given so far, all points happened to be up and to the right of the program zero point. This area up and to the right of the program zero point is called a quadrant (in this case, quadrant number one). It is not uncommon on CNC machines that end points needed within the program fall in other quadrants. When this happens, at least one of the coordinates must be specified as minus.

## 4 Understanding Absolute Versus Incremental Motion

All discussions to this point assume that the absolute mode of programming is used. The most common CNC word used to designate the absolute mode is G90. In the absolute mode, the end points for all motions will be specified from the program zero point. For beginners, this is usually the best and easiest method of specifying end points for motion commands. However, there is another way of specifying end points for axis motion.

In the incremental mode (commonly specified by G91), end points for motions are specified from the tool's current position, not from program zero. With this method of commanding motion, the programmer must always be asking "How far should I move the tool?" While there are times when the incremental mode can be very helpful, generally speaking, this is the more cumbersome and difficult method of specifying motion and beginners should concentrate on using the absolute mode.

Be careful when making motion commands. Beginners have the tendency to think incrementally. If working in the absolute mode (as beginners should), the programmer should always be asking the question "To what position should the tool be moved?" This position is relative to program zero, not from the tools current position.

Aside from making it very easy to determine the current position for any command, another benefit of working in the absolute mode has to do with mistakes made during motion commands. In the absolute mode, if a motion mistake is made in one command of the program, only one movement will be incorrect. On the other hand, if a mistake is made during incremental movements, all motions from the point of the mistake will also be incorrect.

## 5 Assigning Program Zero

Keep in mind that the CNC control must be told the location of the program zero point by one means or another. How this is done varies dramatically from one CNC machine and control to another. One (older) method is to assign program zero in the program. With this method, the programmer tells the control how far it is from the program zero point to the starting position of the machine. This is commonly done with a G92 (or G50) command at least at the beginning of the program and possibly at the beginning of each tool.

Another, newer and better way to assign program zero is through some form of offset. Commonly machining center control manufacturers call offsets used to assign program zero fixture offsets. Turning center manufacturers commonly call offsets used to assign program zero for each tool geometry offsets. More on how program zero can be assigned will be presented during key concept number four.

## 6  Other Points about Axis Motion

To this point, our primary concern has been to show you how to determine the end point of each motion command. As you have seen, doing this requires an understanding of the rectangular coordinate system. However, there are other concerns about how a motion will take place. Fore example, the type of motion (rapid, straight line, circular, etc.), and motion rate (feedrate), will also be of concern to the programmer. We'll discuss these other considerations during key concept number three.

## 7  Telling the Machine what to do — the CNC Program

Almost all current CNC controls use a word address format for programming. (The only exceptions to this are certain conversational controls.) By word address format, we mean that the CNC program is made up of sentence — like commands. Each command is made up of CNC words. Each CNC word has a letter address and a numerical value. The letter address (X, Y, Z, etc.) tells the control the kind of word and the numerical value tells the control the value of the word. Used like words and sentences in English, words in a CNC command tell the CNC machine what it is we wish to do at the present time.

One very good analogy to what happens in a CNC program is found in any set of step by step instructions. Say for example, you have some visitors coming in from out of town to visit your company. You need to write down instructions to get from the local airport to your company. To do so, you must first be able to visualize the path from the airport to your company. You will then, in sequential order, write down one instruction at a time. The person following your instructions will perform the first step and then go on to the next until he or she reaches your facility.

In similar manner, a manual CNC programmer must be able to visualize the machining operations that are to be performed during the execution of the program. Then, in step by step order, the programmer will give a set of commands that makes the machine behave accordingly.

Though slightly off the subject at hand, we wish to make a strong point about visualization. Just as the person developing travel directions must be able to visualize the path taken, so must the CNC programmer be able to visualize the movements the CNC machine will be making before a program can be successfully developed. Without this visualization ability, the programmer will not be able to develop the movements in the program correctly. This is one reason why machinists make the best CNC users. An experienced machinist should be able to easily visualize any machining operation taking place.

Just as each concise travel instruction will be made up of one sentence, so will each instruction given within a CNC program be made up of one command. Just as the travel instruction sentence is made up of words (in English), so is the CNC command made up of CNC words (in CNC language).

The person following your set of travel instructions will execute them explicitly. If you make a mistake with your set of instructions, the person will get lost on the way to your company. In similar fashion, the CNC machine will execute a CNC program explicitly. If there is a mistake in the program, the CNC machine will not behave correctly.

**Program:**

O0001 (Program number)

N005 G54 G90 S400 M03 (Select coordinate system, absolute mode, and turn spindle on CW at 400 RPM)

N010 G00 X1. Y1. (Rapid to XY location of first hole)

N015 G43 H01 Z. 1 M08 (Instate tool length compensation, rapid in Z to clearance position above surface to drill, turn on coolant)

N020 G01 Z-1. 25 F3. 5 (Feed into first hole at 3. 5 inches per minute)

N025 G00 Z. 1 (Rapid back out of hole) N030 X2. (Rapid to second hole)

N035 G01 Z-1. 25 (Feed into second hole)

N040 G00 Z.1 M09 (Rapid out of second hole, turn off coolant)
N045 G91 G28 Z0 (Return to reference position in Z)
N050 M30 (End of program command)

While the words and commands in this program probably do not make much sense to you (yet), remember that we are stressing the sequential order by which the CNC program will be executed. The control will first read, interpret and execute the very first command in the program. Only then will it go on to the next command. Read, interpret, execute. Then on to the next command. The control will continue to execute the program in sequential order for the balance of the program. Again, notice the similarity to giving any set of step by step instructions.

As stated programs are made up of commands and commands are made up of word. Each word has a letter address and a numerical value. The letter address tells the control the word type. CNC control manufacturers do vary with regard to how they determine word names (letter addresses) and their meanings. The beginning CNC programmer must reference the control manufacturer's programming manual to determine the word names and meanings. Here is a brief list of some of the word types and their common letter address specifications.

O — Program number (Used for program identification)
N — Sequence number (Used for line identification)
G — Preparatory function
X — X axis designation
Y — Y axis designation
Z — Z axis designation
R — Radius designation
F — Feedrate designation
S — Spindle speed designation
H — Tool length offset designation
D — Tool radius offset designation
T — Tool Designation
M — Miscellaneous function (See below)

As you can see, many of the letter addresses are chosen in a rather logical manner (T for tool, S for spindle, F for feedrate, etc.). A few require memorizing.

There are two letter addresses (G and M) which allow special functions to be designated. The preparatory function (G) specifies is commonly used to set modes. We already introduced absolute mode, specified by G90 and incremental mode, specified by G91. These are but two of the preparatory functions used. You must reference your control manufacturer's manual to find the list of preparatory functions for your particular machine.

Like preparatory functions, miscellaneous functions (M words) allow a variety of special functions. Miscellaneous functions are typically used as programmable switches (like spindle on/off, coolant on/off, and so on). They are also used to allow programming of many other programmable functions of the CNC machine tool.

To a beginner, all of this may seem like CNC programming requires a great deal of memorization. But rest assured that there are only about 30~40 different words used with CNC programming. If you can think of learning CNC manual programming as like learning a foreign language that has only 40 words, it shouldn't seem too difficult.

Decimal point programming

Certain letter addresses (CNC words) allow the specification of real numbers (numbers that require portions of a whole number). Examples include X axis designator (X), Y axis designator (Y), and radius designator (R). Almost all current model CNC controls allow a decimal point to be used within the specification of each letter address requiring real numbers. For example, X3.0625 can be used to specify a position along the X axis.

On the other hand, some letter addresses are used to specify integer numbers. Examples include the spindle speed designator (S), the tool station designator (T), sequence numbers (N), preparatory functions (G), and miscellaneous functions (M). For these word types, most controls do NOT allow a decimal point to be used. The beginning programmer must reference the CNC control manufacturer's programming manual to find out which words allow the use of a decimal point.

Other programmable functions

All but the very simplest CNC machines have programmable functions other than just axis motion. With today's full blown CNC equipment, almost everything about the machine is programmable. CNC machining centers, for example, allow the spindle speed and direction, coolant, tool changing, and many other functions of the machine to be programmed. In similar fashion, CNC turning centers allow spindle speed and direction, coolant, turret index, and tailstock to be programmed. And all forms of CNC equipment will have their own set of programmable functions. Additionally, certain accessories like probing systems, tool length measuring systems, pallet changers, and adaptive control systems may also be available that require programming considerations.

The list of programmable functions will vary dramatically from one machine to the next, and the user must learn these programmable functions for each CNC machine to be used. In key concept number two, we will take a closer look at what is typically programmable on different forms of CNC machine tools.

## Lesson 28  Planar Linkages

## 1 Introduction

### 1.1 What are Linkage Mechanisms?

Have you ever wondered what kind of mechanism causes the wind shield wiper on the front window of car to oscillate (Fig. 28. 1 a) The mechanism, shown in Fig. 5. 1b, transforms the rotary motion of the motor into an oscillating motion of the windshield wiper.

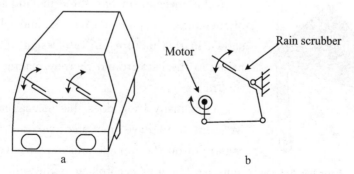

Fig. 28.1  Windshield wiper

Let's make a simple mechanism with similar behavior. Take some cardboard and make four strips as shown inFig. 28. 2a.

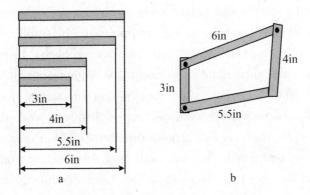

Fig. 28.2　four bar linkage mechanism

Take 4 pins and assemble them as shown in Fig. 28.2b.

Now, hold the 6in. strip so it can't move and turn the 3in. strip. You will see that the 4in. strip oscillates.

The four bar linkage is the simplest and often times, the most useful mechanism. As we mentioned before, a mechanism composed of rigid bodies and lower pairs is called a linkage (Hunt 78). In planar mechanisms, there are only two kinds of lower pairs — revolute pairs and prismatic pairs.

The simplest closed-loop linkage is the four bar linkage which has four members, three moving links, one fixed link and four pin joints. A linkage that has at least one fixed link is a mechanism. The following example of a four bar linkage was created in SimDesign.

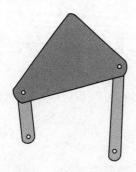

Fig. 28.3　Four bar linkage in SimDesign

This mechanism has three moving links. Two of the links are pinned to the frame which is not shown in this picture. In SimDesign, links can be nailed to the background thereby making them into the frame.

How many DOF does this mechanism have? If we want it to have just one, we can impose one constraint on the linkage and it will have a definite motion. The four bar linkage is the simplest and the most useful mechanism.

Reminder: A mechanism is composed of rigid bodies and lower pairs called linkages (Hunt 78). In planar mechanisms, there are only two kinds of lower pairs — turning pairs and prismatic pairs.

## 1.2 Functions of Linkages

The function of a link mechanism is to produce rotating, oscillating, or reciprocating motion from the rotation of a crank, and vice versa (Ham et al. 58). Stated more specifically linkages may be used to convert.

Continuous rotation into continuous rotation, with a constant or variable angular velocity ratio;

Continuous rotation into oscillation or reciprocation (or the reverse), with a constant or variable velocity ratio;

Oscillation into oscillation, or reciprocation into reciprocation, with a constant or variable velocity ratio.

Linkages have many different functions, which can be classified according to the primary goal of the mechanism.

Function generation: the relative motion between the links connected to the frame;

Path generation: the path of a tracer point;

Motion generation: the motion of the coupler link.

## 2 Four Link Mechanisms

One of the simplest examples of a constrained linkage is the four-link mechanism. A variety of useful mechanisms can be formed from a four-link mechanism through slight variations, such as changing the character of the pairs, proportions of links, etc. Furthermore, many complex link mechanisms are combinations of two or more such mechanisms. The majority of four-link mechanisms fall into one of the following two classes:

- ◆ the four-bar linkage mechanism;
- ◆ the slider-crank mechanism.

## 2.1 Examples

**Parallelogram Mechanism:** In a parallelogram four-bar linkage, the orientation of the coupler does not change during the motion. The figure illustrates a loader. Obviously the behavior of maintaining parallelism is important in a loader. The bucket should not rotate as it is raised and lowered.

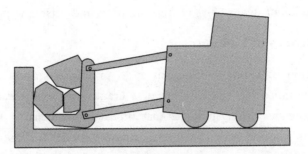

Fig. 28.4　Front loader mechanism

**Slider-Crank Mechanism:** The four-bar mechanism has some special configurations created by making one or more links infinite in length. The slider-crank (or crank and slider) mechanism shown below is a four-bar linkage with the slider replacing an infinitely long outputlink.

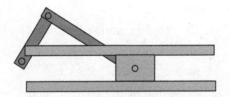

Fig. 28.5　Crank and Slider Mechanism

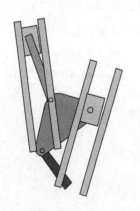

Fig. 28.6　Crank and Piston

This configuration translates a rotational motion into a translational one. Most mechanisms are driven by motors, and slider-cranks are often used to transform rotary motion into linear motion.

**Crank and Piston:** You can also use the slider as the input link and the crank as the output link. In this case, the mechanism transfers translational motion into rotary motion. The pistons and crank in an internal combustion engine are an example of this type of mechanism. The corresponding SimDesign file is simdesign/combustion.sim.

You might wonder why there is another slider and a link on the left. This mechanism has two dead points. The slider and link on the left help the mechanism to overcome these dead points.

**Block Feeder:** One interesting application of slider-crank is the blockfeeder (Fig. 28. 7).

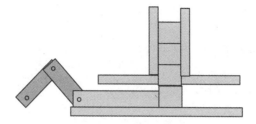

Fig. 28.7  Block Feeder

## 2.2  Definitions

In the range of planar mechanisms, the simplest group of lower pair mechanisms are four bar linkages. A four bar linkage comprises four bar-shaped links and four turning pairs as shown in Fig. 28. 8.

The link opposite the frame is called the coupler link, and the links which are hinged to the frame are called side links. A link which is free to rotate through 360 degree with respect to a second link will be said to revolve relative to the second link (not necessarily a frame). If it is possible for all four bars to become simultaneously aligned, such a state is called a change point.

Fig. 28.8  Four bar linkage

Some important concepts in link mechanisms are:

**Crank:** A side link which revolves relative to the frame is called a crank;

**Rocker:** Any link which does not revolve is called a rocker;

**Crank-rocker mechanism:** In a four bar linkage, if the shorter side link revolves and the other one rocks (i. e., oscillates), it is called a crank-rocker mechanism;

**Double-crank mechanism:** In a four bar linkage, if both of the side links revolve, it is called a double-crank mechanism.

Double-rocker mechanism: In a four bar linkage, if both of the side links rock, it is called a double-rocker mechanism.

### 2.3 Classification

Before classifying four-bar linkages, we need to introduce some basic nomenclature.

In a four-bar linkage, we refer to the line segment between hinges on a given link as a bar where:

$s$ = length of shortest bar

$l$ = length of longest bar

$p$, $q$ = lengths of intermediate bar

Grashof's theorem states that a four-bar mechanism has at least one revolving link if

$$s + l <= p + q \tag{28.1}$$

and all three mobile links will rock if

$$s + l > p + q \tag{28.2}$$

The inequality 28.1 is Grashof's criterion.

All four-bar mechanisms fall into one of the four categories listed in Table 28.1.

Table 28.1  Classification of Four-Bar Mechanisms

| Case | $1+s$ vers. $p+q$ | Shortest Bar | Type |
| --- | --- | --- | --- |
| 1 | < | Frame | Double-crank |
| 2 | < | Side | Rocker-crank |
| 3 | < | Coupler | Doubl rocker |
| 4 | = | Any | Change point |
| 5 | > | Any | Double-rocker |

From Table 28.1 we can see that for a mechanism to have a crank, the sum of the length of its shortest and longest links must be less than or equal to the sum of the length of the other two links. However, this condition is necessary but not sufficient. Mechanisms satisfying this condition fall into the following three categories:

When the shortest link is a side link, the mechanism is a crank-rocker mechanism. The shortest link is the crank in the mechanism.

When the shortest link is the frame of the mechanism, the mechanism is a double-crank mechanism.

When the shortest link is the coupler link, the mechanism is a double-rocker mechanism.

### 2.4 Transmission Angle

In Fig. 28.9, if AB is the input link, the force applied to the output link, CD, is transmitted through the coupler link BC. (That is, pushing on the link CD imposes a force on the link AB, which is transmitted through the link BC.) For sufficiently slow motions (negligible inertia forces), the force in the coupler link is pure tension or compression (negligible bending action) and is directed along BC. For a given force in the coupler link, the torque transmitted to the output bar (about point D) is maximum when the angle β between coupler bar BC and output bar CD is $\pi/2$. Therefore, angle BCD is called transmission angle.

$$\alpha_{max} = |\ 90° - \beta\ |_{min} < 50° \tag{28.3}$$

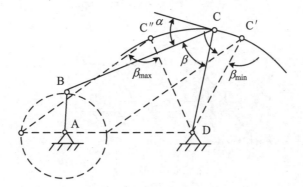

Fig. 28.9 Transmission angle

When the transmission angle deviates significantly from $\pi/2$, the torque on the output bar decreases and may not be sufficient to overcome the friction in the system. For this reason, the deviation angle $\alpha = |\ \pi/2 - \beta\ |$ should not be too great. In practice, there is no definite upper limit for $\alpha$, because the existence of the inertia forces may eliminate the undesirable force relationships that is present under static conditions. Nevertheless, the following criterion can be followed.

### 2.5 Dead Point

When a side link such as AB in Fig. 28.10, becomes aligned with the coupler link BC, it can only be compressed or extended by the coupler. In this configuration, a torque applied to the link on the other side, CD, cannot induce rotation in link AB. This link is therefore said to be at a dead point (sometimes called a toggle point).

In Fig. 28.11, if AB is a crank, it can become aligned with BC in full extension along the line AB1C1 or in flexion with AB2 folded over B2C2. We denote the angle ADC by $\phi$ and the angle DAB by $\theta$. We use the subscript 1 to denote the extended state and 2 to denote the flexed state of links AB and BC. In the extended state, link CD cannot rotate clockwise without stretching or compressing the theoretically rigid line AC1. Therefore, link CD cannot move into the forbidden zone below C1D, and $\phi$ must be at one of its two extreme positions; in other words, link CD is at an extremum. A second extremum of link CD occurs with $\phi = \phi 1$.

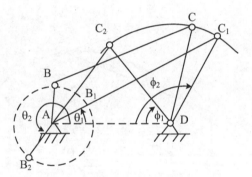

Fig. 28.10  Dead point

Note that the extreme positions of a side link occur simultaneously with the dead points of the opposite link.

In some cases, the dead point can be useful for tasks such as work fixturing (Fig. 28.11).

In other cases, dead point should be and can be overcome with the moment of inertia of links or with the asymmetrical deployment of the mechanism (Fig. 28.12).

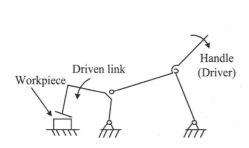
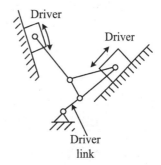

Fig. 28.11　Work fixturing

Fig. 28.12　Overcoming the dead point by asymmetrical deployment (V engine)

## 2.6　Slider-Crank Mechanism

The slider-crank mechanism, which has a well-known application in engines, is a special case of the crank-rocker mechanism. Notice that if rocker 3 in Fig. 28.13a is very long, it can be replaced by a block sliding in a curved slot or guide as shown. If the length of the rocker is infinite, the guide and block are no longer curved. Rather, they are apparently straight, as shown in Fig. 28.13b, and the linkage takes the form of the ordinary slider-crank mechanism.

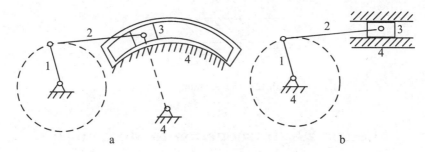

Fig. 28.13　Slider-Crank mechanism

## 2.7　Inversion of the Slider-Crank Mechanism

Inversion is a term used in kinematics for a reversal or interchange of form or function as applied to kinematic chains and mechanisms. For example, taking a different link as the fixed link, the slider-crank mechanism shown in Fig. 28.14a can be inverted into the mechanisms shown in Fig. 28.14b, c, and d. Different examples can be found in the application of these mechanisms. For example, the mechanism of the pump device in Fig. 28.15 is the same as that in Fig. 28.14b.

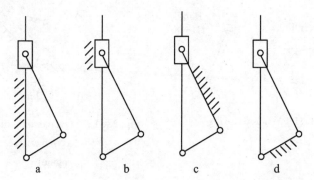

Fig.28.14  Inversions of the crank-slide mechanism

Keep in mind that the inversion of a mechanism does not change the motions of its links relative to each other but does change their absolute motions.

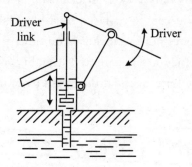

Fig.28.15  A pump device

# Lesson 29   Introduction to Mechanical Engineering Literature

## 1  Science Citation Index

Science Citation Index provides researchers, administrators, faculty, and students with quick, powerful access to the bibliographic and citation information they need to find relevant, comprehensive research data. Overcome information overload and focus on essential data from over 3,700 of the world's leading scientific and technical journals across 100 disciplines.

Also available through Web of Science and the online version, SciSearch as Science Citation Index Expanded, which covers more than 6,650 journals across 150 disciplines.

With Science Citation Index, you can:
- Find high-impact articles from peer-reviewed, influential journals.
- Uncoverrelevant results in related fields.
- Keep up with the latest developments in your field, helping you pursue successful research and grant acquisition.
- Identify potential collaborators with significant citation records.

### 1.1 Why Choose Science Citation Index?

**Comprehensive and Relevant Coverage:** Every journal included in *Science Citation Index* has met the high standards of an objective evaluation process that eliminates clutter and excess and delivers data that is accurate, meaningful and timely.

**Cited Reference Searching:** Track prior research and monitor current developments, see who is citing your work, measure the influence of colleagues' work, and follow the path of today's hottest ideas. Navigate forward, backward and through the literature, searching all disciplines and time spans to discover information with impact.

**KeyWords Plus:** Enhance the power of cited reference searching by searching across disciplines for all the articles that have cited references in common.

**Cover-to-cover indexing:** With *Science Citation Index*, you can access every significant item from a journal, including original research articles, reviews, editorials, chronologies, abstracts, and more.

**A full range of disciplines:** Find information in areas such as agricultural, biological, and environmental sciences, engineering, technology, applied science, medical and life sciences, and physical and chemical sciences.

### 1.2 Related Interest

**Web of Science:** Provides quick, powerful access to the world's leading citation databases, with authoritative, multidisciplinary coverage from nearly

9,300 of the highest impact journals worldwide, including Open Access journals. You'll find current and retrospective coverage in the sciences, social sciences, arts, and humanities, with coverage available to 1900. You can search five databases simultaneously within *Web of Science*, as well as any other databases you subscribe to through *ISI Web of Knowledge*.

**Science Citation Index Expanded**: Over 6,650 major journals across 150 disciplines, to 1900.

**Social Sciences Citation Index**: Over 1,950 journals across 50 social science disciplines, as well as 3,500 of the world's leading scientific and technical journals, to 1956.

**Arts & Humanities Citation Index**: Over 1,160 arts and humanities journals, as well as selected items from over 6,000 scientific and social sciences journals.

**Index Chemicus**: Over 2.6 million compounds, to 1993.

**Current Chemical Reactions**: Over one million reactions, to 1986, plus INPI archives from 1840 to 1985.

**ISI Web of Knowledge**: Quickly find, analyze, and share information in the sciences, social sciences, arts, and humanities with this premier research platform. Whether you're writing a paper, looking for potential collaborators, analyzing research performance or evaluating your library's collection, *ISI Web of Knowledge* is built to accommodate your style of discovery and analysis.

## 2　Engineering Village

Engineering Village is the premier web-based discovery platform meeting the information needs of the engineering community. By coupling powerful search tools, an intuitive user interface and essential content sources, Engineering Village has become the globally accepted source of choice for engineers, engineering students, researchers and information professionals.

Engineering Village provides access to today's most important engineering content through one single interface:

◆ Compendex;
◆ Engineering Index Backfile;
◆ Inspec;
◆ Inspec Archive;
◆ NTIS;

- Referex;
- Patents from USPTO and espcenet;
- Ei Patents
- EncompassLIT
- EncompassPAT
- GEOBASE
- Chimica
- CBNB
- PaperChem;
- GeoRef.

Engineering Village provides:
- Combined database searching of all databases including deduplication;
- Personalized e-mail alerts;
- The ability to save searches and create personalized folders;
- Easy, Quick & Expert Search options, all of which allow you to save and combine searches;
- The ability to choose preferred output formats (citation, abstracts or detailed) for Selected Record scts, which can then be viewed, printed, saved, downloaded or e-mailed;
- Open URL linking to Endeavor Link Finder Plus, Ex Libris SFX, Serials Solutions Article Linker, and Innovative Interfaces Web Bridge for local holdings checking and full text option presentation;
- Links to full-text using CrossRef;
- Links to document delivery services;
- Context sensitive help;
- Reference Services: Ask a Librarian & Ask an Engineer;
- RSS Feeds and Faceted Searching;
- Tags & Groups.

### 2.1 Compendex

Compendex is one of the most comprehensive engineering literature databases available to engineers. With 12 million records across 190 engineering disciplines, Compendex delivers the comprehensive, precise information and insights that researchers need. Available on Engineering Village, users get results that are consistently accurate. Relevant. Up-to-date. And easy to find. Users know that when they search with Compendex, valuable information is not overlooked. Thousands of new records are added weekly and are indexed according to the Engineering Index Thesaurus. And with email and RSS alerts on new records in areas of interest, users stay up-to-date on new developments.

Compendex covers subjects in every engineering discipline including:

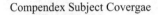

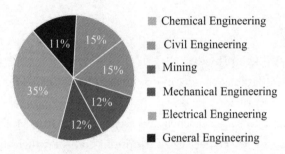

Fig. 29.1

- ◆ Chemical Engineering;
- ◆ Civil Engineering;
- ◆ Electrical Engineering;
- ◆ Mechanical Engineering;
- ◆ Mining Engineering.

Since 1970, Compendex has been the engineering database of choice for researchers, students, faculty and engineering professionals around the world. In fact, 98% of the top 50 US engineering schools currently subscribe to Compendex.

## 2.2 Engineering Index Backfile

The Engineering Index Backfile provides a comprehensive, historical view of engineering developments and innovations described in literature from 1884～1969. Over 1.7 million records have been digitized from the original Engineering Index print indexes. Information is fully searchable, for easy user access to original records chronicling virtually every major engineering breakthrough from the late 19th to 20th centuries. Available on Engineering Village, the combined searching capability of Compendex and the Ei Backfile offers the most comprehensive resource for engineering available anywhere.

## 3　ISI Web of Knowledge

Welcome to the *ISI Web of Knowledge* tutorial. This tutorial will give you an overview of the product and how to use it in your research.

Use the Next Page and Previous Page navigation arrows in the banner to move through the tutorial. You can also click a section title (for example, My Journal List) to go directly to that topic.

**Introduction** — *ISI Web of Knowledge* is an integrated Web-based platform that provides high-quality bibliographic content and the tools to access, analyze, and manage research information. The tools include:

- ◆　All Databases Searching;
- ◆　My endNote web;
- ◆　My citation alerts;
- ◆　My journal list;
- ◆　My saved searches;
- ◆　View / Manage marked lists;
- ◆　Print, email, export, and save bibliographic information;
- ◆　Links to full text.

**Note:** Use the all databases search function to search for records across multiple *ISI Web of Knowledge* databases in your subscription service. For example, if you have a subscription to *Web of Science*, *Current Contents Connect*, and *BIOSIS Previews*, then the system searches across all three products when you perform an all databases search.

**User Registration and Sign In** — To take full advantage of all the features in *ISI Web of Knowledge* such as My Citation Alerts and My Journal List, register and always sign in when you start a new search session.

**All Databases Search** — This feature allows you to search across all product databases in your institution's subscription. For example, if you have a subscription to *Web of Science*, *Current Contents Connect*, and *BIOSIS Previews*, then the system searches across all three databases when you perform an all databases search.

Search for records using topic terms, author names, publication names, and publication years.

In one or more search fields, enter words or phrases connected by Boolean search operators (and, or, not, same). Use wildcard operators to search for plurals and variant spellings.

**Note** — To search a single database such as *Web of Science* or *Current Contents Connect*, click the Select a Database tab, and then the needed database to search.

**Results** — This page shows the records retrieved by your search. It provides many features to aid your research, including:

◆ Search within Results;
◆ Refine Results;
◆ Sort by;
◆ Output Records;
◆ Analyze Results.

Be aware that only records in your product subscription will appear in the results set. For example, if you have a subscription to *Web of Science* and *Current Contents Connect*, then you will see records from these two products.

**My Preferences (Edit My Information)** — Use this feature to update your contact information (e-mail address, password, and name) and to set up automatic sign in.

To access this feature, click the Preferences link that appears on the Search page in the right-hand column under the My Web of Knowledge section.

To use this feature, you must be a registered user and you must sign in.

**My Preferences (Select a Starting Application)** — Use this feature to select a starting application in your product subscription. The selected product immediately appears when you begin a new search session.

Be aware that you must select the Automatic Sign In feature from the Edit My Information page for this feature to work.

To use this feature, you must be a registered user and you must sign in.

**My Saved Searches** — After you perform a search, you can save your search queries as a search history file. Later, you can open the file to continue your research.

To save a search history to our server, you must be a registered user and you must sign in.

**My Saved Searches** — The Open / Manage Saved Searches page allows you to manage and run your saved searches. You can also turn on alerts, update your e-mail address, change the history name, and change the history description.

**Did you know** — when alerting is turned on, the system searches the latest update to the database and sends all relevant results to you by e-mail. Your organization must subscribe to alerting to save a search history as an alert.

Be aware that alerting is not available for all databases saved searches.

To use this feature, you must be a registered user and you must sign in.

**My Citation Alerts** — A citation alert notifies you by e-mail whenever an article has been cited by a new article. The alert is active for one year. You may renew the alert at any time.

This feature requires a subscription to *Web of Science*.

To use this feature, you must be a registered user and you must sign in.

**My Cited Articles List-Modify Settings** — Go to this Web page to remove an article from your citation alerts list, change your e-mail address, or select a different delivery format.

To use this feature, you must be a registered user and you must sign in.

**My Journal List** — This features allows you to manage a list of frequently viewed journals. You can also set up alerts for journals. With alerting turned on, the system sends you the most recent table of contents by e-mail.

This feature requires a subscription to Current Contents Connect.

To use this feature, you must be a registered user and you must sign in.

**My Journal List-add Journals** — Use this feature to add journals to your journal list and to set up table of contents e-mail alerts.

There are three ways to search for journals:

(1) Search Full Journal Titles;

(2) Select Journals Alphabetically;

(3) Browse Journal Titles by Subject.

**My Journal List** — Modify Settings — Use this feature to:

(1) Remove journals from your list;

(2) Change your e-mail address;

(3) Change your e-mail format;

(4) List journals on your home page;

(5) Set up table of contents e-mail alerts.

**4  Journal of ASME Transactions**

(1) *Journal of Applied Mechanics*
(2) *Journal of Biomechanical Engineering*
(3) *Journal of Computational & Nonlinear Dynamics*
(4) *Journal of Electronic Packaging*
(5) *Journal of Energy Resources Technology*
(6) *Journal of Fluids Engineering*
(7) *Journal of Fuel Cell Science and Technology*
(8) *Journal of Heat Transfer*
(9) *Journal of Pressure Vessel Technology*
(10) *Journal of Solar Energy Engineering*
(11) *Journal of Computing and Information Science in Engineering*
(12) *Journal of Dynamic Systems, Measurement and Control*
(13) *Applied Mechanics Reviews*
(14) *Journal of Engineering for Gas Turbines and Power*
(15) *Journal of Engineering Materials and Technology*
(16) *Journal of Mechanical Design*
(17) *Journal of Manufacturing Science and Engineering*
(18) *Journal of Mechanisms and Robotics*(New in 2009)
(19) *Journal of Offshore Mechanics and Arctic Engineering*
(20) *Journal of Tribology*
(21) *Journal of Turbomachinery*
(22) *Journal of Vibration and Acoustics*
(23) *Journal of Medical Devices*
(24) *Applications in Thermal Science and Engineering*(New in 2009)

# Lesson 30  English Paper Writing Guide

This paper presents some of the most common Chinese-English habits observed from over 200 English technical papers by Chinese writers. The habits are explained and in most cases, example text from an actual paper is given along with preferred text. An attempt is made to explain how to correct and prevent such mistakes. In some cases, a possible explanation of why the habit occurs is also given. This paper can serve as an individual guide to editing technical papers especially when a native English-speaking editor is unavailable.

# 1 Introduction

Most Chinese universities require their doctoral and master candidates in technical and scientific fields to publish at least one English paper in an international journal as a degree requirement. However, many factors make this task difficult to accomplish. First, previous English studies may not have focused enough on writing, let alone technical writing. Current studies may not include English, causing the writers English fluency level to decline. Second, most writers have never lived in an English-speaking country. Third, due to the special aspects of technical writing, even native English-speaking engineering students have a technical writing course as part of their study.

Too often, students' papers are returned unaccepted because of poor English writing. If available, students may have their papers edited by a native English speaker. However, this can get expensive for a department that has many students with each paper typically needing to be edited twice. Hiring someone to edit papers is difficult, costly and only puts a patch over the problem. A native English speaker can do a good job at getting rid of most of the grammatical mistakes. However, if this person does not have a technical background, particularly in the area of the papers he is editing, he is unable to get rid of all of the mistakes and make sure that the meaning is clear. He cannot recognize the incorrect translation of technical terms for which there is a standard word. Such mistakes will not be picked up by the processor's spelling and grammar checker. In addition, if they are not familiar with the topic or field, they may not grasp the meaning of the entire article and fail to make critical edits.

Hiring a person with a technical background similar to that of the papers being edited is a better option. Nevertheless, while a person with a technical background may be able to edit the paper sufficiently, he may not be able to explain to the writer how to prevent such mistakes in the future. Besides, it is difficult for most Chinese universities to hire such staff simply for editing. Universities may consider inviting a visiting scholar who will edit papers in addition to doing research or teaching as part of an exchange.

Although editing may be the fastest way to publish papers, it does little in the way of teaching the writers how to prevent common mistakes and colloquial habits that prevent a clear understanding of the writer's ideas. Writers who have already obtained an impressing command of the English language can only truly benefit if they are made aware of their common mistakes and colloquial habits and how to prevent them.

**Purpose**

The purpose of this report is to introduce the most common habits in Chinese-English writing as noted from the over 200 papers I have edited. The habits include grammar mistakes, colloquialisms, and formatting problems and in most cases prevent a clear understanding of the writer's ideas. A few of the habits, such as writing extremely long sentences, can be corrected with careful use of the MS Word grammar and style checker. However, most habits, such as missing articles, go unnoticed by automatic grammar checking devices. Still, Chinese-English colloquial habits are not recognized by such software tools.

**Structure**

The common habits are presented in two sections. The first section lists the habits that, in my opinion, need the most attention. These habits interrupt the flow of the paper making it difficult to understand and occur most frequently. In this section, the habits are explained, example sentences from actual papers are given to show the habits, and the sentences are rewritten to show the correct way to write them. In the case of missing articles, a flow chart is also given to aid in choosing the correct articles.

In the second section, an additional list of habits is given. In some cases, example sentences are given. In other cases, advice is given. The second section is very useful in becoming familiar with small nuances.

Not all of the common habits I observed are presented mainly because they can only be dealt with on an individual basis. For example, writers had difficulty titling their papers and naming new technical ideas to express their contents and functions concisely. This problem frequently occurred but it can only be addressed individually. Once writers are aware of their habits, they would be able to write better technical English articles.

**Section 1**

**"a, an, the"**

The most common habit is the omission of articles a, an, and the. This occurs because Mandarin has no direct equivalent of articles and the rules for using them are somewhat complicated for a non-native speakers.

Articles signal that a noun will follow and that any modifiers between the article and the noun refer to that noun (a big blue bicycle / the first award). A and an are indefinite articles; the is a definite article. Every time a singular noncount noun, a common noun that names one countable item, is used the noun requires some kind of determiner.

**Mistake** *The*, *a*, and *an* are 1) omitted where they are required, 2) used where they are not needed or contribute to wordiness, 3) used wrongly in place of the correct article.

**Examples of incorrect usages:**

**Incorrect** Fig. 2 shows the distribution of relative velocity on surface of main and splitter blades[15]. (see Appendix of Lesson 30)

**Correct** Fig. 2 shows the distribution of relative velocity on the surface of the main and splitter blades[15].

**Incorrect** The software Power SHAPE is chosen to be a 3D modeling tool; it is good at dealing with free surfaces and curves[4].

**Correct** The software Power SHAPE is chosen to be the 3D modeling tool; it is good at dealing with free surfaces and curves[4].

There was only one 3D modeling tool used in this study, therefore "3D modeling tool" is specific and requires the article *the*.

**Incorrect** A theoretical method for calculating the inner flow-field in centrifugal impeller with splitter blades and investigation of the interactions between main and splitter blades is presented in this paper. The vortices are distributed on the main and splitter blades to simulate the effects of flows. Systematical study of number and distribution of vortices is conducted[15].

**Correct** A theoretical method for calculating the inner flow-field in a centrifugal impeller with splitter blades and an investigation of the interactions between main and splitter blades is presented in this paper. The vortices are distributed on the main and splitter blades to simulate the effects of flows. A systematical study of the number and distribution of vortices is conducted[15].

**Incorrect** Theoretically, remanufacturing could fully take advantage of resources contained in EOF product thereby minimizing impact on environment to the greatest extent compared to landfill or recycling of materials; consequently it contributes greatly to resource conservation[16].

**Correct**　　Theoretically, remanufacturing could fully take advantage of resources contained in an EOF product thereby minimizing the impact on the environment to the greatest extent compared to landfill or recycling of materials; consequently it contributes greatly to resource conservation[16].

**Definitions:**

**Articles**　　Also called determiners or noun markers, articles are the words *a*, *an*, and *the*. *A* and *an* are indefinite articles, and *the* is a definite article. Articles signal that a noun will follow and that any modifiers between the article and the noun refer to that noun. (a cold, metal chair/ the lightning-fast computer).

**Determiners**　　A word or word group, traditionally identified as an adjective, that limits a noun by telling how much or how many about it. (expression of quantity, limiting adjective, marker) They tell whether a noun is general (*a* tree) or specific (*the* tree). *The* is a definite article. Before a noun, *the* conveys that the known refers to a specific item (*the* plan). *A* and *an* are indefinite articles. They convey that a noun refers to an item in a nonspecific or general way (*a* plan).

**Common nouns**　　A noun that names a general group, place, person, or thing: dog, house.

**Count noun**　　A noun that names an item or items that can be counted: radio, streets, idea, fingernails.

**Noncount nouns**　　A noun that names a thing that cannot be counted: water, time.

**Specific noun**　　A noun understood to be exactly and specifically referred to; uses the definite article *the*.

**Nonspecific noun**　　A noun that refers to any of a number of identical items; it takes the indefinite articles *a*, *an*.

**Very Long Sentences**

Very long sentences are especially common in Chinese-English writing because the writers often translate directly from Chinese to English. Although, in Chinese writing it is acceptable to put several supporting ideas in on sentence to show their relationship, in English the main idea and each supporting idea is typically written in separate sentences.

One can usually recognize a very long sentence by its length-sixty words or more. However, sentences of smaller lengths can also be too long if they contain multiple statements that confuse the main idea. Long sentences can be avoided by limiting each sentence to one or two topics. Semicolons should be used where the writer really wants to emphasize the relationship between ideas.

**Too long**  According to the characteristic of fan-coil air-conditioning systems, this paper derives the cooling formula of fan-coil units based on the heat transfer theories and puts forward a new method to gauge cooling named Cooling Metering on the Air-side, which can monitor the individual air-conditioning cooling consumption during a period of time by detecting the parameters of inlet air condition-temperature and humidity-of the fan-coil air-conditioning system as well as the parameters of inlet cooling water provided by the chiller.

**Correct**  This paper derives the cooling formula of fan-coil units based on the characteristics of fan-coil air-conditioning systems and heat transfer theories, and puts forward a new method to gauge cooling called Cooling Metering on the Air-side. The new method can monitor individual air-conditioning cooling consumption during a period of time by detecting the condition of inlet air-temperature and humidity-of the fan-coil air-conditioning system as well as the parameters of the inlet cooling water provided by the chiller.

**Too long**  The gear transmission is grade seven, the gear gap is 0.00012 radians, the gear gap has different output values corresponding to any given input value, non-linearity of the gear gap model can be described by using the phase function method, the existing backlash block in the non-linear library of the Matlab/zdimulink toolbox can be used, the initial value of gear gap in the backlash block is set to zero[9].

**Correct**  The gear transmission is grade seven. The gear gap, which is 0.00012 radians, has different output values corresponding to any given input value. The non-linearity of the gear gap model can be described by using the phase function method. The existing backlash block in the non-linear library of the Matlab/zdimulink toolbox can be used; the initial value of gear gap in the backlash block is set to zero.

Another type of super-long sentence that frequently occurs in technical papers is that of a list. The writer wants to give a large amount of data, usually parameter values, and puts this information into one long, paragraph-sized sentence. However, the best way to give such type and quantity of information is to tabulate it (put it in a bulleted list).

**Too long**   where m is the mass of the heavy disk mounted at the mid-span of a massless elastic shaft, e is the eccentricity of the mass center from the geometric center of the disk, $\varphi$ is the angle between the orientation of the eccentricity and the $\xi$ axis, k$\xi$ and k$\eta$ are the stiffness coefficients in two principal directions of shaft respectively, c is the viscous damping coefficient of the shaft and the disk, $c_i$ is the inner damping coefficient of shaft, $\omega$ is the rotating speed, $\xi$ s and $\eta$ s are the components of initial bend in directions of $\xi$, $\eta$ axes respectively: $\xi$ s= rb cos$\theta$, $\eta$s = rb sin$\theta$.

**Correct**   Where m is the mass of the heavy disk mounted at the mid-span of a massless elasticshaft, e is the eccentricity of the mass center from the geometric center of the disk, $\varphi$ is the angle between the orientation of the eccentricity and the $\xi$ axis, k$\xi$ and k$\eta$ are the stiffness coefficients in the two principal directions of the shaft, c is the viscous damping coefficient of the shaft and the disk, $c_i$ is the inner damping coefficient of the shaft, $\omega$ is the rotating speed, $\xi$ s and $\eta$ s are the components of initial bend in directions of $\xi$, $\eta$ axes, respectively: $\xi$ s = rb cos$\theta$, $\eta$s = rb sin$\theta$.

**Too long**   The clear height of the case is 6.15 meters; the thickness of the roof is 0.85 meters; the thickness of the bottom is 0.90 meters, the overall width is 26.6 meters, the overall length of the axial cord is 304.5 meters, the length of the jacking section is about 148.8 meters; the weight of the case is about 24127 tons[3].

| Clear | • Case clearance height | 6.15 meters |
|---|---|---|
| | • Roof thickness | 0.85 meters |
| | • Bottom thickness | 0.90 meters |
| | • Overall width | 26.6 meters |
| | • Overall length of the axial cord | 304.5 meters |
| | • Length of the jacking section | 148.8 meters (approx.) |
| | • Weight of the case | 24127 tons (approx.) |

**Prefacing the Main Idea of a Sentence by Stating the Purpose, Location or Reason First**

Chinese writers often preface the main topic of a sentence by first stating the purpose, location, reason, examples and conditions as introductory elements. However, this has the effect of demoting the importance of the main idea and making the reader think the author is indirect. Bring the main idea to the beginning of the sentence stating any locations, reasons, etc., afterwards.

**Incorrect**  For the application in automobile interiors, this paper studies the nesting optimization problem in leather manufacturing[5].

**Correct**  This paper studies the nesting optimization problem in leather manufacturing for application in automobile interiors.

**Incorrect**  Especially when Numerical Control (NC) techniques[4] are widely used in industry and rapid prototype methods[5-6] bring a huge economical benefits, the advantage of constructing 3D model[7-9] becomes extremely obvious[2].

**Correct**  The advantage of constructing a 3D model[7-9] becomes extremely obvious especially when Numerical Control (NC) techniques[4] are widely used in industry and rapid prototype methods[5-6] bring a huge economical benefits.

**Incorrect**  Inside the test box, the space was filled with asbestos[15].

**Correct**  The space inside the test box was filled with asbestos.

**Incorrect**  In practice, we employed this approach to dispose of a wheelhouse subassembly of one kind of auto-body, and the results show that this method is feasible[16].

**Correct**  We employed this approach to dispose of a wheelhouse subassembly of one kind of auto-body, and the results show that this method is feasible.

**Incorrect** To ensure sheet metal quality as well as assembly quality, CMMs are widely used in automotive industry production[16].

**Correct** CMMs are widely used in automotive industry production to ensure sheet metal quality as well as assembly quality.

## Tendency of Placing Phrases Which Indicate Time at the Beginning of a Sentence

**Incorrect** When U is taken as the control parameter, the BDs for $\Delta = 0.0$, $0.001$, $0.005$ are shown in Fig. 8.

**Correct** Fig. 8 shows the BDs for $\Delta = 0.0$, $0.001$, and $0.005$ when U is taken as the control parameter.

## Place the Most Important Subject at the Beginning of the Sentence for Emphasis

**Incorrect** Based on the triangulation structure built from unorganized points or a CAD model, the extended STL format is described in this section[4].

**Correct** The extended STL format is described in this section based on the triangulation structure built from unorganized points or a CAD model.

**Incorrect** The 3D dentition defect and restoration element models are designed precisely with complicated surfaces[4].

**Correct** The 3D dentition defect and restoration element models with complicated surfaces are designed precisely.

## "which/ that"

The antecedent (noun or pronoun) to which *which* refers is not specific, causing confusion.

Antecedent The noun or pronoun to which a pronoun refers.

"The Shijiazhuang south road underground bridge possesses the largest jacking force, which is built at 1978(10680t)." ["Shijiazhuang south road underground bridge possesses the largest jacking force which is built at 1978(10680t)."]

Absolute truths in paleontology are often elusive, and even the filmmakers were surprised at the fierce arguments that split the scientists when an initial brainstorming session was else.

**"Respectively" and "Respective"**

Respectively refers back to two or more persons or things only in the order they were previously designated or mentioned. If two lists are given, respectively pairs the list entries according to the order in which they are given. In this case the use of respectively is to allow the writer to give a lot of information without confusing the reader or writing several short sentences. Respectively is usually at the end of the sentence. In both cases, mentioning the order must be important to the meaning of the sentence otherwise it is not used.

For example: Bobby, Nicole and Daren wore red, green and blue coats, respectively.

|  List 1 |  | List 2 |
| --- | --- | --- |
| Bobby | wore | a red coat. |
| Nicole | wore | a green coat. |
| Daren | wore | a blue coat. |

Respective to two or more persons or things only in the order they were previously designated or mentioned.

The uses of these two words are usually incorrect or confusing as in the following examples.

(1) Respectively is misplaced in the sentence; it is put before the nouns to which it refers.

**Incorrect** Equations 2 ~ 6 can be respectively linearized as: ... (equations given) [13]

**Correct** Equations 2 ~ 6 can be linearized as: ... (equations given) ... , respectively.

**Incorrect** The weights of the two experts are respectively 0.600 and 0.400[19].
**Correct** The weights of the two experts are 0.600 and 0.400, respectively.

(2) Respectively is inserted to express that there is a certain order in which something was done. However, the order is already implied elsewhere in the sentence or does not need to be expressed because it does not add value to

meaning of the sentence.

**Incorrect**  If both the core technology score and core quality score of a bottleneck process are, respectively, below certain scores, then we refer to strategy 1, otherwise, if either is, respectively, above a certain score, then we refer to strategy 2. Similarly, if the core technology and core quality are, respectively, above a certain score, then we refer to strategy 3, otherwise, if either is, respectively, below a certain score, then we refer to strategy 4[19].

**Correct**  If both the core technology score and core quality score of a bottleneck process are below certain scores, then we refer to strategy 1, otherwise, if either is above a certain score, then we refer to strategy 2. Similarly, if the core technology and core quality are above a certain score, then we refer to strategy 3, otherwise, if either is below a certain score, then we refer to strategy 4.

**Incorrect**  Then, the rows of vortex due to both of the long and short blades are transformed into two singularities on the $\zeta$-plane and integrate the induced velocity along the blades respectively[20].

**Correct**  Then, the rows of vortex due to both of the long and short blades are transformed into two singularities on the $\zeta$-plane and integrate the induced velocity along the blades.

(3) In addition to 2, it is unclear to what "respectively" refers.

**Incorrect**  The dynamic characteristics of a rotor with asymmetric stiffness or with initial warp have been studied before respectively [1-4].

**Correct**  The dynamic characteristics of a rotor with asymmetric stiffness or with initial warp have been studied before [1-4].

**Incorrect**  The inlet and outlet temperature of the air cooler were measured using two thermocouples respectively[17].

**Correct**  The inlet and outlet temperature of the air cooler were measured by using two thermocouples.

"In this paper", "in this study"

Two errors occur when these phrases are used. The first is overuse. In some papers written by Chinese, these phrases can occur as much as twice per page. In papers written by native English writers these phrases are reserved for primarily two uses

(1) In the introduction and conclusion to emphasize the content of the paper.

(2) In the body of the paper, after referring to work not done by the author such as in other journal articles or in standard.

Therefore, if either phrase occurs more than three times in a paper, its use is questionable. Actually, the reader is aware that the work presented is by the author (unless the author states otherwise) so there is no reason to repeat these phrases.

The second error is more subtle. The two phrases are interchanged.

**Awkward**  In this paper, IDEAS was used to ...

**Correct**  In this study, IDEAS was used to ...

**Awkward**  In the paper, a SZG4031 towing tractor is used as the sample vehicle, it components equivalent physical parameters are obtained by UG design and testing[9].

**Correct**  In this study, a SZG4031 towing tractor is used as the sample vehicle, it components equivalent physical parameters are obtained by UG design and testing.

The "study" is the work the author(s) did. The paper is the mode to present this work and is what the reader is holding/ reading. Keep in mind the writer can also use other phrases such as "in this research", and "this paper present".

**Numbers and Equations**

Two very common errors are those concerning the presentation of Arabic numerals, and equations. Chinese writers usually write Arabic numerals instead of spelling out the word. The use of Arabic numerals, itself, is not an error however; they should never be used at the beginning of sentences.

**Incorrect**  12 parameters were selected for the experiment.

**Correct**  Twelve parameters were selected for the experiment.

In addition, Arabic numerals are overused. Arabic numerals should be used to give data in technical papers, however they should not be used to give general information.

**Incorrect**  All 3 studies concluded that the mean temperature should be 30℃.

**Correct**  All three studies concluded that the mean temperature should be 30℃.

This probably stems from the fact that Mandarin is a symbolic language and not alphabetic. Thus, the writer will find it easier to write a symbol that expresses the idea instead of the word. This problem is even more serious when equations are used in place of words in a way that is not practiced by native English speakers. Consider the following examples.

Equations should be introduced as much as possible, not inserted in place of words. Most journals, like the International Journal of Production Research, discourage the use of even short expressions within the text.

**Incorrect**  If the power battery SOC > SOClo and the driving torque belongs to the middle load …

**Correct**  If the power battery SOC is greater than SOClo and the driving torque belongs to the middle load …

**Incorrect**  All 3 studies concluded that the mean temperature should be 30℃.

**Correct**  All three studies concluded that the mean temperature should be 30℃.

**Format**

**Paragraphs**

A paragraph is a group of sentences that develop one topic or thought. Paragraphs are separated to indicate the end of one idea or thought and the beginning of another. All English paragraphs start on a new line with an indent of about one inch or with an extra line between the two paragraphs. The latter is more typical for business writing.

Chinese students are often puzzled by separating paragraphs; the may perform one of two error. One error occurs when the writer fails to distinguish between two paragraphs. Although the new paragraph starts on a new line, there is no indentation, therefore, the reader in is not aware of the change in paragraphs or ideas. The second error occurs when a paragraph is preceded by a single sentence on a single line. The single line is indented along with the succeeding paragraph as in example #. This commonly occurs in Chinese texts but is never done in English.

**"Figure" and "Table"**

The abbreviations for figure and table are Fig. and Tbl, respectively. However, the abbreviation of table is rarely seen in text. One can also write fig.

for figure. However, one should choose one convention and use it throughout the paper. You should not switch between, Figure, figure, Fig, or fig. In addition, abbreviations are not used at the beginning of sentences and a space belongs between the word/ abbreviation and the number.

**Incorrect**   Figure. 6, Figure6, Fig. 6, Tbl10

**Correct**   Figure 6, Fig. 6, Tbl. 10

**Variables**

Variables, especially those of the English alphabet, should be italicized in technical papers to distinguish them from English words. Of course, this depends on the style required by the journal.

**Capitals**

Be careful that capitals are not in the middle of the sentence.

**Incorrect**   In table 1, The mark ...

**Correct**   In table 1, the mark ...

**"Such as" and "Etc."**

Such as and etc. are commonly misused by Chinese-English writers. Such as means "for example" and implies that an incomplete list will follow; etc. means "and so on" and is used at the end of a list to show it is not complete. Therefore, using such as and etc. together is redundant.

**Incorrect**   Studies of methodology and process of implementing remanufacturing mainly focus on durable products such as automobile motors, printers, and etc[11].

**Correct**   Studies of methodology and process of implementing remanufacturing mainly focus on durable products such as automobile motors, and printers.

Such as means that an incomplete list will be given and should not be used when a complete list is given.

**Incorrect**   Compared to traditional industry, Micro-electronic fabrication has three characteristics such as high complexity, high precision and high automation.

**Correct**   Compared to traditional industry, Micro-electronic fabrication has three characteristics: high complexity, high precision and high automation.

## Section 2

(1) Some words have identical singular and plural forms and do not need an s added on to make them plural. These words include:
- literature (when referring to research);
- equipment;
- staff (referring to a group of people);
- faculty.

(2) Avoid redundancy in the following types of phrases frequently used by Chinese English writers

| Instead of | Say | Or say |
| --- | --- | --- |
| Research work | Research | Work |
| Limit condition | Limit | Condition |
| Knowledge memory | Knowledge | Memory |
| Sketch map | Sketch | Map |
| Layout scheme | Layout | Scheme |
| Arrangement plan | Arrangement | Plan |
| Output performance | Output | Performance |
| Simulation results | Results | Simulation |
| Knowledge information | Knowledge | Information |
| Calculation results | Results | Calculation |
| Application results | Results | Application |

(3) Certain words demand that the noun they modify is plural. These include different, various, and number words.

| Don't write | Instead write |
| --- | --- |
| Different node | Different nodes |
| Various method | Various methods |
| Two advantage | Two advantages |
| Fifteen thermocouple | Fifteen thermocouples |

(4) Never begin an English sentence with abbreviations and Arabic numerals such as Fig. and 8. Instead write Figure and Eight.

(5) Do not write "by this way". Instead write "by doing this", or "using this method".

(6) Never write "How to ..." at the beginning of a sentence. (Don't say it either.)

**No**  How to find the optimal parameter is the main objective.

**Yes**  Determining how to find the optimal parameter is the main objective.

(7) Do write "the results areshown in Figure 2". Do not write "the results are showed as Figure 2".

(8) Italicize variables appearing in the text to differentiate them from words. This is especially important when the variables are English alphabets. Write "The graph shows $t$, $a$, and $C$ as a function of time". Do not write "The graph shows t, a, and C as a function of time".

(9) Refrain from using the word obviously in a technical paper in the following way

**No**  Obviously, detecting regimes by means of PMH maps is a novel method[8].

**Yes**  Detecting regimes by means of PMH maps is a novel method[8].

(10) International papers should not use location dependant terms such as "at home", "abroad", "here", "our country" because the reader most likely is not Chinese and not in China. Instead, write "in China".

(11) Avoid overusing the phrases "that is to say" and "namely". Instead, try to convey your meaning in one sentence.

(12) Do not use "too" at the end of a written sentence, especially in a technical paper.

## Appendix

[1] Lin Fushen, Meng Guang. Dynamic Behavior of an Unbalanced and Warped Jeffcott Rotor with Asymmetric Stiffness.

[2] Zhang Yuping, Jiang Shouwei. Review and Analysis of 3D Model Reconstruction and Application.

[3] Du Shouji. Long Distance Box-bridge Jacking Research: Report of Starting Research.

[4] Zhang Wenqiang, Yan Heqing, Huang Xuemei, et al. 3D Modeling and Rapid Prototyping for Dentition Defect Restoration.

[5] Zhang Yuping, Jiang Shouwei, Yin Zhongwei. A Generic Approach for Leather Nesting with an Heuristic Simulated Annealing Based Genetic Algorith[J]. Natural Computation, 2009,14(16):303-307.

[6] Hu Xin, Xi Juntong, Jin Ye. Shape analysis and parameterized modeling of a hip joint[J]. J. Comput. Inf. Sci. Eng. ,2003,3(3):260-266.

[7] Li Lijun, Jin Xianlong, Li Yuanyin, et al. A Parallel Solver for Structural Modal Analysis.

[8] Chen Yongguo, Tian Ziping, Miao Zhengqing. Application of Time-frequency Analysis to Fluidization Regimes Recognition in Circulating Fluidized Beds.

[9] Ren Shaoyun, Zhang Jianwu, Gao ChangYun. Modeling and Simulation Analysis of the Torsional Vibration of a FR Driveline System.

[10] Wu Lijun, Chen Huier. Mathematical Model for on-line Prediction of Bottom and Hearth of Blast Furnace by Particular Solution Boundary Element Method.

[11] Jing Xuedong, Zhang Guoqing, Pu Gengqiang, et al. Study on Architecture of Remanufacturing System.

[12] Cai Xiaoping, Jin Chen, Wu Junbiao, et al. Application of Partial Singular Value Decomposition Analysis to Location of Vibration Sources of Elevator.

[13] Ye Yao, Lian Zhiwei, Hou Zhijian. Heat Exchange Analysis of Cooling Coils Based on a Dynamic Model.

[14] Niu Xinwen, Din Han, Xiong Youlun. Assembly Plans Generation Based on Precedence Graphs.

[15] Liu Zhenghua, Tong Tiefeng, Critical Heat Flux of Steady Boiling for Subcooled Water Jet Impingement on the Flat Stagnation Zone[J]. J. Heat Transfer, 2004, 126(2):179-184.

[16] Wang Jian, Lin Zhongqin, Zhang Yizhu. Matching Clearance Analysis for Sheetmetal Assembly.

[17] Deng Dorgquan, Xu Lie. Experimental investigation on the performance of an air cooler under frosting conditions[J]. Applied Thermal Engineering, 2003, 23(7):905-912.

[18] Yin Zhongwei, Jiang Shouwei, Iso-phote based adaptive surface fitting to

digitized points and its applications in region-based tool path generation[J]. Computers in Industry, 2004, 55(1): 15-28.

[19] Gu Zhengling, Wang Liya, Qian Shanyang. An AHP-based Method for Improving the Manufacturing Processes of Mass Customization.

[20] Xu Jie, Gu Chuangang. Numerical Calculation of the Flow-Field in a Centrifugal Impeller with Splitter Blades.

[21] Zhu Zhengli, Yin Chengliang, Zhang Jianwu. Matching and Optimization of HEV Powertrain Based on Genetic Algorithm.

# Referrences

[1] Koichi H. Elementary Knowledge of Metalworking[M]. Japan：National Maritime Research Institute，2002.

[2] 汪永明. 机械设计制造及其自动化专业英语讲义. 马鞍山：安徽工业大学，1999.

[3] McGraw-Hill Science & Technology Encyclopedia：Metal，mechanical properties of metallurgical engineering[M]. New York：The McGraw-Hill Companies Inc，2005.

[4] Justin F. Steels-An Introduction to Heat Treatment. Materials Information Service[EB/OL]. http：//www. azom. com/article. aspx? ArticleID=313.

[5] Manufacturing：Forming [EB/OL]. http：//openlearn. open. ac. uk/mod/resource/view. php? id=198368.

[6] 朱派龙. 机械专业英语图解教程[M]. 北京：北京大学出版社，2008.

[7] Machine tool [EB/OL]. http：//en. wikipedia. org/wiki/Machine_tools.

[8] Tusek J. How to extend tool life [C]//11th international scientific conference achievements in mechanical & materials engineering. Slovenia：Faculty of Mechanical Engineering，University of Ljubljana.

[9] Cutting tool (machining) [EB/OL]. http：//en. wikipedia. org/wiki/Cutting_tool_(machining).

[10] 章跃. 机械制造专业英语[M]. 北京：机械工业出版社，2009.

[11] Engineering tolerance [EB/OL]. http：//en. wikipedia. org/wiki/Tolerances.

[12] John R W. Machining Fundamentals[M]. South Hlland：Goodheart-Willcox Co，2004.

[13] Dan W. Introduction to Artificial Intelligence & Expert Systems[M]. New Jersey：Prentice Hall，1990.

[14] Expert system [EB/OL]. http：//en. wikipedia. org/wiki/Expert_System.

[15] Winifred L，Ijomah，Christopher A. Development of Design for Remanufacturing Guidelines to Support Sustainable Manufacturing[J]. Robotics and Computer-Integrated Manufacturing，2007，23(8)：712-719.

[16] Garcia E J. The Evolution of Robotics Research[J]. Robotics & Automation Magazine，2007，14(1)：90-103.

[17] Kahney, Leander. Grandiose Price for a Modest PC. *Wired*. Lycos[EB/OL]. http://www.wired.com/news/culture/0,60349-0.html.
[18] Personal computer [EB/OL]. http://en.wikipedia.org/wiki/Personal_computer #Computers_at_home
[19] Daniel K. Programmable Automation Technologies[M]. New York: Industrial Press, 2010.
[20] Lawrenceville. Introduction to fluid power [M]. New Jersey: Meridian Education Corp. 2006.
[21] MGalal R. Fluid power engineering [M]. New York: The McGraw-Hill Companies Inc, 2009.
[22] James J. Introduction to Fluid Power [M]. New York: Delmar Thomson Learning, 2002.
[23] Patrick J K. Fluid power systems [M]. Orland Park, Ill: American Technical Publishers, 2010.
[24] http://hydraulicspneumatics.com.
[25] John S C. Fluid power circuits and controls: fundamentals and applications [M]. Boca Raton : CRC Press, 2002.
[26] Peng Z. Referex Mechanical Engineering and Materials. Advanced Industrial Control Technology [M]. Burlington: William Andrew, Inc, 2010.
[27] Tan K K. Drives and Control for Industrial Automation [M]. London: Springer-Verlag Ltd, 2011.
[28] Computer-aided design[EB/OL]. http://en.wikipedia.org/wiki/Computer-aided_design.
[29] Jan H Bohn, Arvid M. Computer-aided engineering in Access Science[M]. New York: McGraw-Hill Companies, 2008.
[30] Raphael B and Smith I F C. Fundamentals of computer aided engineering[M]. New York: John Wiley, 2003.
[31] Computer-aided process planning [EB/OL]. http://en.wikipedia.org/wiki/Computer-aided_process_planning.
[32] Kenneth C. Computer-aided process planning [EB/OL]. http://www.npd-solutions.com/capp.html.
[33] Engelke, William D. How to Integrate CAD/CAM Systems: Management and Technology[M]. Boca Raton: CRC press,1987.
[34] Help, Definitions, Glossary, Advice, CAM: Computer Aided Manufacturing [EB/OL]. http://www.bestpricecomputers.co.uk/glossary/computer-aided-

manufacturing. htm.

[35] Paul T K. Agile Manufacturing: Forging New Frontiers[M]. Menlo Park: Addison-Wesley, 1994.

[36] Serope K, Steven R S. Manufactureing Engineering and Technology[M]. New Jersey: Prentice Hall, 2001.

[37] What are Rapid Prototyping Technologies? [EB/OL]. http://www.cheshirehenbury.com/rapid/what.html.

[38] Rapid prototyping [EB/OL]. http://en.wikipedia.org/wiki/Rapid_prototyping.

[39] Paul T K. E-manufacturing and E-Manufacturing Benefits [EB/OL]. http://www.cheshirehenbury.com/emanufacturing/index.html.

[40] Biren P. Concurrent Engineering Fundamentals[M]. Englewood: Prentice Hall, 1996.

[41] Rosenblatt A, Watson G. Concurrent Engineering[J]. IEEE Spectrum, 1991.

[42] Nanotechnology [EB/OL]. http://en.wikipedia.org/wiki/ Nanotechnology

[43] Lee Lerner K. Nanotechnology [M]. The Gale Group Inc, 2004.

[44] John T. Reaching For A Smarter Factory [EB/OL]. http://www.industryweek.Com/articles/reaching_for_a_smarter_factory_14779.aspx

[45] Training material for CNC, CNC Concepts, Inc. [EB/OL]. http://www.cncci.com/index.html

[46] Berard S J, Waters E O, Phelps C W. Principles of Machine Design[M]. New York: Ronald Press, 1955.

[47] Web of Science [EB/OL]. http://thomsonreuters.com/products_ervices/science/science_products/a-z/web_of_science/.

[48] Engineering Village: basic of Searching on Compendex [EB/OL]. http://www.biblioteca.mincyt.gov.ar/material_instructivo/EngVillCompendex.pdf

[49] Ei Village 2 [EB/OL]. http://zh.wikipedia.org/wiki/ %E5%B7%A5%E7%A8%8B%E7%B4%A2%E5%BC%95

[50] Overview and Description[EB/OL]. http://www.isiwebofknowledge.com.

[51] Felicia Brittman. The Most Common Habits from more than 200 English Papers written by Graduate Chinese Engineering Students [EB/OL]. http://wenku.baidu.com/view/ 8667fd4669eae009581bec68.html.